Carolyn Forster is a best-selling quilting author, with over 175,000 books sold worldwide. She started making quilts when she was a teenager, and her passion for patchwork and quilting led her to study Textiles at Bath Spa University, UK.

Since then, she has taught patchwork and quilting both in the US and UK, and has had her quilts featured in a number of books and magazines, including *Today's Quilter* and French magazine *Magic Patch*. Carolyn lives in Kent, UK.

www.carolynforster.co.uk

@quiltingonthego

Also by Carolyn Forster

978-1-78221-940-8

978-1-78221-821-0

978-1-78221-671-1

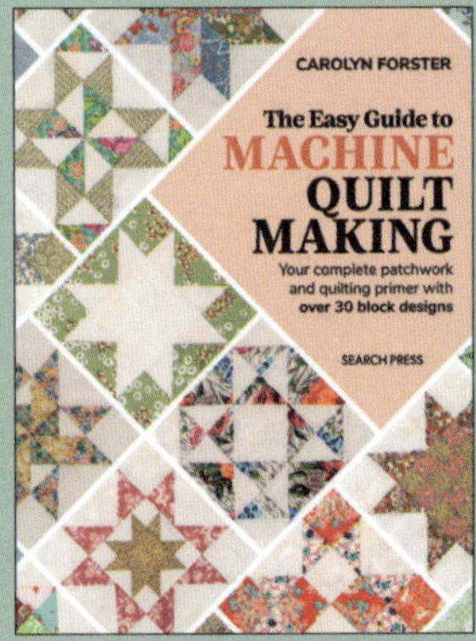

978-1-78221-994-1

978-1-80092-082-8

978-1-80092-258-7

978-1-80092-355-3

1930s QUILTS

Dedication

In memory of Marion Drake.

CAROLYN FORSTER

1930s QUILTS

Explore the creativity
of the Great Depression era
with 10 stunning step-by-step quilts

Contents

06 Foreword
by Kate Hebert, Chief Curator
at American Museum & Gardens, Bath, UK

10 Hello and Welcome

12 A Small History of 1930s Quilts

30 **THE QUILT PROJECTS**

32 Using Solids
36 Ric-Rac Baskets Quilt

44 Fine Hand Quilting
46 Scrap Basket Quilt

54 Complex Piecing
56 Grandmother's Prize Quilt

64 Using White Fabric
66 Endless Chain Quilt

72 Friendship and Community
76 Friendship Garden Quilt

84 Embroidering Quilts
86 Embroidered Linen Squares Quilt

92 Black Accents
94 Split Nine-Patch Quilt

100 Using Feedsacks
102 Five-Patch Star Quilt

108 Using Small Scraps
110 Scrap Doll Quilt

116 Redwork Embroidery
120 Redwork Cot Quilt

126 Patchwork and Quilting Basics

186 Templates

198 Thanks

199 Index

Foreword

by Kate Hebert, Head Curator at American Museum & Gardens, Bath, UK

As the world emerged from the devastation of the First World War, the 1920s brought a period of economic prosperity to the western world. Alongside this growth came major advances in manufacturing, technology, arts and culture, and society—and at the start of the decade, the 19th amendment to the Constitution finally granted women the right to vote (although it was many more years until most women benefited from this). For many the Roaring Twenties was a period of extravagance, but this came to an abrupt end with the Wall Street Crash of 1929, and what followed was a period of economic depression.

Following the crash, unemployment in America rose to record highs. With many unable to support themselves, those affected by the depression turned to the federal government for help. During his 1932 presidential campaign, Franklin Delano Roosevelt promised a "New Deal" to help Americans out of the financial crisis. Following his inauguration in 1933, President Roosevelt implemented his New Deal, providing both financial support and employment opportunities.

Roosevelt's wife, First Lady Eleanor Roosevelt, played an active role in supporting her husband's New Deal. She used her influence to spearhead craft training projects through the Works Progress Administration during the Great Depression. The aim of the project was to encourage Americans to revive traditional craft skills, including quiltmaking (in which there was a resurgence of interest during this time of thriftiness). The collection at the American Museum & Gardens in Bath, UK, includes a postage-stamp style quilt made by an unknown quilter and presented to the First Lady—shown opposite.

The quilt is characteristic of those made between the 1920s and the 1940s. The scrap-bag style quilt perfectly showcases the bright new pastel-colored cottons that became available after the First World War. The shift in colors was made possible by advances in synthetic dyes, which introduced a whole new palette of colors that were markedly different from those that preceded them. The 1920s saw a bold change in color ranges as bright and cheerful pastel designs became fashionable. Quilts made using these new fabrics and colors had a brighter and fresher appearance than their 19th century counterparts.

> "Carolyn's passion for Depression era quilts shines through (...) this book..."

"Trip Around the World" quilt by unknown maker; USA; c. 1935; 75in (191cm) wide x 75in (198cm) tall; AM&G: 2001, no. 154.

The quilt is composed of 1in (2.5cm) squares cut from multicolored patterned cottons that have then been set on point by machine. The pieced squares are arranged in bands to form the "Trip around the World" pattern. The quilt is filled with light batting / wadding, backed with green cotton, and bound with cream cotton. Each square has been hand-quilted a ¼in (5mm) from its edge, known as outline or echo quilting.

> “[It’s] like having a quilting expert right there with you, guiding you every step of the way.”

“Bow Tie” quilt by unknown maker; USA; c. early 20th century; 64in (162.5cm) wide x 75in (190.5cm) tall; AM&G: 2001, no. 129.

This is a pieced quilt top of Bow Tie blocks alternating with squares of patterned fabric. The backing, a floral pink fabric, has a border of single patches running around all edges (see the detail, opposite top). A variety of patterned cottons has been used for the patchwork. There is thick batting / wadding inside, and all layers have been hand-tied together with red cotton thread.

The popularity of these printed cottons from what we now call the "Depression era" has endured, and many of the historic fabrics are available as modern reproductions today. For those of us who aren't fortunate to have our own period example, this book offers inspiration and practical guidance for creating your own version.

Carolyn's passion for Depression era quilts shines through in this book, which explores the history of the period and identifies the key stylistic elements found in most Thirties quilts. Each of these elements is presented as a different project and chapter in the book, with the introductory section providing context and explaining how each design reflects the style of the early 20th century.

I particularly enjoy the fun and innovative way that Carolyn draws inspiration from antique quilts while adding her own unique twist. She encourages us all to use these projects as a starting point to explore our own ideas, rather than simply replicating what has been done before. This is especially evident in the Embroidered Linen Squares Quilt (see page 86) where Carolyn uses blocks cut from vintage embroidered tablecloths as the focal point of a quilt. This project celebrates the skills of past needlewomen by re-purposing items that aren't generally used today.

The Patchwork and Quilting Basics section at the end of the book provides a wealth of tips, advice and short cuts or alternative construction methods. The clear instructions and helpful photographs are like having a quilting expert right there with you, guiding you every step of the way. I for one will be hunting out a grapefruit spoon the next time I safety-pin the layers of a quilt together!

Hello and Welcome

One of the most frequent questions I am asked about my quilting journey, is when did I start making quilts?

And the answer is when I was in my teens. I had always loved crafting—from making the weekly Blue Peter projects, knitting, and crochet to cross-stitching, and making dolls' clothes from a fabric scrap bag we had (my mum sewed lots of our clothes, so there was always fabric, as well as the idea that you could make whatever it was you wanted).

My first ever quilt was actually a design from a cross-stitch book, and I stitched it from squares—English Paper Piecing (EPP) style. Little did I know I was already working in a fashion similar to 1920s and 1930s needlework designer, Anne Orr.

There was a wonderful independent bookshop near my family home where I would spend my pocket money on books. I started searching the shelves for books about quilts, and at that time they were few and far between. However, they did have a copy of Ruby Short McKim's *101 Patchwork Patterns*. This book, first published in 1931, contained lots of old patchwork patterns from America, and this fascinated me. It was the first patchwork book that I bought, and it was magical. I wanted to make all the blocks in it. I didn't really know what the actual quilts would look like in real life, as all the drawings in the book were in black and white, so I simply traced the patterns and stitched the blocks with my dress scraps. And sometimes it all worked out and other times it didn't... So, the next book I bought was all about drafting patchwork patterns; this time, I knew it would all fit together. And that's where I started!

I saw some quilts from the 1930s at the American Museum and Gardens in Bath, UK, when I was studying at the college in Bath, and these really spurred me on. It was around this time that I saw one of my first books on old quilts from the US. This book talked about the lives of the women who stitched the quilts, and on the cover was a quilt from the 1930s, or the Revival Period (1910–1940). Finally, I was able to see the quilt designs in color, and I became hooked on the palette and fabrics from this period, as well as the patterns. The fabric colors were fresh—mainly pastels and solids—with hints of black quilting and embroidery. They weren't the dark reds, greens, browns, and creams from the mid- to late 1800s; they were literally a breath of fresh air!

I wanted to make my quilts in these bright, fresh fabrics. When I started to look more closely at what was available to us quilters in the UK at that time, fabric ranges from the US were beginning to emerge, as well as reproduction fabrics seen in the quilts from this period. This meant I could buy both, and add these American elements to my stitching. Sometimes I'd mix and match reproduction and modern-day fabrics (albeit ones that had a similar feel) to give my quilts a unique flavor, but one that was still reminiscent of 1930s quilts.

Blocks and ideas that I wanted to try would be stitched as a "try-out" in this fresh color palette, and quickly I found this colorway very comfortable and pleasing to work with. It seemed so easy to use that, even if my eventual quilt did not get made in those fabrics, I had enough try-out blocks that complemented each other to end up in a quilt together (inadvertently becoming examples of the frugal, waste-not want-not approach often seen in my beloved 1930s quilts). So, for me, the 1930s color palette became my go-to when stitching new ideas.

As my interest grew, and I traveled to the US more, I was thrilled to learn I could buy the actual fabrics from the 1930s and put them in my quilts!

During all the years that I have sewn quilts, 1930s or Depression-era quiltmaking in the US (which actually loosely covers a wider period that spans from the early 1900s to the late 1940s) has continued to fascinate me. This period, with its excitement, the historical events that occurred, and how those events affected women and quiltmaking, still offers me endless inspiration.

In this book, my interest is not to reproduce quilts and patterns from the period—and if that is your taste, there are lots of books available to help you do this authentically. Instead, I'm celebrating the stunning fresh designs that evolved in such a turbulent period by interpreting them through a collection of quilt projects; this way, I'm not only highlighting the incredible workmanship of the quiltmakers of the period, but demonstrating how their work is still relevant—and looks just as wonderful—today. I'm hoping also that a subject that has inspired me for so long might be something that inspires you too.

And if you're wondering, yes: I'm still pawing through my Ruby Short McKim book today.

A Small History of 1930s Quilts

I've always referred to the quilts that inspire me, and the period they belong to, as the Thirties. However, the qualities that distinguish these quilts from others before and after them come from a wider period than that. The events that happened before the economic crash of 1929, chartering what historians now call the Depression era, and continued to happen after 1940, all equally affected and influenced how "1930s" quilts were made, thus making it harder to firmly pin down their iconic features to a 10-year period.

Many designs and patterns prior to the 1930s were similar to what we would consider a "Thirties style", and remade often; so, it is inaccurate to say that, because a block was seen in a newspaper column in 1930, the quilt was made then. Furthermore, since women were encouraged to "cut and clip" (i.e. cut patterns out of magazines and keep them for future use), personal scrapbooks were created that would have been referred to in years to come; this meant newspaper editors could even ask readers to send in old patterns, which were then often renamed as a "new" pattern.[1] Lastly, we all know how a stash of fabric scraps can build over time, and that a quilt might start to be stitched one year, but not necessarily finished that same year; these same things were experienced by the makers of old. What was once a feedsack may have been cut up and used for a garment, which was then handed down and then eventually found its way into a quilt. This means a finished quilt from the Thirties may have been made from scraps collected a decade or more beforehand, and quilts made in the Forties may have the fabrics and style of quilts from the Thirties.

I'm going to try to fill in the gaps in and around the 1930s, so that we can have a glimpse at the things that will have influenced quilts and their makers at that time.

---

[1] *Merikay Waldvogel, "Also Known as Patty Shannon", Quilter's Newsletter Magazine, October 2004 issue, p. 38*

AND

Merikay Waldvogel, Soft Covers for Hard Times: Quiltmaking and the Great Depression, *(Rutledege Hill Press: Nashville, 1990), p. 20*

“Pieced Fans” quilt by Katy Clark Elmore; Chula, Missouri; c. 1937; 79in (201cm) wide x 86in (218cm) tall; AM&G: 1980, no. 70.

Pieced fans in multicolored cottons with white backgrounds, set diamond-wise, create 7in (17.75cm) square blocks. The quilt has been backed with white cotton, and the fans outline (or echo) quilted. Unusually, the lower edge of the quilt is scalloped, adding interest and extra texture. The whole quilt has been bound with striped cotton. There is a light filling. This is one of a pair of quilts made by Elmore for twin beds.

PRE-1930s

The influence of Colonial Revival

The quilts that I love are part of what is now known as the Colonial Revival movement, which was prevalent in art and design from around the 1880s to 1950s, reaching a peak in the 1920s and 1930s.[2] This movement's ethos, to put it simply, looked back on and admired the "simpler times" before the American Civil War (1861–1865).

Colonial Revival was brought about primarily by the Centennial Exposition held in the city of Philadelphia in Pennsylvania, USA, in 1876. Created to tie in with the anniversary of the country's Declaration of Independence (and partly to encourage nationhood after a period of internal war), this "expo" or fair showcased innovations, art, and culture from around the world. The expo was visited by millions, and the design trends that gripped the visitors included embroideries from the Royal School of Needlework in London, UK, and artifacts in the East Asian pavilions.[3]

The English embroideries on show were works based on the designs and aesthetics of William Morris, whose cleaner, simpler, more naturalistic designs moved away from the heavy, cluttered, ornate Victorian design and interiors trends prevalent at the time. The East Asian pavilions were fascinating to visiting citizens (Japan being particularly intriguing, as the country had only opened its doors to the US in 1854), and much of it was seen as novel. To visitors, the art and designs of India, China, and Japan were reminiscent of pre-Industrial times, and were seen as exotic but familiar, natural yet sophisticated, ornate yet sincere and uplifting.[4]

---

[2] Roderick Kiracofe, The American Quilt, A History of Cloth and Comfort 1750–1950 (Clarkson N. Potter: New York, 1993), p. 209

[3] Kiracofe, The American Quilt, A History of Cloth and Comfort 1750–1950, p. 166

[4] Kiracofe, The American Quilt, A History of Cloth and Comfort 1750–1950, p. 140

"Cherry Trees" quilt by Naomi Beckworth; Oregon; c. 1930; 79in (200cm) wide x 81in (206cm) tall; AM&G: 1997, no. 110.

The Cherry Tree design—a reinvention of the Tree of Life motif—was popular at the beginning of the 20th century. Commercial patterns were available for quilts and embroideries. In 1922 the Ladies Home Journal sold a transfer pattern of this quilt design. The quilt pattern makers Bucilla also produced a kit (albeit a simplified version). The resemblance of this quilt to others in The Art Institute of Chicago and at the Denver Art Museum implies that this example was made using such a kit or commercially produced transfer pattern.

US designers were not only inspired by what they saw at the Centennial Exposition, but their desire to reflect the style of the simpler, pre-Civil War times was also influenced by, and a reaction to, the fast-changing world around them. The rapidity of the modern industrialized life and the technology developed—from railroads and roadworks to telephones and light bulbs—left some feeling unsettled and uneasy, especially as it had even brought about the displacement of some people too: many born in rural communities moved to the cities for better jobs and, with that, better income. There was a desire to lessen the impact of the current changes and social realities, and so there was a sense of nostalgia for the times before the Civil War and an impetus to emulate the past. The Colonial Revival movement was often seen as "anti-modern" for these very reasons.[5]

This feeling heightened after The First World War (1914–1918), when a sense of patriotism made some Americans look back at all that was good in this now idolized pre-war period.[6] American colonial heritage arts and crafts started being collected by museums. In 1924 the Metropolitan Museum of Art in New York opened its new wing for colonial arts and crafts. Millionaires, keen to make their mark, went about creating museums themselves. In 1928 John Rockefeller bought land that had been Virginia's colonial capital, and announced the restoration of Colonial Williamsburg as a historical site—a "shrine... [to] the American Revolution".[7] This literally gave a space for colonial arts and crafts to be shared, viewed, and celebrated.

While millionaires turned to opening museums and buying land to celebrate colonial revival, the middle classes turned to furnishing their homes with it.[8] Hand-made items with a simpler aesthetic grew in popularity, as they created a sense of stability and a reconnection to the past. They were the antithesis of the growing number of mass-produced, factory-made goods. But this meant crafts such as quiltmaking, with its artistic simplicity and sentimentality, became very appealing.

---

[5] *Sara Nephew, My Mother's Quilts: Designs from the Thirties (That Patchwork Place: Washington, 1988), p. 6*

[6] *Barbara Brackman, "Quilts at Chicago's World's Fairs", Uncoverings 1981: Research Papers of the American Quilt Study Group, Vol. 2, ed. Sally Garouette, website link: <https://digitalcommons.unl.edu/cgi/viewcontent.cgi?article=1025&context=aqsg-uncoverings>, p. 68*

[7] *"Nationwide Comments on the Restoration of Williamsburg", Culpeper Exponent, Vol. 48, No. 28, 18 October 1920, electronic scan via website: <https://www.virginiachronicle.com/?a=d&d=TCX19281018.1.5&e=-------en-20--1--txt-txIN--------- >, p. 5*

AND

Anders Greenspan, "Colonial Williamsburg", 7 December 2020, Encyclopedia Virginia: Virginia Humanities, via website: <https://encyclopediavirginia.org/entries/colonial-williamsburg>

"Star of Bethlehem" quilt by Bertha (Tanner) Robertson; Yakima, Washington; c. 1928; 91in (227cm) wide x 92in (233cm) tall; AM&G: 1993, no. 166.

Bertha Robertson has pieced the large star from individual diamond shapes and applied it to a white border. The triangles have been arranged so that bands of color radiate from the center. A floating border composed of dark red diamonds and white triangles frames the central star. The quilt is lightly padded, and backed and bound with plain white fabric. Robertson has outline quilted the diamonds and filled the white sections with quilted feather vines.

---

8 Xenia E. Cord, "Marketing Quilt Kits in the 1920s and 1930s", *Uncoverings 1995: Research Papers of the American Quilt Study Group*, Vol. 16, ed. Virginia Gunn, website link: <https://digitalcommons.unl.edu/cgi/viewcontent.cgi?article=1011&context=aqsg-uncoverings>, p. 140

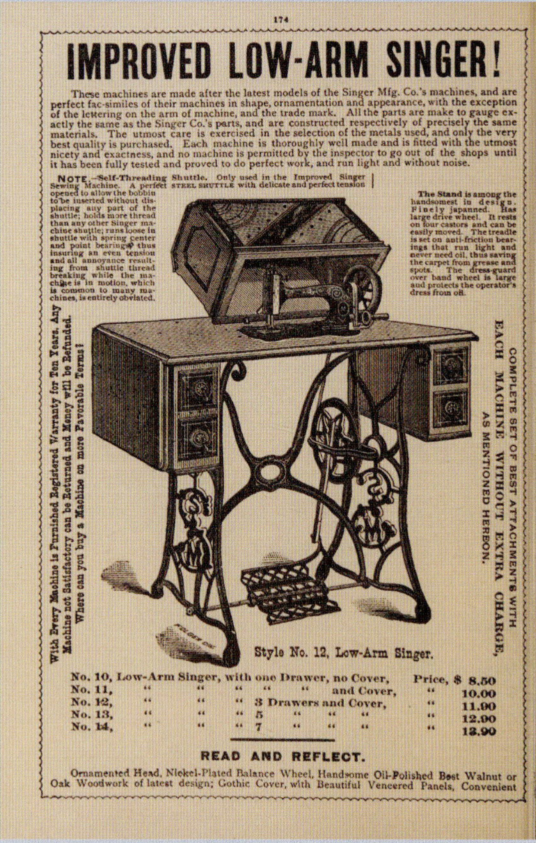

174

IMPROVED LOW-ARM SINGER!

These machines are made after the latest models of the Singer Mfg. Co.'s machines, and are perfect fac-similes of their machines in shape, ornamentation and appearance, with the exception of the lettering on the arm of machine, and the trade mark. All the parts are make to gauge exactly the same as the Singer Co.'s parts, and are constructed respectively of precisely the same materials. The utmost care is exercised in the selection of the metals used, and only the very best quality is purchased. Each machine is thoroughly well made and is fitted with the utmost nicety and exactness, and no machine is permitted by the inspector to go out of the shops until it has been fully tested and proved to do perfect work, and run light and without noise.

NOTE.—Self-Threading Shuttle. Only used in the Improved Singer Sewing Machine. A perfect STEEL SHUTTLE with delicate and perfect tension opened to allow the bobbin to be inserted without displacing any part of the shuttle; holds more thread than any other Singer machine shuttle; runs loose in shuttle with spring center and point bearings, thus insuring an even tension and all annoyance resulting from shuttle thread breaking while the machine is in motion, which is common to many machines, is entirely obviated.

The Stand is among the handsomest in design. Finely japanned. Has large drive wheel. It rests on four castors and can be easily moved. The treadle is set on anti-friction bearings that run light and never need oil, thus saving the carpet from grease and spots. The dress-guard over band wheel is large and protects the operator's dress from oil.

With Every Machine is Furnished Registered Warranty for Ten Years. Any Machine not Satisfactory can be Returned and Money will be Refunded. Where can you buy a Machine on more Favorable Terms!

COMPLETE SET OF BEST ATTACHMENTS WITH EACH MACHINE WITHOUT EXTRA CHARGE, AS MENTIONED HEREON.

Style No. 12, Low-Arm Singer.

No. 10,	Low-Arm Singer, with one Drawer, no Cover,	Price, $ 8.50
No. 11,	" " " " " and Cover,	" 10.00
No. 12,	" " " 3 Drawers and Cover,	" 11.90
No. 13,	" " " 5 " " "	" 12.90
No. 14,	" " " 7 " " "	" 13.90

READ AND REFLECT.

Ornamented Head, Nickel-Plated Balance Wheel, Handsome Oil-Polished Best Walnut or Oak Woodwork of latest design; Gothic Cover, with Beautiful Veneered Panels, Convenient

Above: *Page 174 of the Sears, Roebbuck and Co. Consumers Guide 1894.*

Below: *"Making a quilt in Scranton, Iowa, home. The ladies will give the quilt to a needy family" by photographer John Vachon (1914–1975), April 1940, Farm Security Administration—Office of War Information Photograph Collection (Library of Congress), website link: <https://www.loc.gov/pictures/item/2017810133/>*

Technological advancements

Ironically, it was new technologies and the moving forward of industry (all the things the Colonial Revival movement fought against) that helped makers have greater access to a wider variety of fabrics, colors, patterns, and notions more than ever before, making the quilting industry very modern.

After the First World War, the USA developed its own print and dye industry, opening up new colors and prints but also making it easier for fabrics to be bought.[9] The Art Nouveau movement also influenced fabric design and, with new tech, anything now could be printed on fabric.[10]

Direct mail-order catalogues, a phenomenon established in the US by Tiffany & Co™ in 1845,[11] allowed consumers to be able to buy items they could only buy previously if they visited a town or city. Sears, Roebuck and Co.'s first catalogue was vast (its 1894 catalogue was 322 pages in extent), and from it consumers could buy watches, jewelry, bicycles, sewing machines, clothing, and more—and at a much cheaper price than from the rural, general stores.[12] The expansion of the American railway between 1860 and 1910 increased the number of mail-order catalogues, and resulted in better communications and postal service. This now meant those who lived more rurally,

[9] *Marin F. Hanson, "Modern, Yet Anti-Modern: Two Sides of Late-Nineteenth and Early-Twentieth Century Quiltmaking", Uncoverings 2008: Research Papers of the American Quilt Study Group, Vol. 16, ed. Laurel Horton, pp. 17–19*

[10] *Melinda Watt, "Timeline of Art History: Nineteenth-Century European Textile Production", October 1, 2024, The Met Museum: Essays, website link: <https://www.metmuseum.org/essays/nineteenth-century-european-textile-production>*

which amounted to at least a third of the population during that period, had more access to goods—including fabrics and other sewing requirements.[13]

In 1925, the Sears brand expanded beyond its catalogue and opened its first department store in Chicago. The department store could offer almost anything to anyone under one roof. This made shopping much easier; even if they didn't buy anything, the store was an attractive day out in itself.

One obvious convenience was the sewing machine being used to make these "old" quilts. Although invented back in 1840, and commonplace in the 1860s, at the turn of the 20th century the number of makers who owned machines increased—partly due to department stores and mail-order catalogues, but also because they could now be purchased on installment plans, making them more affordable.[14]

The sewing machine liberated stitchers: since clothes could be sewn on the machine instead of by hand, they had more time to sew other projects—including quilts. This extra time meant a stitcher could hand-piece blocks if desired, but often the blocks were then put together on the machine. In turn, this saw an increase in the popularity of repeat-block quilt designs.[15]

Community and nationhood

During the American Civil War women were encouraged to make quilts for the home, to save blankets for those fighting. While there was no need to make quilts after the war, many women still made them as a creative outlet. If quilts weren't needed for their own homes, makers made quilts for fundraisers and for American Red Cross auctions.

There was also the community that the craft created. Quilting Bees were still something that rural women could look forward to, and in the cities women with time on their hands (due to the labor-saving devices) were also looking to get out of the house and find some company.

---

[11] *"1845: Tiffany publishes the first direct mail catalogue in the U.S. and introduces Americans to luxury goods", The Tiffany & Co. Timeline, website link: <https://www.tiffany.com/world-of-tiffany/the-world-of-tiffany-timeline/>*

[12] *Sears, Roebuck and Co. Consumers Guide (Sears, Roebuck and Co., 1894), via Internet Archive: <www.archive.org>, book URL: <https://archive.org/details/bwb_SO-ATP-483/mode/2up>*

[13] Robert Shaw, American Quilts: The Democratic Art, 1780–2007 (Sterling: New York, 2009), p. 159

[14] Thomas K. Woodard and Blanche Greenstein, Twentieth Century Quilts: 1900–1950 (E.P. Dutton: New York, 1988), p. 7

[15] Marin F. Hanson, "Modern, Yet Anti-Modern: Two Sides of Late-Nineteenth and Early-Twentieth Century Quiltmaking", Uncoverings 2008: Research Papers of the American Quilt Study Group, Vol. 16, ed. Laurel Horton, pp. 17–19

Pattern boom

Following the American Civil War, and on the back of the Centennial Exposition, more patterns and books were being published about quilts and their history.[16]

Initially, old quiltmaking patterns before the American Civil War were re-printed by magazines and newspapers, and the quilts made from them copied the colors and fabrics of the old quilts.[17] But, as more interest in the quilting world grew, there was a greater interest in exploring new patterns, fabrics, and colors.

Ladies' Art Company was one such publisher to take advantage of this. Established in 1889 in St Louis, Missouri, it was the first company to offer block patterns with individual names in a mail-order catalogue. By 1928, there were 530 designs in the published booklet to order from.[18] These patterns were often referenced by other designers thereafter. You could buy patterns for 10 cents each, and they were supplied as printed outlines on tracing paper, with a separate 3in (7.75cm) square card with a colored image of the block on it. From 1912, Ladies' Art Co. started offering quilt kits too; readers could buy just the perforated pattern, or the pattern with fabric, or even fabric with the pattern printed on it.[19]

Kits played a huge role in the Colonial Revival, and moved quiltmaking away from the traditional folk group craft in a domestic setting to a professional, commercial art form, with quilts bearing intricate surface designs.[20] Besides the speed and ease the kits offered (which would contain pre-cut fabrics, and sometimes even partly assembled blocks, as well as pattern templates), and thanks to a level of marketing around them, they asserted popular quilting and patchwork styles, along with color schemes, that would become a standard during this period.[21] But behind the mostly corporate background of the kits was a more empowering message: they were a reaffirmation of women's domestic and artistic skills, and their importance in influencing the art and craft movement.[22]

So now that the quilting industry was gaining traction, the women who stitched could also be the women who could influence it.

Carlie Sexton was one such woman. Born into a working-class family, Sexton supported herself by doing clerical work at a magazine publisher, then combined her passion for quiltmaking with her

---

[16] *Examples include:*

Marie Webster, Quilts: Their Story and How to Make Them *(Doubleday Page & Company: New York, 1916)*

Ruth Finley, Old Patchwork Quilts and the Women Who Made Them *(J. B. Lippincott Company: Philadelphia, 1929)*

Carrie Hall and Rose Kretsinger, Romance of the Patchwork Quilt in America *(The Caxton Printers, Limited: Idaho, 1935*

[17] *Elizabeth V. Warren and Sharon L. Eisenstat*, Glorious American Quilts: The Quilt Collection of the Museum of American Folk Art *(Penguin Studio in association with Museum of American Folk Art: New York, 1996)*, p. 91

[18] *Woodard and Greenstein*, Twentieth Century Quilts: 1900–1950 *(E.P. Dutton: New York, 1988)*, p. 20

[19] "Quilt kits", *Ladies' Art Company website: <https://ladiesartcompany.com/?page_id=99>*

[20] Cord, "Marketing Quilt Kits in the 1920s and 1930s", p. 139

[21] Cord, "Marketing Quilt Kits in the 1920s and 1930s", pp. 139–142

[22] Cord, "Marketing Quilt Kits in the 1920s and 1930s", pp. 139–142

Above:
A selection of stitching ephemera, including Aunt Martha® iron-on transfers (a company founded in the 1930s, and still in business today), and templates for fabric yo-yos or Suffolk puffs, and home-made templates for a double wedding ring quilt. Magazines of the time, like the one shown, featured patterns for the characteristic traycloth embroidery.

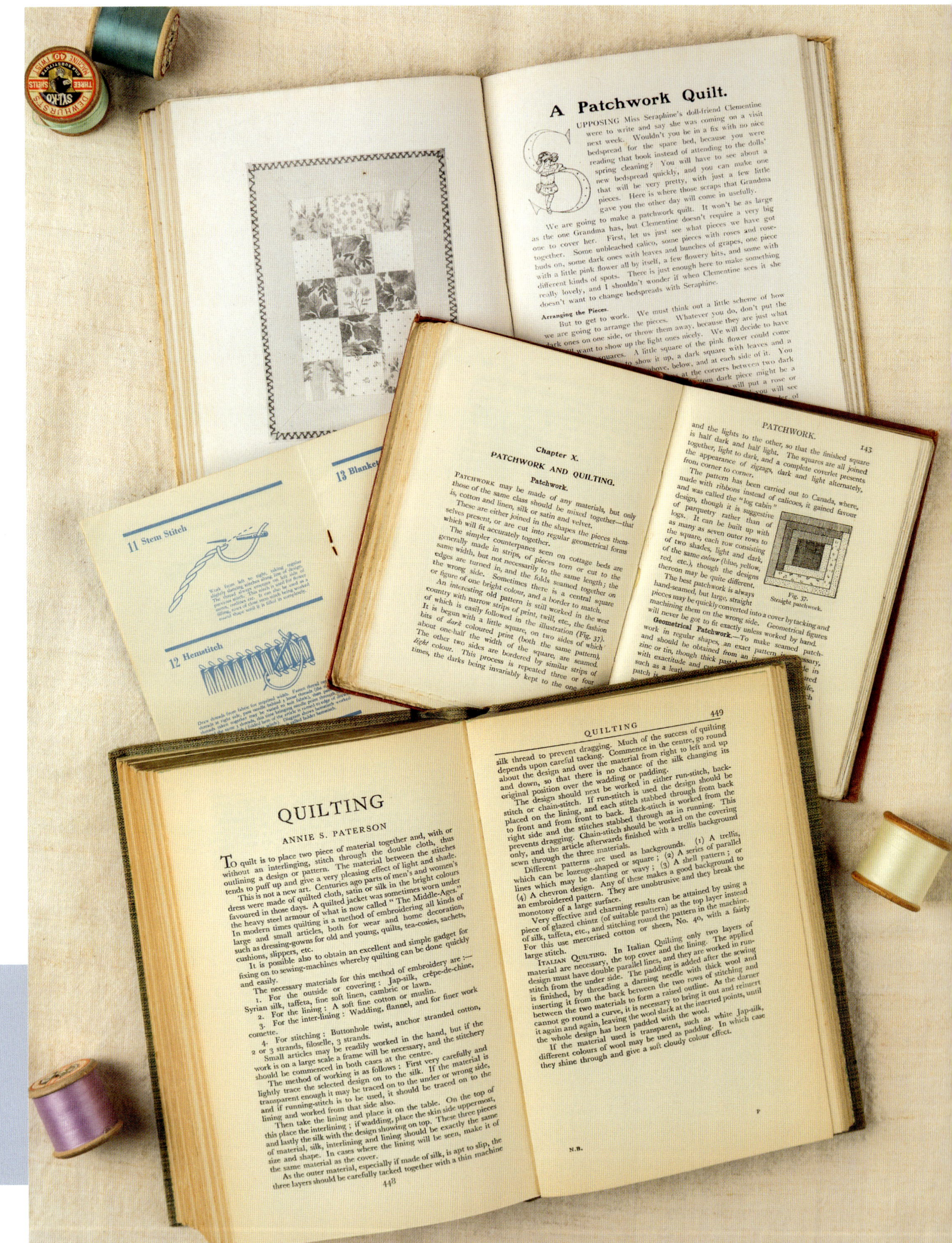
A Patchwork Quilt.
Arranging the Pieces.
11 Stem Stitch
12 Hemstitch
13 Blanket
Chapter X.
PATCHWORK AND QUILTING.
Patchwork.
PATCHWORK.
143
Fig. 37.
Straight patchwork.
QUILTING
ANNIE S. PATERSON
448
QUILTING
449

knowledge of printing to create her pamphlets of quilt patterns.[23] In the 1920s Sexton published three small books on quilting—*Quaint Quilts* (1922), *Early American Quilts* (1924) and then *Old Fashioned Quilts* (1928).[24] These became reference books for the next half century (and interestingly, are still looked at today), giving us a snapshot of how patchwork and quiltmaking were viewed at that time.

Carrie Hall, co-author of the milestone book, *The Romance of the Patchwork Quilt in America* (1935), is another. Originally a dressmaker, in the 1920s Hall saw her garment-making business declining, but noticed the quilt revival explosion. So, she set about making a book of all the block patterns she could find—a huge undertaking, as the final printed book contained over 800 blocks.[25] Hall then displayed and had talks about these blocks, and on the history of quiltmaking, in a lecture circuit at department stores and women's groups. Hall's lectures became well-known, all the more because she wore a colonial moiré dress throughout. In 1938, Hall donated her physical block samples, and the research material behind them, to The Spencer Museum of Art at the University of Kansas.

By the end of the 1920s, the pattern and kit business was vast. Makers Nancy Cabot, Ruby Short McKim, Anne Orr and Marie Webster, as well as the Ladies' Art Company, the newspaper *Kansas City Star*, and the brand Mountain Mist® were all names that the sewist would recognize and associate with quiltmaking and quilt designs. These names all succeeded in the market as customers wanted new designs, fabrics, sewing machines, and mass-produced kits and patterns. And, ironically, many makers seeking the simple, colonial style embraced quiltmaking kits for their modernity and progressiveness.

Nevertheless, there was a fear that, with more designs published, certain quilt blocks would lose their regionality. Sharing block patterns was by no means a new concept: quilters had always shared blocks, but the process had been much slower as before they were published in papers and journals, and when the railways weren't as extensive.

Opposite:
A collection of books all printed in and around the 1930s. In the Thirties, there were lots of general needlework compendiums available to buy, such as the ones shown. These compendiums included chapters on quilting and patchwork as well as basic embroidery stitches often seen in the redwork panels or to enhance appliqué within a quilt.

[23] Susan Price Miller, "Carlie Sexton and Her Quiilt Pattern Business", *Uncoverings 1996: Research Papers of the American Quilt Study Group*, Vol. 17, ed. Virginia Gunn, website link: <https://kora.quiltindex.org/files/35-90-202/Uncoverings1996-A3.pdf>, p. 30

[24] Price Miller, "Carlie Sexton and Her Quilt Pattern Business", p. 35

[25] Diane Hammill, , "Carrie Hall", Quilters Hall of Fame, website link: <https://quiltershalloffame.net/carrie-hall>

THE 1930s

Depression Era

In October 1929, the stock market crashed at the New York Stock Exchange on Wall Street, catalyzing a 10-year period of recession in the United States —North America's longest economic downturn in history—now infamously known as the Great Depression. This economic instability, and the fallout from it, cast a shadow over most of the 1930s in the United States.

This is when you might think the quilting industry might take a downturn too. But not only is quiltmaking a beacon of inspiration to quilters today, it actually seemed to spur on stitchers during this difficult period. Patchwork and quilting were seen as ways to save money, use what resources you already had, and be productive; but, it also meant makers could satisfy creative and social needs, too. As Marie Webster wrote in her book of quilts: "...the care in piecing, the patience in quilting; all make for feminine contentment and domestic happiness".[26] Perhaps a forerunner of the creative mindfulness we see today?

Bright fabrics and fresh, airy quilt designs emerged in the Thirties for a few reasons. The main trigger was improvements in technology:[27] before the First World War, Germany was one of the largest suppliers of synthetic dyes in the western world, but dyes from Germany were banned when war broke out. The drab utilitarian colors available during war time forced American manufacturers to invest time and money in improving the production of synthetic dye on home soil. By the late 1920s, the manufacturing processes in the US had improved so much that hundreds of new colors and prints could be produced successfully and inexpensively.[28]

A healthy textile industry churning out inexpensive fabric in colorful shades naturally impacted home-decorating trends, and in turn influenced the quilting market.[29] Anne Orr, a popular quilt designer from the 1930s, was one such designer who took her color cues from the home designs that were in style.[30] But quilters turned to brighter, cheerful fabrics for a deeper purpose too—for their uplifting qualities. Robert Cogswell sums this up neatly in his foreword to Merikay Waldvogel's book, *Soft Covers for Hard Times*: "Quilt designers introduced a full palette of pastel colors, art nouveau stylings... The dream-like and sometimes luxuriant visual qualities of such designs contrasted sharply with the reality of hard times, making them akin to the escapist fare that

[26] *Marie Webster*, Quilts: Their Story and How to Make Them *(Doubleday Page & Company: New York, 1915), book available via Project Gutenberg, website link: <https://www.gutenberg.org/files/24682/24682-h/24682-h.html>, p. xv*

[27] *Woodard and Greenstein*, Twentieth Century Quilts: 1900–1950, *p. 8*

[28] *Woodard and Greenstein*, Twentieth Century Quilts: 1900–1950, *p. 8*

[29] *Waldvogel,* Soft Covers for Hard Times: Quiltmaking and the Great Depression, *p. 23*

[30] *Waldvogel,* Soft Covers for Hard Times: Quiltmaking and the Great Depression, *p. 24*

the film industry served Depression-era audiences through lavish Busby Berkeley production numbers, optimist rags-to-riches plots and comedic treatments of despair."[31]

There were some key players in the Thirties that not only ensured the survival of quiltmaking, but enabled it to flourish: the brands Mountain Mist® and Aunt Martha®, the newspaper *Kansas City Star*, Ruby Short McKim (sometime women's editor and design contributor to said newspaper), the Chicago World's Fair of 1933, and feedsacks.

Several companies still did well in this time of economic downturn, not just because there was a need for the product and service they sold, but because they adapted to the difficult economic landscape and accommodated the limited income of their customers.

Stearns & Foster Company, founded in 1846, sold batting / wadding for quilts. In 1928 they established **Mountain Mist®**—a range of batting / wadding that was "100 per cent new cotton fiber with no second-hand material" in attractive, colorful wrappers.[32] In 1929, the range's sales manager, Frederick Hooker, decided to print free patchwork and appliqué templates on the inside of these wrappers, complete with quilt patterns.[33]

The free patterns, attractive wrappers, and the option to buy an extra quilt pattern (so long as a coupon printed on the wrapper was supplied with the money) made Mountain Mist® batting / wadding not only recognizable but popular with consumers. The quilt designs were mainly traditional, but the wrappers featured modern ones too on occasion. Hooker was also careful to show only solid rather than printed fabrics in the illustrations of the finished blocks, avoiding the issue with the discontinuation of fabric collections (and a change in the customers' tastes) and giving the patterns a longer lifespan.[34] Department stores followed Hooker's marketing advice to host quilt exhibits and demonstrations alongside stock of Mountain Mist®, to great success,[35] and not only did these displays incentivize folks to buy the batting / wadding, but they added exciting and social elements to quiltmaking too.

Aunt Martha® was another company that did well, despite the recession. Officially known as The Colonial Company, it become known as (and eventually

[31] Waldvogel, Soft Covers for Hard Times: Quiltmaking and the Great Depression, p. XV

[32] *Merikay Waldvogel, "The Origin of Mountain Mist® Patterns", Uncoverings 1995: Research Papers of the American Quilt Study Group, Vol. 16, ed. Virginia Gunn, website link: <https://quiltindex.org//view/?type=page&kid=35-90-193>, p. 98 and p. 99*

[33] *Waldvogel, "The Origin of Mountain Mist® Patterns", p. 98*

[34] *Waldvogel, "The Origin of Mountain Mist® Patterns", p. 125 and p. 126*

[35] *Waldvogel, "The Origin of Mountain Mist® Patterns", p. 98*

trademarked the alias) "Aunt Martha" after a Chicago editor decided the brand's newspaper features needed a more grandmotherly name with the right touch of Colonial history.[36] Established in the early 1930s in Kansas City, Missouri, Aunt Martha® began as a cottage industry specializing in cut-to-size quilt blocks and patches, but changed its model and started selling paper patterns, since these sold more successfully in the tougher climate.[37] The brand advertised its designs around the country in newspapers and magazines, and notably its adverts read more like editorial columns: while the adverts promoted the company's products and mail-order service, they also included some charming quilt lore.[38] Popular then in its appeal, it is one of the only companies from this period still running today—now as Colonial Patterns.

***Kansas City Star* (KCS)**, a regional newspaper based in Missouri, played its part in the promotion of patchwork and quilting, with its regular columns on quiltmaking and block patterns to stitch. These in turn would be syndicated to other papers, increasing the reach of the patterns and its designers.[39] The patterns were published from 1928 to 1961, amounting to hundreds and hundreds of blocks over this time-frame. Many of the original designs were created by the newspaper's editors or design team, with some even solicited from readers; others were reworked traditional patterns that were simply renamed and/or re-colored years later.[40] There's a particular charm to these block patterns, and they embody the "quilt fever" of the 1930s; however, often the look overrode the practicalities of the pattern (for example, some of the templates for a block were changed in scale to fit the page they were printed on), and important information (such as the finished block size or seam allowance to use) were overlooked.

Ruby Short McKim was perhaps the best known editor and quilt designer for *KCS* (followed by Eveline Foland, Marie Folard and Eda Marie Dunn). Her patterns were in the paper from 1928 to 1930. She then set up her own business—McKim Studios—with her husband and in 1931 published her first and only book, *101 Patchwork Patterns*. It's McKim Studios' patterns and kits, and the patterns McKim published through *KCS*, that put patchwork on the map in this period—and kept it there. Their influence can be demonstrated by how their names, and their impact on quiltmaking, are still talked about today.

---

36 "About us", Colonial Patterns website, link: <https://colonialpatterns.com/about-us/>

37 "About us", Colonial Patterns website, link: <https://colonialpatterns.com/about-us/>

38 "About us", Colonial Patterns website, link: <https://colonialpatterns.com/about-us/>

39 Jill Sutton Filo, "Ruby Short McKim", American Patchwork and Quilting Magazine, February 1998 issue, p. 42 (article based "Ruby Short McKim: The Formative Years", published in Uncoverings 1996: Research Papers of the American Quilt Study Group, Vol. 17)

40 Sutton Filo, "Ruby Short McKim", p. 42 (article based on "Ruby Short McKim: The Formative Years", published in Uncoverings 1996: Research Papers of the American Quilt Study Group, Vol. 17)

AND

E. Duane Elbert and Rachel Kamm Elbert, History from the Heart: A Two-Century Heritage of Illinois Quilts and Quiltmaking, Quilt Paths Across Illinois (Rutledge Hill Press: Nashville, 1993), p. 159

The **Chicago World's Fair** in 1933 played a large role in the quilt revival of this decade, and to quilt historians is particularly special due to the national quilt contest it held. This event holds a window up to what was fashionable at this time, as there are physical examples of what quilters were using and buying for their quiltmaking.

While there was a national quilt contest at the Chicago World's Fair in 1893,[41] the 1933 contest was unique: as it was sponsored by Sears, Roebuck and Co., it was heavily advertised across the US via newspapers, radio and the Sears' catalogue; there were also prizes for the quilts amounting to $7500, which included a grand prize of $1000 (approximately $25,000 today) for the winning quilt[42]. In a period of economic trouble, such a large amount of money triggered nationwide quiltmaking. As Merikay Waldvogel puts it, "People who had never quilted before decided to try. Husbands and boyfriends helped make the quilts. Adept quilters did their very best work... [and] local Sears stores... sold fabric, supplies, and patterns [too]."[43] It's thought that around 24,000 quilts in total were entered into the Sears contest.

Above:
A selection of feedsack fabrics. The printed label on the cloth gradually switched to a paper label that could be soaked off, enabling homemakers to use the feedsacks for household sewing and quiltmaking. For more information about using feedsack fabrics in quilts, see pages 28, 64, and 100–101.

[41] *Brackman, "Quilts at Chicago's World's Fairs", p. 68*

[42] *Merikay Waldvogel, "1933 Sears National Quilt Contest Discoveries", Quilt Index, website link: <https://quiltindex.org/view/?type=specialcolls&kid=33-133-2>*

[43] *Waldvogel, "1933 Sears National Quilt Contest Discoveries"*

The quilts came from all economic backgrounds, and interestingly many were made from expensive, specially bought fabrics.[44] While it's true that the Depression impacted the affordability of fabrics—and many makers did use fabric scraps and incorporated printed feedsacks into their quilt designs (more on that in a moment)—it's clear from the surviving quilt samples that many sewists were still buying yardage to create their best work. It's worth remembering that kits with new designs were being sold successfully at that time, so there was some money around to be spent on what mattered to people.

Although traditional quilt designs were still the majority entered, and the winners of the top prizes, there was a special category for original quilt designs that reflect the "Century of Progress" theme of the fair. So, innovation was being rewarded. Many of the prize-winning quilts that are still around today, and on display, still have their green ribbons from the fair, indicating the level of prestige the competition held in the eyes of the quilters.

And, finally, **feedsacks**. In the past, flour and animal feed were purchased in bulk inside large cotton sacks. As the economy spiraled downwards, feedsacks began to be seen as free fabric by the thrifty seamstress. Lye soap was used to wash out the trademarks and words printed on the fabric, and just like that makers had fabric they could use for curtains, quilt backing, clothing, and other household use.[45] As the Thirties progressed, it became apparent that cotton sacks would be replaced with paper bags. To keep the cotton sacks relevant and create a demand, and to appeal to these home sewers, the bag industry started to print decorative designs on their cotton sacks. These fabrics ended up in quilts, as well as clothes and homewares, and the popularity of printed bags was so great that bag companies eventually moved toward paper labels, so consumers didn't have to remove any printed words on the fabric.[46]

These printed feedsacks now epitomize the whole Depression era of quilting, and in fact more were probably used after the Second World War when fabrics were rationed, and folks still had them in their scrap bags. Thousands of designs are thought to have been printed on feedsacks between the 1930s and 1950s.[47] To me, there's a fairy-tale quality to the feedsack story: something so humble as a cotton bag for flour or grain is used to put someone's ideas into reality, to stitch their own creation, and ends up in a cherished quilt for all of us to admire decades and decades later.

---

[44] *Barbara Brackman and Merikay Waldvogel, "1933 World's Fair Quilt Contest—and its aftermath", PieceWork magazine, July/August 1995 issue, p. 76*

[45] *Linzee Kull McCray,* Feed Sacks: The Colourful History of a Frugal Fabric *(Uppercase: Calgary, 2016), p. 112*

[46] *Edie McGinnis, "The History of 1930s Fabrics", Missouri Star Quilt Co. blog, website link: <https://blog.missouriquiltco.com/the-history-of-reproduction-fabrics/>*

[47] *Kull McCray,* Feed Sacks: The Colourful History of a Frugal Fabric *(Uppercase: Calgary, 2016), p. 44*

CONCLUSION

When researching the quilts and quilters of the Great Depression, I could see evidence of makers still having the urge to stitch and create, despite the financial hardships many faced. It isn't hard to imagine that making something both useful and beautiful, and to absorb yourself in stitching, would be something of a comfort in trying times, and lift one's spirits.

Yet despite the colorful and inspiring qualities of quilts from the Revival period, this high of quiltmaking did not continue.

The advent of World War Two, and the years that followed, brought great social change and economic upheaval to American society.[48] The US government set up an office to control national prices, wages and the production of consumer goods, to combat inflation; production of consumer goods switched to the manufacturing of weapons and war materials; and rationing of fabric meant clothes—and quilts—became simpler in style.[49]

During the Depression, quiltmaking had given women a sense of accomplishment when there was time to spare and money was tight. But the War's huge increase in munitions production meant that, while women still quilted, quiltmaking as an industry slowed down since many women went to work in factories as the men went to war.[50] Handiwork was not something for which women had as much time.

After the end of the Second World War, things were different and quiltmaking continued to take a downward turn. The War revitalized American industry, and improved the circumstances of a large proportion of the nation, to the extent that it brought about the end of the Great Depression. The system of organized production and large-scale labor, and the rapid growth of technology and science during the period, meant there was not only a populace earning good wages, but there were now more manufactured goods for them to spend their money on.[51] The new industry, and the new America it created, proved alluring. If quiltmaking took a back seat, it was not only down to time; women were not aspiring to make quilts as much as they were before the war.

That's not to say quilts weren't being made at all during this period, and in many ways the quilts only differ slightly from those made before. Perhaps more "V for Victory" designs were seen, but women were still using up their scrap bags, upcycling feedsacks, and had their clipped or purchased patterns from the previous decade: the rationing of fabric meant the designs and influences behind Depression era quilts continued into the late 1940s.[52]

---

[48] *Claudia Goldin, "The Role of World War II in the Rise of Women's Work", American Economic Review, Vol. 81, No. 4 September 1991, pp. 741–742*

[49] *Christopher J. Tassava, "The American Economy during World War II", Economy History Association, website link: <https://eh.net/encyclopedia/the-american-economy-during-world-war-ii>*

[50] *Tassava, "The American Economy during World War II", Economy History Association*

[51] *Tassava, "The American Economy during World War II", Economy History Association*

[52] Kiracofe, The American Quilt, A History of Cloth and Comfort 1750–1950, p. 199

The Quilt Projects

Since falling in love with the quilts of this period and then having the opportunity to share them with you, it was interesting to think about how that might look. Rather than just say, "Well, this is a quilt and it speaks to me", I've focused on 10 characteristics that I've observed from quilts of this period.

By looking at the quilts in this way, I have identified the different elements that have defined these quilts for me. I hope that these characteristics may inspire you in deciding what you like about the quilts from this period, too.

In this chapter I will highlight a theme or quality (be that "Using Solids" or "Friendship and Community"), show some historical examples of what I mean, and then introduce a quilt design I've made influenced by those elements.

Of course, there is nothing stopping you from using your own color palette and stash fabrics; the very nature of Thirties quilts means their designs can adapt to what's accessible to the maker, opening each design up to countless creative possibilities.

HISTORICAL TECHNIQUE NO. 1

Using Solids

The use of new dye colors to produce solid fabrics is one of the defining characteristics in this period. Historians often refer to "That Green" or "That Pink", as that is how they will be able to place the quilt in this time period. When you look back at how the dyes and colors changed you can see why they were seen as so different and fresh from what had gone before.

Up until the 1920s, the fabrics and colors used in quiltmaking were similar to those used in the late 1800s—heavy dark colors, with only unbleached muslin / calico to break them up. Despite synthetic dyes becoming more widely available, offering more variety of colors, quiltmakers wanted to emulate the quilts of an earlier period, and so continued to use fabrics and colors that were characteristic of that time.

Opposite:
Appliqué quilt from the collection of Marion Drake; quilt size 86in (218.5cm) wide x 104in (264.25cm) tall.

The machine-appliquéd blocks are hand embroidered, as are the stems. The blocks are put together using a version of Quilt-As-You-Go. This quilt has no lining or batting / wadding but is fully finished; so it's more like a finished top than a coverlet.

However, a change came about because of the First World War. Before the war, Germany was the world leader in the production of synthetic dyes, which were not only cheaper and more stable than natural colors, but offered a greater variety of shades too. With England blockading Germany, from whom the US was originally importing dyes, there was a "dye famine". Initially, the low availability of dyes led to fabric designs having a lot of white areas and pale colors, to cut down on the amount of dye needed. Then, American dye companies began developing their own dye recipes, to mitigate the shortage,[1] and new, seemingly novel colors continued to be produced even after the end of the war. Makers were being spoiled with vivid pinks, periwinkle blues, and seafoam greens; warm yellows and greens, lavender, and rose pink all added to the newness and modernity.

The designers of the time made ample use of and popularized these new solids in their latest pieced and appliquéd quilt designs, often only using them in their floral appliqué designs and kits. Renowned quilt designer Anne Orr used solids extensively in her cross-stitch-style pieced quilts.

As with many quilts sewn, these solids crept into makers' scrap quilts over time and this expands our understanding of Depression-era quilts from the 1930s. Kits from the 1930s did include pre-cut fabrics, but many quilt makers added the new solids in with prints they already had.

[1] Madelyn Shaw, "The 'new vogue for black and white' during World War I dye shortages", National Museum of American History, Smithsonian website, link: <https://americanhistory.si.edu/blog/new-vogue-black-and-white-during-world-war-i-dye-shortages>

* * *

Opposite:
"Swans and Lily Pads" quilt from the collection of Carolyn Forster; quilt size 49in (124.5cm) wide x 63in (160cm) tall.

This unfinished top still has the pattern line markings on it, which were either printed or traced onto the background fabric. The swans, flowers, and lily pads are appliquéd by hand; the embroidery stitches in black thread are holding the pieces in place. The blocks are machine-pieced together.

Right:
"Fritallaries" quilt from the collection of Carolyn Forster; quilt size 70½in (179cm) wide x 88in (223.5cm) tall.

The quilt is almost completely made up of solids except for a single printed-fabric flowerhead that changes in each block. It features very fine hand quilting, and there is cotton batting / wadding on the inside.

Ric-Rac Baskets Quilt

DESIGNED & MADE BY CAROLYN FORSTER; MACHINE-QUILTED BY TRUDI WOOD

BACKGROUND

A basket block is pretty much a classic in the patchwork world, and there are so many variations on this popular pattern. My version here is based on a quilt of the period that I saw on the internet (the way that phrase just rolls out of the keyboard nowadays!)—a far cry from when I started sewing, when if it wasn't printed in my Ruby Short McKim book it did not exist!

The version I saw appealed to me because of the ric-rac handles, which is such a fun addition to the quilt. This traditional woven trim, produced from the mid-1800s and replacing the original crocheted zigzag braid, was used mainly in dressmaking, and was often embroidered in place with decorative stitches. Like many things, over time, the makers became more inventive with how they attached and eventually used their ric-rac—from stitching it on as a lace to positioning and stitching it to the work to look like little birds and flowers.

Ric-rac trimming can be found on other vintage quilts, often part of flower designs. I can see where the idea for ric-rac flowers might have come from: Baltimore appliqué quilts from the mid-1800s were an elaborate form of the album quilt—quilts with blocks that had light-colored patches which were then inscribed with the names of the individuals who made the quilt. Baltimore quilts were often sewn for Christian religious leaders in the Baltimore area (hence the name) when they were moving to new churches or across the USA, or retiring. Album quilts can also be comprised of less fancy blocks and include piecing, but the Baltimore quilts were often very elaborate: their appliqué work may have featured buildings and monuments from the city, and the fabrics for the floral appliqué blocks themselves were often ruched and textured to create 3D effects. Ric-rac seemed like the next step, creating a nice texture but with less work.

The setting of the basket blocks makes nice use of the popular solids of the 1930s. It is easy to add some white or cream when designs need spaces for the eye to rest, but having some color here adds richness to the quilt. Pick the solids which work best with your print fabric. You could just pick one if you have a favorite, but this design is good for when you can't decide—I've used two, for instance. The solid fabrics complement the ric-rac basket handles, which are solid colors themselves; the trims are stitched down with embroidery stitches, and provide a nice counterbalance for the baskets within the solid squares.

Ric-Rac Basket Quilt design—print fabrics for the checkerboard setting corners are shown in peach.

MEASUREMENTS

Quilt size:
68½in (174cm) square

Basket block finished size:
12in (30.5cm) square,
and 17in (43.45cm) when on-point

REQUIREMENTS

Basket blocks:
White / cream background
60in (1.55m) x WOF

Print
Sixteen different prints, one Fat Quarter of each

OR

Eight different prints, one Fat Quarter of each

Ric-rac
Per basket, you'll need a 15in (38cm) length of ¾in (2cm) wide ric-rac, in one or more colors—I used black, purple, and bright green

Embroidery
Cotton perle no. 12 in at least two different colors—I used black, purple, and bright green (to mirror the color of the ric-rac)

OR

Stranded embroidery cotton floss in at least four different colors, depending on your ric-rac color choice

Size 6 Embroidery needle

Checkerboard setting corners:
Print
70in (177.75cm) x WOF

Plain Blue
28¾in (73cm) x WOF

Plain Purple
41¼in (104.75cm)

Batting / wadding:
78in (200cm) square

Backing:
156in (400cm) x WOF

Binding:
17½in (45cm) x WOF

Everything else:
Trimming template (see page 187)

Ric-rac placement template (see page 187)

FABRIC CUTTING

Basket blocks:
Background
- Cut three 10⅞in (27.75cm) x WOF strips. Sub-cut into eight 10⅞in (27.75cm) squares, then cut diagonally into sixteen HSTs.
- Cut two 6⅞in (17.5cm) x WOF strips. Sub-cut into eight 6⅞in (17.5cm) squares. Cut diagonally into sixteen HSTs.
- Cut two 6½in (16.5cm) x WOF strips. Sub-cut into thirty-two 6½x 2½in (16.5 x 6.5cm) rectangles.

Print
Cut the following from each printed fabric –
- One 10⅞in (27.75cm) square. Sub-cut into two HSTs—if you are using sixteen different fabrics discard one; if you are using eight prints, keep all HSTs. Use the trimming template on page 187 to draw a line across one corner of the fabric, and trim off with scissors.
- One 2⅞in (7.25cm) square. Sub-cut into two HSTs.

Note: If you are cutting two baskets from one print then you will need both large triangles and to cut a second small square to then sub-cut into HSTs.

Checkerboard setting corners:
Print
For Blue corners –
- Cut ten 2⅝in (6.75cm) x WOF strips. Sub-cut into one hundred and twenty-eight 2⅝in (6.75cm) squares.

For Purple corners –
- Cut five 2⅝in (6.75cm) x WOF strips. Sub-cut into sixty-four 2⅝in (6.75cm) squares.
- Cut five 3in (7.75cm) x WOF strips. Sub-cut into sixty-four 3in (7.75cm) squares, then cut these across the diagonal to make 128 HSTs.

Plain Blue
- Cut five 2⅝in (6.75cm) x WOF strips. Sub-cut into sixty-four 2 5/8in (6.75cm) squares.
- Cut five 3in (7.75cm) x WOF strips. Sub-cut into sixty-four 3in (7.75cm) squares, then sub-cut diagonally into 128 HSTs.

Plain Purple
- Cut fifteen 2⅝in (6.75cm). Sub-cut into one hundred and twenty-eight 2⅝in (6.75cm) squares.

Backing:
Cut into two equal lengths. Trim off the selvages / selvedges and stitch the two lengths together along the longest edges. Press the SA open.

Binding:
Cut seven 2½in (6.5cm) x WOF strips. Join the short ends with a bias join to make a continuous length (see page 179). Trim the SA to ¼in (5mm) and press open. Fold in half along the length, WS together, and press.

METHOD

Basket blocks

Step One Using the ric-rac positioning template on page 187, trace the curved placement line for the ric-rac onto the RS of a large background HST. Pin the ric-rac over the line, covering it, and allowing its ends to cross over the SA.

Step Two Using cotton perle no. 12 (or three strands of stranded cotton) in your first shade, secure the ric-rac in place with herringbone stitch. This effectively couches down the ric-rac. Place the stitches into the "dips" of the ric-rac, as shown in the photo opposite. Using a second shade, finish the embroidery work by stitching a French knot over the center of each ric-rac "point".

Step Three Along the bias edge, stitch a large printed-fabric HST with a trimmed-off corner to the large background triangle with the ric-rac, RS together. Press the SAs toward the printed-fabric HST.

Step Four Stitch the small printed-fabric triangles (they should be the same print as the large printed-fabric triangle) to the short ends of two of the background rectangles—one triangle to a short end of the first rectangle, and one triangle to the opposite short end of the second rectangle. Note, there will be an overhang at the triangle points (**A**)—do not trim these off. Press the SAs toward the triangles.

Step Five Stitch the rectangle-triangle units either side of the basket triangle unit , as shown in **B**. Press the SAs toward the rectangles.

Step Six Stitch the smaller background HST to the base of the basket (**C**). Press the SAs toward the smaller background HST.

Step Seven Repeat Steps 1–6 to make 16 basket blocks in total. If you need guidance on colors to use, please refer to this quilt's diagram on page 38.

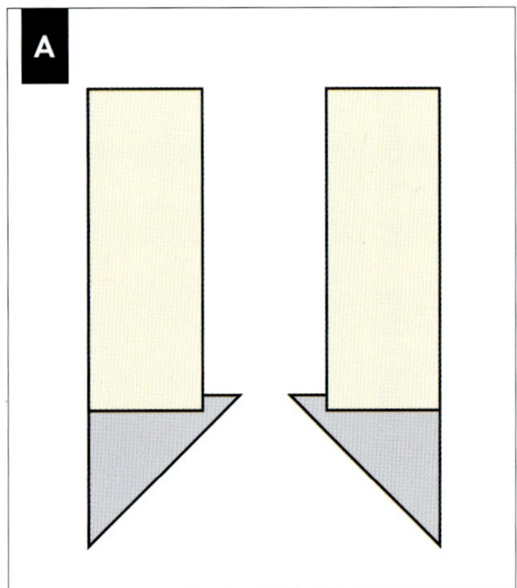

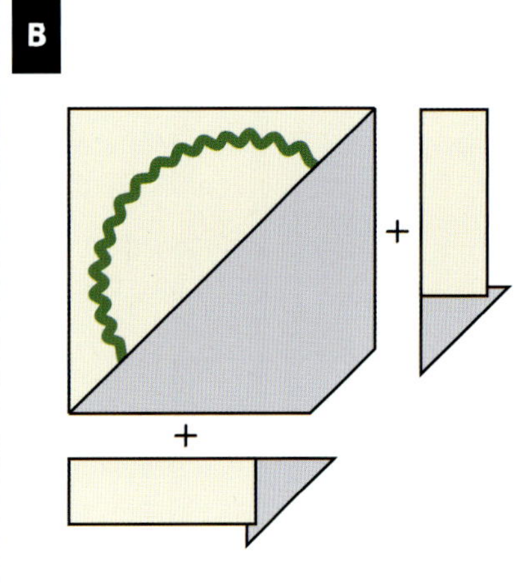

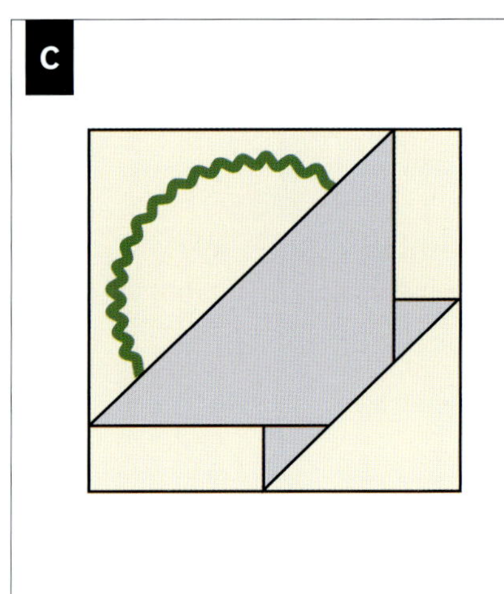

Checkerboard setting corners

Step Eight If you haven't already, divide the setting-corner fabrics into two piles—one for the Blue corners and one for the Purple corners. Note that the Blue corners will have the printed squares at their right-angle, whereas as the Purple corners will have solid purple squares at their right-angle.

Step Nine Start with the Purple corners. You will need 32 finished corner units, four for each corner of eight basket blocks. Lay out the squares and triangles as per the construction diagram below (**D**). Note the solid purple square at the right-angled corner. Stitch the shapes in each row together first, RS facing. Press the SAs in alternating directions. Then, sew the rows RS together (**D**). Press the SAs open this time.

Step Ten Repeat Step 9 with the Blue corners (**E**). Again, you will need 32 finished corner units, four for each corner of eight basket blocks. Note the printed square at the right-angled corner.

Step Eleven To sew the corners to the basket blocks, you'll need to prepare the basket blocks and corners first. Mark the halfway points on the sides of the basket blocks that are closest to the ric-rac handle by folding each block in half along these edges, finger-pressing to crease then unfolding. You will not need to finger-press the other two edges, as you can use the seams halfway along the diagonals as your center marks.

Step Twelve Before stitching, decide which color corner units to "frame" around each basket block. For this quilt layout I used one colorway per basket block.

Step Thirteen Take one basket block in the blue colorway. Place one of its Blue corner units along one side of the basket block, lining up the mid-points, then pin RS together. Stitch from end to end, raw edge to raw edge. Press the SA open. Sew another Blue corner unit in the same way on the opposite side of the basket block (**F**).

Step Fourteen Sew the two other Blue corner units to the remaining sides of the basket block in the same way.

Step Fifteen Repeat Steps 13 and 14 to make eight basket blocks in total with Blue corners.

Step Sixteen Using the Purple corners, repeat Steps 13 and 14 to make eight basket blocks in total.

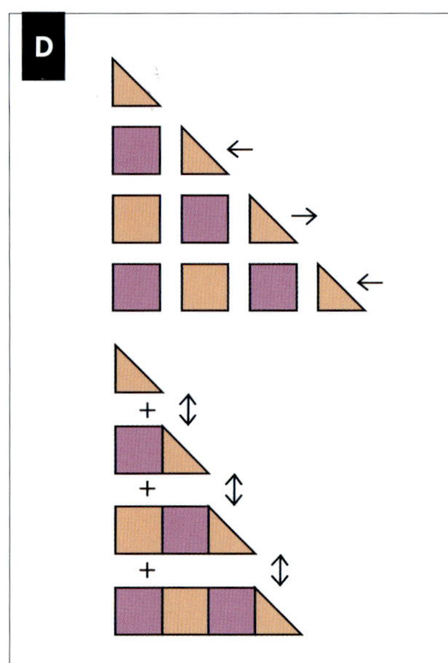

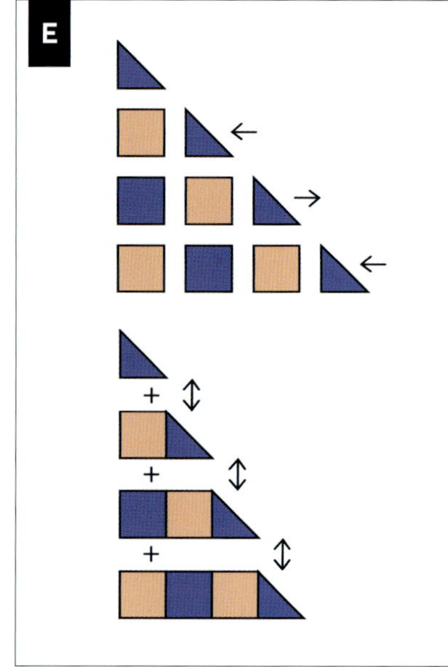

Assembly and finishing

Step Seventeen Lay the basket blocks out in four rows of four blocks, alternating the colors of the checkerboard corners. Stitch the blocks together in rows, RS facing and pinning at seam junctions that might not knit neatly together. Press the SAs open.

Step Eighteen Now sew the rows together, again pinning at seam junctions. Press the SAs open.

Step Nineteen Prepare your quilt layers: place the backing RS down, center the batting / wadding over the top then center the quilt top over these, RS up. Baste / tack the layers together using your chosen method (see pages 162–165), ready to quilt.

Step Twenty Quilt your quilt sandwich as desired. I used the Baptist Fan design (see pages 168 and 169 for more information about the design, see page 189 for the fan template) and quilted by machine, but you could hand-quilt instead. Take a look at the quilting section of this book for other ideas (see pages 166–177).

Step Twenty-one Once quilted, remove the basting / tacking stitches then trim the edges and square up. Bind the quilt with your chosen method (see pages 180–183), then add a label to finish (see page 185).

HISTORICAL TECHNIQUE NO. 2

Fine Hand Quilting

From the time of the first European settlers in America, "homesteading"—i.e. being self-sufficient, from doing small-scale farming and food preservation to craft work—had been a way of life and survival for women.

For a long time, needlework served mainly a practical purpose, and was used for stitching clothing or household linens, or to mend. Until the advent of the sewing machine and other labor-saving devices, much sewing was of a utilitarian nature. That wasn't to say makers weren't skilled—far from it. Rather, they lacked the time and access to materials. Quilts allowed for some decorative outlet, and we can see wonderful examples of fine hand quilting on preserved quilts, even if they were made from scraps and then the layers simply hand-tied.

The hand quilting designs during the Thirties were really not very different from those that had gone before. Fine hand quilting seemed to be reserved for quilts designed to be displayed, rather than quilts for regular use in the home, as the elaborate and intricate designs would have required a great deal of time and effort to create.

When quilt kits and patterns were becoming popular, it was feared that this production-line approach would rid quiltmaking its technical art and skills (see Carrie Hall's writing at the time of the publication of her book with Rose Kretsinger, *The Romance of the Patchwork Quilt in America*). In fact, it likely proved to be the contrary. The kits encouraged more people to get quilting, and they would have included those who had few sewing skills. The kits gave makers a standard to aspire to. Furthermore, with local county-fair quilt competitions, and then subsequently the Sears competition at the Chicago World's Fair, there were more opportunities to show others your achievements, and be rewarded for them, whether that be with money or a rosette.

Opposite, top:
"French Bouquet" (AKA "Old Time Bouquet") quilt from the collection of Marion Drake; quilt size 91½in (232.5cm) wide x 99in (251.5cm) tall.

This pattern appeared in the 1930s, designed by Florence La Ganke under the pen name of Nancy Page (by which it is better known), a and it was often sold within a kit. As well as offering wonderful designs to show off one's appliqué skills, there was lots of space to show off the maker's hand quilting.

Opposite, bottom:
This is a close-up of the border on the "Cottage Tulips" quilt (as seen on page 55), which is based on the "Cottage Tulips" pattern that appeared in the Kansas City Star newspaper in 1931. The maker has emphasized the floral nature of the quilt by hand-quilting "scrolls" of flowers. The pattern itself is intricate to piece, and the maker's skill is highlighted by the outline quilting around her perfect piecing.

Above:
"French Baskets" quilt by Alzona Maria (Conrad) Green; New York; 1932; 77in (195.5cm) wide x 91in (231cm) tall; AM&G: 1997, no. 122.

Alzona Maria Green (1853–1947) created the quilt top from a pattern by Marie Webster. Alzona signed and dated the quilt, and you can see her text, embroidered with blue thread, in the bottom-left corner. According to the donors, Green sent the quilt top to Iowa, where it was then quilted by members of an Amish church. The details shows the fine hand-quilting stitches, including a feather wreath that is repeated across the quilt top.

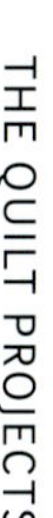

Scrap Basket Quilt

DESIGNED, MADE AND HAND-QUILTED BY CAROLYN FORSTER

BACKGROUND

As much as we admire the tiny stitches and the designs in vintage quilts, we might not aspire to that level or wish to take that much time over hand quilting. But it is nice to say we have tried. This quilt block gives us a little taster of hand stitching and that lovely scrunchy look (achieved after washing a hand-stitched quilt) that only fine hand quilting offers.

First the patches are outline quilted (sometimes known as "echo quilting") by following the seam lines, and then the crisp white background has a quilt pattern of a trailing vine with leaves (see the detail on page 51). The motif itself is inspired by the quilting in the sashing of a simple nine-patch design from an issue of the *Kansas City Star* from 1932.

The quilt sample opposite has been washed, and you can see that it now has that cozy vintage feel we associate with the old quilts we have admired within these pages.

If hand quilting a whole quilt is something you feel is out of reach, just do one block and turn it into a pillow cover—you'll then have trod a little in those past quilters' footsteps!

It is a scrappy quilt, so very little of each fabric is needed, making this project a great stash buster. To create some harmony in an otherwise scrappy design, I've kept the baskets in one color.

Scrap Basket Quilt design.

MEASUREMENTS

Quilt size:
64½in (163.75cm) square

Block size, finished:
12in (30.5cm) square

Block size with frame, finished:
16in (40.75cm) square

REQUIREMENTS

Blocks:

Red "basket" prints
Sixteen different red prints, one Fat Eighth (11 x 9in / 28 x 23cm) of each—*note this amount allows for a different basket color for each block; however, if you want to repeat a fabric in another basket, you'll need only eight prints in total*

Scrap "flowers"
At least five 3⅞in (10cm) x WOF strips

Cream background
61½in (156.25cm) x WOF of muslin / calico

Frames:
Sixteen different fabrics, one 5in (12.75cm) x WOF strip of each

Batting / wadding:
74in (188cm) square

Backing:
148in (376cm) x WOF

Binding:
17½in (45cm) x WOF

Notions:
28wt cotton thread, for hand quilting

Size 10 Betweens or Embroidery needle, for hand quilting

Everything else:
Quilting design templates (see page 188)

FABRIC CUTTING

Blocks:

Red "basket" prints
Cut the following from each printed fabric –

- Cut one 6⅞in (17.5cm) square. Sub-cut into two HSTs—*note you will only need one of these if you have sixteen different fabrics.*
- Cut one 3⅞in (10cm) square. Sub-cut into two HST—*note if you are using only eight fabrics, cut two squares, then sub-cut each into HSTs.*

Scrap "flowers"
Cut the following from each fabric –

- Sub-cut the five strips into forty-eight 3⅞in (10cm) squares—*leave these squares as is, since we will be using a sew-then-cut method later to make HST units.*

Cream background

- Cut seven 3⅞in (10cm) x WOF strips. Sub-cut five strips into forty-eight 3⅞in (10cm) squares. *Leave these squares as is, since we'll be using a sew-then-cut method later to make HST units.* Cut the remaining two strips into sixteen 3⅞in (10cm) squares. Sub-cut these into thirty-two HSTs.
- Cut three 6½in (16.5cm) x WOF strips. Sub-cut these into thirty-two 3½ x 6½in (9 x 16.5cm) rectangles.
- Cut two strips 6⅞in (17.5cm) x WOF. Sub-cut these into eight 6⅞in (17.5cm) squares, then sub-cut the squares into sixteens HSTs.

Frames:
Cut the following from each printed fabric –

- Cut two 2½in (6.5cm) x WOF strips. Sub-cut one into two 2½ x 12½in (6.5 x 31.75cm) strips, then sub-cut the other strip into two 2½ x 16½in (6.5 x 42cm) strips.

Backing:
Cut into two equal lengths. Remove the selvages / selvedges and stitch the two lengths together along the longest edges. Press the SA open.

Binding:
Cut seven 2½in (6.5cm) x WOF strips. Join the short ends with a bias join to make a continuous length (see page 179). Trim the SA to ¼in (5mm) and press open. Fold in half along the length, WS together, and press.

METHOD

Basket blocks

Step One Start by making 96 HST units: draw a diagonal line from one corner to the opposite corner on the WS of a cream square; pin the cream square to a scrap "flower" print square RS together; stitch ¼in (5mm) away from the drawn line, on each side (**A**); cut along the drawn line through all layers to create two HST units. Press the SAs toward the printed fabric.

Step Two Lay out six different colored HST units in three rows as shown in diagram **B**, adding a background HST at the ends of rows 2 and 3. Note that the background triangles sit in the top left-hand corner of the HST units.

Step Three Stitch the units in each row RS together, pressing the SAs open.

Step Four Stitch all three rows together, RS facing. Press the SAs open.

Step Five Stitch a large red-print triangle to the base as shown in diagram **C**: start by folding the red-print triangle in half along its bias edge, finger-pressing a crease then opening it out. Match the crease mark of the red-print triangle and the central seam of the scrappy block then pin and sew RS together. Press the SAs toward the red-print triangle.

Step Six Stitch the small red-print triangles to the short ends of the two background rectangles (**D**). Note the different orientation of the small red-print triangles on each rectangle. Press the SAs toward the triangles. Sew the rectangle-triangle strips to the scrappy-triangles block, RS together—one along the bottom edge, one along the right-hand side. The red-print triangles should sit in the bottom-right corner of the block. Press the SAs toward the rectangles.

Step Seven Finish the block with a large background triangle: start by folding the background triangle in half along its bias edge, finger-pressing a crease then opening it out. Match the crease mark of the large background triangle to the central seam junction on the scrappy block then pin and sew RS together (**E**). Press the SAs toward the large background triangle.

Step Eight Repeat Steps 2–7 to make 16 basket blocks in total.

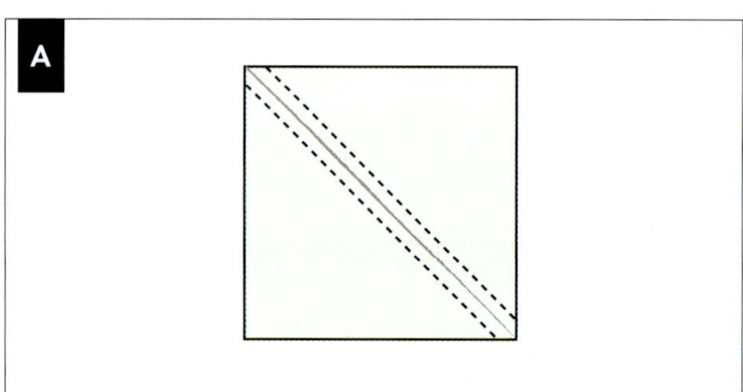

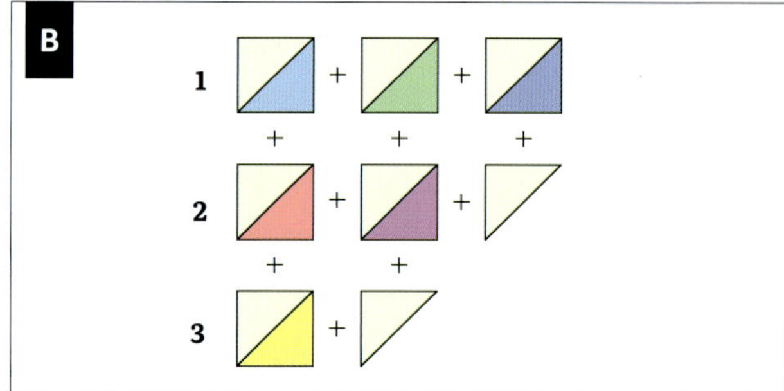

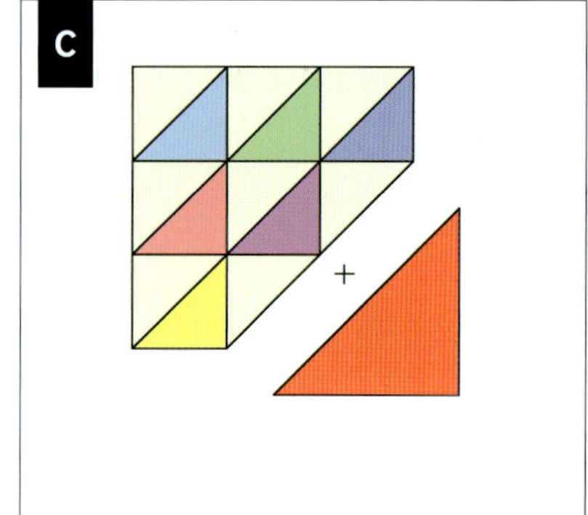

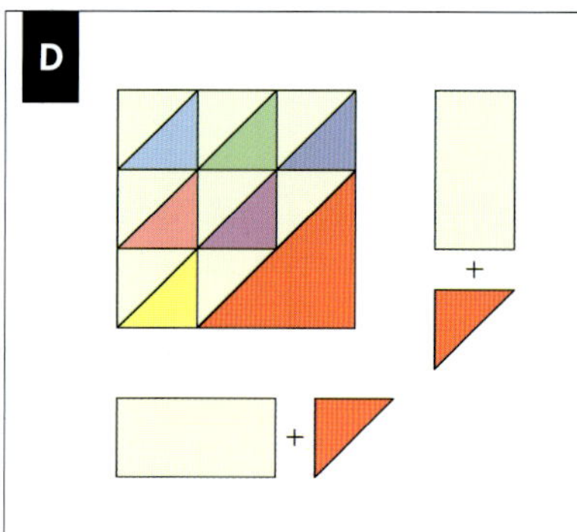

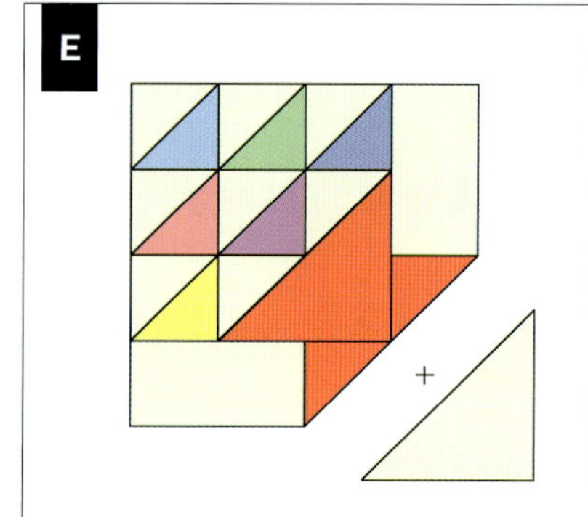

Adding frames

Step Nine Before adding the frames, you need to decide on the arrangement of your quilt top, and the orientation of the basket blocks within each row. This is important, as the positions of the framing strips rotate and alternate within each row. All of my blocks "point" toward the top-left corner. Remember, there are four blocks in each row, and four rows in total.

Step Ten Once you've decided, start by adding the shorter frames first. In rows 1 and 3 they go on the top and bottom edges for the first and third blocks, and on the left- and right-hand sides for the second and fourth blocks (**F**). Do the opposite for the blocks in rows 2 and 4. Press the SAs toward the frames. Then add long frames, again pressing the SAs toward the frames. Frame all sixteen blocks.

Assembly and finishing

Step Eleven Arrange the blocks into four rows of four blocks, making sure that the framing strips alternate long and short.

Step Twelve Sew the blocks in each row together, RS facing. Press the SAs toward the long framing strips.

Step Thirteen Sew the rows RS together. Press the SAs in the same direction, either up or down.

Step Fourteen Prepare your quilt layers: place the backing RS down, center the batting / wadding over the top then center the quilt top over these, RS up. Baste / tack the layers together using your chosen method (see pages 162–165), ready to quilt.

Step Fifteen Next, hand quilting. Referring to diagram **G** and using the templates on page 188, mark your design on each block. The leafy designs are placed within the background rectangles and large background triangle; the rest of the quilting lines consist of stitching within each shape, ¼in (5mm) away from the seams and ¼in (5mm) inside the inner edges. For extra interest, I stitched four lines through the "basket" section of the block, approximately 1in (2.5cm) away from the 90-degree corner of the red-print triangle—two parallel, and two perpendicular; this is optional.

Step Sixteen Once quilted, remove the basting / tacking stitches then trim the edges and square up. Bind the quilt with your chosen method (see pages 180–183), then add a label to finish (see page 185).

HISTORICAL TECHNIQUE NO. 3

Complex Piecing

Kits, the local and national quilt competitions taking place during this time, and the availability of time-saving sewing equipment like sewing machines, meant that women were inspired and able to do more quiltmaking than before. This also meant makers had the skills—or had the opportunity to improve them—to sew more complicated shapes and create intricately pieced quilts.

The quilt opposite, stitched from the Cottage Tulips pattern beside it, is one such quilt. It would have required an enormous amount of skill to get right—and still does today. Curves and set-in seams all demand a level of practice and concentration.

Even the pattern itself indicates this: typical of patterns from this time, there were very few instructions, there was no grain line indicated on the templates, and often there was no information on the seam allowances (occasionally, the written instructions would casually mention some details). From time to time, there would be some fabric color suggestions. This meant most of the time the maker was very much expected to know what to do, and have the confidence to choose a color palette also. This is so different to the amount of information we get or would expect in patterns today.

Examples of templates can be seen on page 21, including two for a mini Double Wedding Ring (DWR) quilt—these have been drawn on sandpaper for durability, and are the finished size plus a seam allowance. The sewist would be expected to stitch the ¼in (5mm) seam allowance by eye in this case.

Patterns that required more skill such as the DWR and the Cottage Tulips opposite would all have been contenders in county fairs due to the way the blocks are pieced.

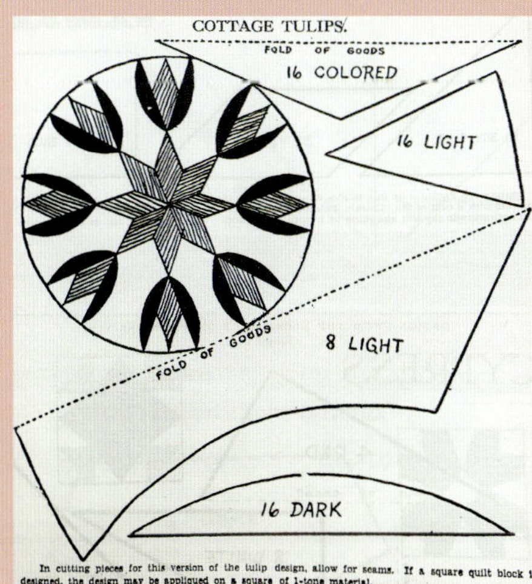

Top left:
The original Cottage Tulip pattern , printed in Rita Weiss's Quilt blocks from the Kansas City Star (American School of Needlework: 1987), which is now out of print.

Top right:
"Cottage Tulips" quilt from the collection of Carolyn Forster; quilt size: 78½in (199.5cm) wide x 94½in (240cm) tall.

This quilt was made from a pattern that appeared in the Kansas City Star newspaper in 1931. The piecing is exceptional, with equally intricate hand quilting that is original in design (see more of the border on page 44). Without doubt the quilt was made by a very experienced person.

Bottom right:
Close up of the 16in (40.75cm) square block from the above quilt. The original pattern printed in the Kansas City Star newspaper doesn't actually give the size of the finished block, but it does note it is for experts and that care should be taken. Interestingly, it also suggests that it could be appliquéd on to a background and that the tulips should suggest colour options. If only pattern writing was as straightforward today!...

Grandmother's Prize Quilt

DESIGNED, HAND-PIECED AND HAND-QUILTED BY CAROLYN FORSTER

BACKGROUND

Although there are only three templates for this block, the hand sewing of them requires some concentration as there are many set-in seams. If set-in or Y-seams is a new technique for you, you'll be well practiced once you've made this quilt! It's techniques like these that would set the best needlewomen above the rest, and worthy of a 1930s prize.

The block for this quilt is based on one from a book by Jan Halgrimson, *Great Scrap Bag Quilts* (Weaver-Finch Publications: Washington, 1980). Although the book is from the early Eighties, the block patterns inside it have an older feel, and the particular style of this quilt is similar in design to the Poinsettia and Double Friendship patterns often attributed to the 1930s newspaper and journal columnist, Laura Wheeler. (Although "Laura Wheeler" was a pseudonym used by "Old Chelsea Station Needlecraft Service"—a fictional name for the actual syndicate of the patterns, Graphic Enterprises Inc., as their mailing address was at Old Chelsea Station in New York—to sell quilt patterns through local newspapers.)†

Upon researching the block in this quilt, I came up against some dead ends. "Grandmother's Prize" is the name given by Halgrimson, and while there are dozens of blocks from the Thirties with the prefix "Grandmother"—reflecting the love of nostalgia during the quilt revival period—I couldn't find the design or the pattern under that name anywhere else. So, we will have to run with Halgrimson's name.

The original design had colored scraps only at the center star in the block; the corner pieces were cream. I soon realized that if I went down that route, I would not be making much of a dent in my scrap pile!

The nice thing about this quilt is that although the individual star-shaped blocks themselves are lovely, when they are joined together a second star motif appears, creating an impressive linked star design. Have fun playing about with fabric placement in this quilt—why not make the center stars in one print and the framed corner stars in another? As usual with patchwork, there are lots of creative possibilities!

I have hand-pieced each quilt block, then sewed them together and finished off the rest of quilt on the sewing machine; however, you can put the whole quilt together on a machine if you'd prefer that. Personally, I like to have the opportunity to indulge in a little bit of slow-stitching, and it makes for a nice on-the-go project, too.

For the quilting, I've opted for a utility big-stitch quilting design composed of cross-hatched lines, worked using a thicker thread for boldness and speed. The spacing is dictated by the block grid itself, and the widest spaced lines are marked initially with a long rotary-cutting ruler and a Hera marker; the lines in between can often be quilted by eye.

I didn't want a border, and regular binding seemed too narrow, so the wide binding on this quilt is a nice compromise between the two. By using the same fabric as the one used for the B/BR pieces, it acts as a unifying frame to the stars.

† *Kiracofe*, The American Quilt, A History of Cloth and Comfort 1750–1950, *pp.* 219 *and* 247

Grandmother's Prize Quilt design.

MEASUREMENTS

Quilt size:
63½in (161.25cm) square

Block size, finished:
12in (30.5cm) square

REQUIREMENTS

Blocks:

Colorful scraps
These can be cut from scraps—they must be at least 3¾in (9.5cm) square

OR

Seventeen strips 3¾in (9.5cm) x WOF

OR

Thirty-four strips 3¾in (9.5cm) x half WOF / 20in (50.75cm)

Blue print star "frames"
44in (111.75cm) x WOF—*note the extra fabric needed under the binding section, if you want the latter to be the same print as the "frames"*

Cream background
79in (200.75cm) x WOF

Batting / wadding:
73in (185.5cm) square

Backing:
146in (371cm) x WOF

Binding:
31½in (80cm) x WOF

Notions:

Hand piecing
Size 10 Sharps needle

28wt cotton thread, in a shade that blends

Fine propelling pencil, to mark the WS of the fabric

Patchwork or appliqué pins

Utility / big-stitch quilting
12wt cotton thread

Size 6 Embroidery or Betweens needle

Everything else:
Templates A, B/BR, and C/CR (see page 186)

FABRIC CUTTING

Blocks:

Note on templates—hand-piecing templates like these do not have a SA: they are the finished size. This means you will be drawing around them on the WS of your fabrics, leaving enough space between them to add a ¼in (5mm) SA all around. You can either add this SA with a fine pencil, or by eye when you cut out the templates.

Colorful scraps
Cut two-hundred pieces using Template A.

Note—each 3¾in (9.5cm) x WOF strip will yield twelve pieces, and each 3¾in (9.5cm) x half WOF strip will yield six pieces.

Blue print star "frames"
Cut twenty-five 1¾in (4.5cm) x WOF strips. Then, from these strips, cut the following (note each strip will yield four Template B shapes and four Template BR shapes):

- One-hundred pieces using Template B.
- One-hundred pieces using Template BR (simply flip Template B).

Cream background
Cut fifteen 5¼in (13.5cm) x WOF strips. Then, from these strips, sub-cut the following (note each strip will yield seven Template C shapes and seven Template CR shapes):

- One-hundred pieces using Template C.
- One-hundred pieces using Template CR (simply flip Template C).

Backing:
Cut into two equal lengths. Remove the selvages / selvedges and stitch the two lengths together along the longest edges. Press the SA open.

Binding:
Cut seven 4½in (11.5cm) x WOF strips. Join the short ends with a bias join to make a continuous length (see page 179). Trim the SA to ¼in (5mm) and press open. Fold in half along the length, WS together, and press.

METHOD

Blocks

Step One Start by stitching two Template A shapes together along one of their shorter edges. As you are sewing by hand, place the patches RS together, match up the start and finish of the seam, and pin along the seam in approx. 1in (2.5cm) increments within the SA (**A**).

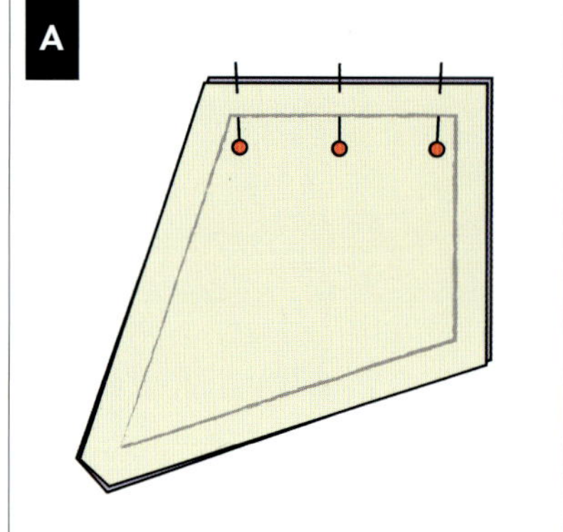

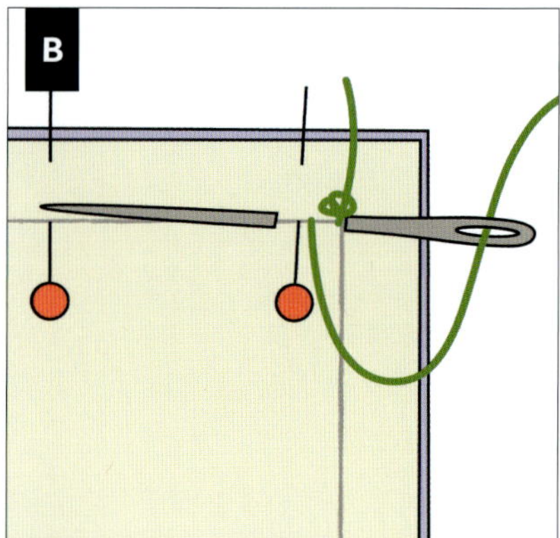

Step Two Thread the sewing needle with the blending 28wt thread then knot the end. Take the needle down at the right-hand corner (left-hand corner, if you're left-handed) then bring the needle up about ⅛in (2mm) along. Make a backstitch by taking the needle down at your starting point (**B**). Then, work small running stitches up to the next pin. Backstitch at the pin (**C**) then remove the pin. Work small running stitches up to the next pin, backstitch at the pin then remove the pin. Continue in this way all the way to the end of the seam. To finish, sew two or three backstitches at the end of the seam line then snip the thread (**D**), leaving a ½in (1.25cm) tail of thread. You will not need to press the SA until the block is complete.

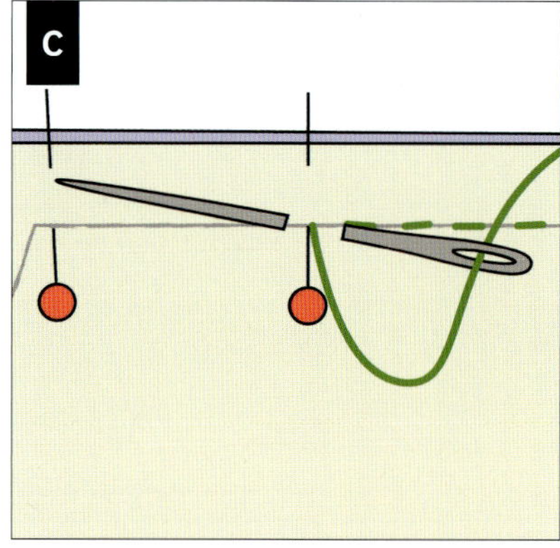

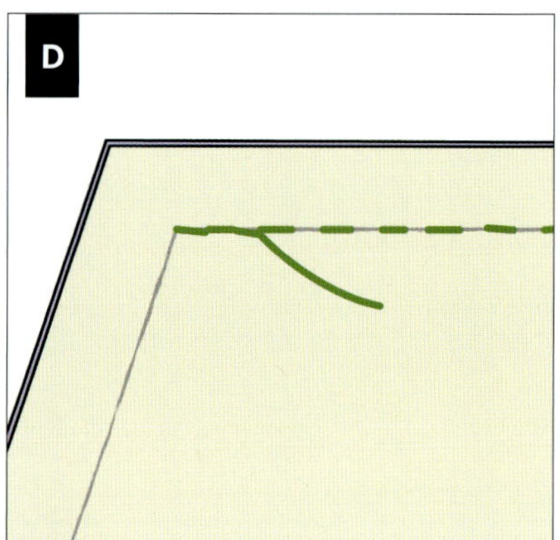

Step Three Repeat Steps 1 and 2 to stitch together another pair of A shapes.

Why backstitch?

I like to backstitch approximately every 1in (2.5cm) along the seam, in addition to small running stitches, as this helps "lock" the seam a little more and prevents the running stitches from being pulled like gathering threads.

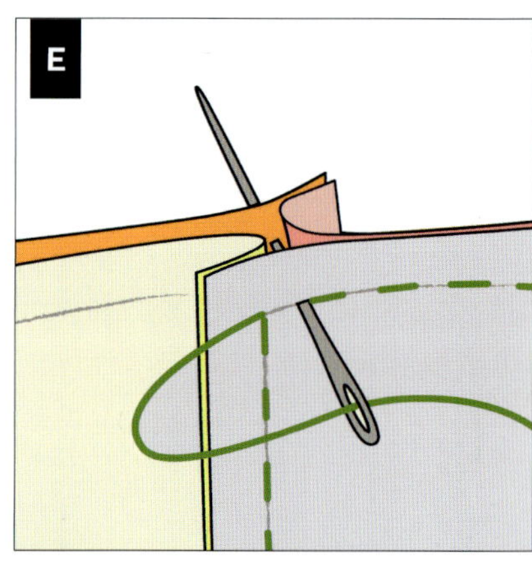

Step Four Now stitch the pairs together. Pin then stitch up to the seam junction in the same way as before. At the end of the seam start making a backstitch, but then take the needle down through both layers diagonally (**E**) and up at the right-hand corner of the patch on the other side of the SA (**F**) to move to the next part of the seam. Start the new section with a backstitch to secure the junction, then sew as before. Finish the seam line with three backstitches. Center complete (**G**). (See also the technique on page 148.)

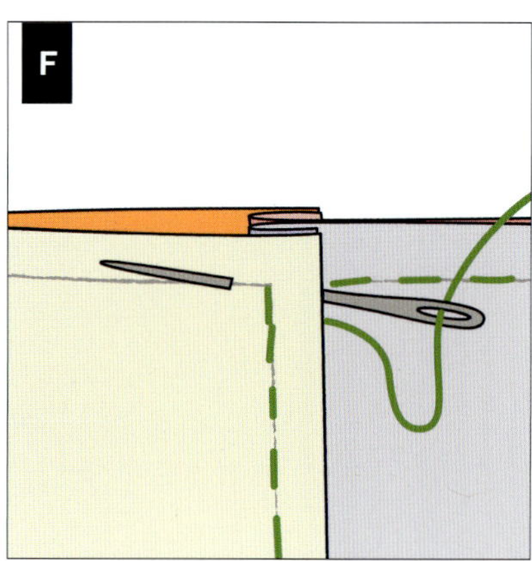

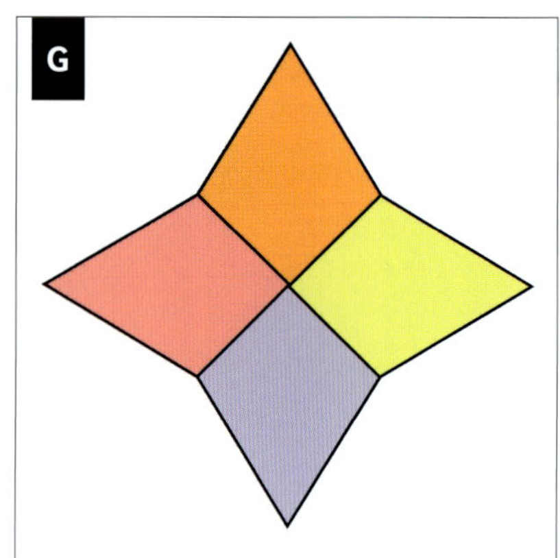

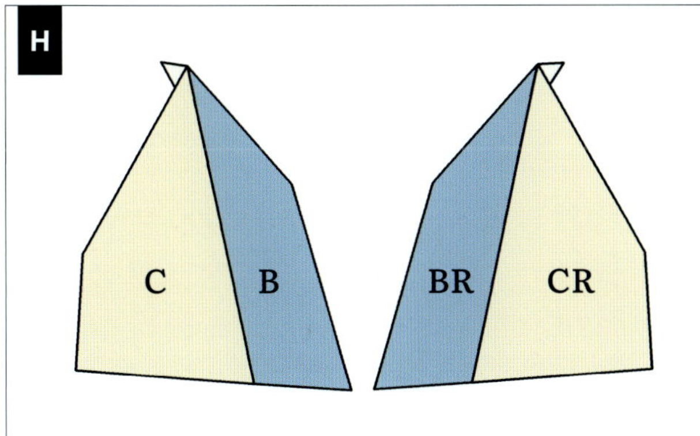

Step Five Using the same process described in Steps 1 and 2, stitch a B shape to a C shape, and a CR shape to a BR shape, joining them along their longest edges (**H**). Make four B/C and four BR/CR units in total.

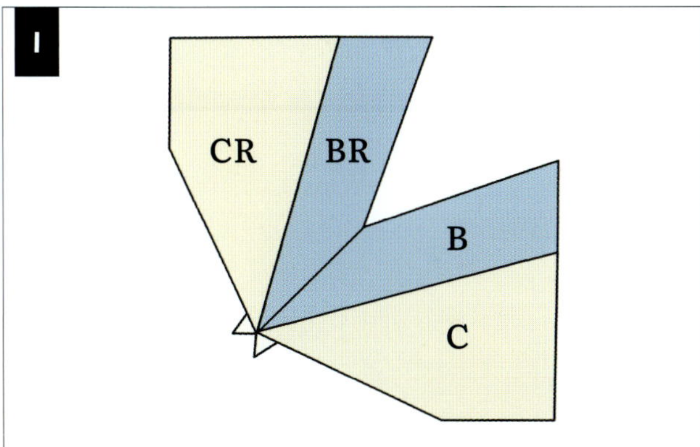

Step Six Join a B/C unit to a BR/CR unit as shown in diagram **I**, following the same process described in Steps 1 and 2. Make four of these in total.

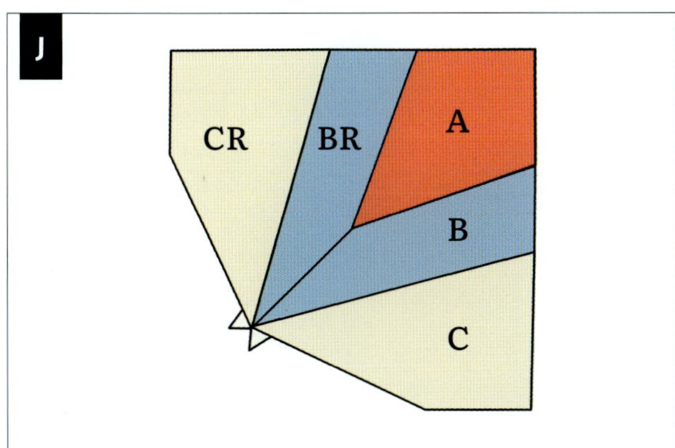

Step Seven Sew (or "set in") a contrasting shape A piece between the B and BR shapes, following the same method detailed in Steps 1–4 (**J**)—see also page 149 where I take you through sewing this Y-seam in detail. Repeat with the other three units. These are the corners.

Step Eight Set two of the corners on opposite sides of the central star from Step 4 (**K**)—see also page 150 for more details. Repeat on the remaining edges of the central star.

Step Nine Now to press the SAs—use diagram **L** to guide you. Start from one corner A piece and press the SA to one side. Repeat all the way round the outer pieces (outer A, B, C, CR, BR) clockwise, pressing in the same direction. Then, press the SAs of the longest edges of the central star in the same direction. Finally, press the shorter edges of the central star in the opposite direction to the outer edges. Pressing in this way ensures the blocks will fit neatly together at the seam junctions in the quilt.

Step Ten Make 25 of these blocks in total. Trim each block evenly to measure 12½in (31.75cm) square.

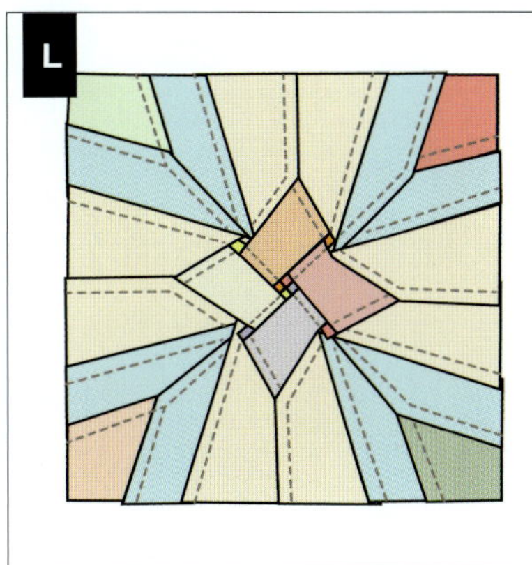

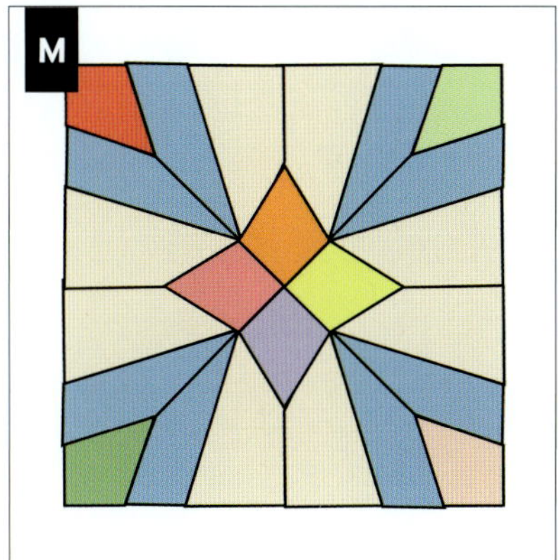

Assembly and finishing

Note: I stitched my blocks together on a sewing machine, but you could hand-sew your own blocks together if you wish.

Step Eleven Arrange the blocks into five rows of five blocks. Stitch the blocks in each row RS together then press the SAs in one direction, alternating the pressing every row.

Step Twelve Now stitch the rows RS together. Press the SAs between rows in one direction.

Step Thirteen Prepare your quilt layers: place the backing RS down, center the batting / wadding over the top then center the quilt top over these, RS up. Baste / tack the layers together using your chosen method (see pages 162–165), ready to quilt.

Step Fourteen Using the diagram you can start to mark the quilting lines. I like to use a Hera marker for this. You can see that they form a grid, which is naturally made by the stars in the quilt. Mark the first lines in one direction at a 45-degree angle (pink lines in **N**), and mark a second set of lines over the top of the first set, again at a 45-degree angle but this time "pointing" in the opposite direction (blue lines in **N**).

Step Fifteen Using the size 6 Betweens or Embroidery needle and 12wt thread, quilt large running stitches over your marked lines. Work the first set of lines first, then stitch the second set of lines over the top in a second layer.

Step Sixteen Once quilted, remove the basting / tacking stitches then trim down the batting / wadding and backing to ¾in (2cm) larger than the patchwork top. Bind the quilt using the wide square-corner binding method—see page 183.

Step Seventeen Add a label to finish—see page 185 for inspiration.

HISTORICAL TECHNIQUE NO. 4

Using White Fabric

Just as they do today, quilters of the past have wanted to make the most of their precious printed fabrics. The easiest and most economical way to do that was to intermingle them with a cheaper fabric, one that would let the prints and overall piecing design (and/or appliqué) shine through.

More expensive fabrics were used primarily for dressmaking; scraps from it were then used for the main patchwork and/or appliqué. The background, borders, cornerstones, and sashing could all be sewn from bleached or unbleached muslin / calico, which was more readily available and could be bought at the general store.

Another advantage to plain, neutral fabrics was that they could show off any hand quilting, thus adding another decorative element to the quilt.

But one of the main appeals of using white fabric during the revival period was the airy, folksy feel it gave to quilts. Unlike the dark, heavy, and almost cluttered look of Victorian quilts (take a look at some examples of crazy patchwork from the Victorian era, and you'll see what I mean!), the whites you see in quilts of the early 20th century exude a lovely, light, fresh simplicity that was becoming popular at the end of the late modern period (c. 1800–1945), which is what makes them so characteristic of quilts during this time period.

When the cost of muslin / calico became prohibitive to some during the Great Depression, as the economic situation worsened, makers had to turn to other sources of white fabric. As we touched on earlier, cotton feedsacks became one of these sources.

Feedsacks could be used as is, turned wrong-side out (so that the printed labeling on the front of the sacks was hidden between the layers of the quilt), or bleached to remove the printed labeling and then and used on the front of the quilt like regular neutrals.

The quilts shown opposite are good examples of letting the fabrics speak for themselves, and being able to see bright clear designs created from the print fabrics.

Top left:
"Tulips" quilt, *from the collection of Carolyn Forster; quilt size 70¾in (179.75cm) wide x 83½in (212cm) tall.*

The quilt has 9in (23cm) square pieced tulip blocks set on point with white fabric as the filling squares and triangles; it is also bound with white fabric.

Top right:
"French Bouquet" (AKA "Old Time Bouquet") quilt *from the collection of Marion Drake; quilt size 91½in (232.5cm) wide x 99in (251.5cm) tall.* *For more details and information, see pages 44–45.*

Bottom right:
"Dresden Plate" quilt *by unknown maker; USA; c. 1930; 71½in (182cm) wide x 90½in (230cm) tall; AM&G: 1979, no. 103.*

This quilt is composed of twenty 16½in (42cm) square blocks, each featuring a scrappy Dresden-plate pattern. Around the edge is a 5in (12.75cm) deep scalloped border that's then bound in green.

Endless Chain Quilt

DESIGNED AND MADE BY CAROLYN FORSTER; MACHINE-QUILTED BY CHRIS FARRANCE

BACKGROUND

This pattern originated in the 1930s through the Laura Wheeler pattern company (appearing in the *The Cincinnati Enquirer* on August 14th, 1933), and became a favorite with quilters as it's great for using up odd scraps.

The design really lets the fabric colors shine, and by using more of the white fabric as a wide border, the colors are emphasized even more.

Traditionally, this quilt is put together in units of four, with all the strip points meeting in the middle—see the bottom-left diagram. The original quilt would have been stitched using the bleached white muslin / calico of the time, or even bleached cotton feedsacks. As noted earlier, the bleaching would have been to get rid of the brand printing on the fabric to make it more acceptable for use on a quilt front.

The Endless Chain is a fun block on its own, and would make a nice sampler mini quilt or placemat. You can either keep the units in the traditional setting or rearrange them to make a star—see the bottom-right diagram. Choose whichever setting appeals, as both will be great and use up all your treasured scraps.

Although this is a scrappy quilt that's great for using up odd pieces left over from other projects, you can take a more planned approached with your fabrics by cutting up newly purchased lengths from bolts or pre-cuts—Jelly Rolls, in particular, are ideal for this.

The odd shaping of the templates make them easy to draw around and cut out, but it does also mean they can be tricky to rotary cut. To cut multiples of the odd shapes with a rotary cutter, first stack up to six layers of scraps on a cutting mat then draw around the template shape on just the top layer. With your rotary cutter and a small ruler (and a Lazy Susan or turntable to help with rotating, if you have one), cut along the drawn lines through all the layers. It's a good idea to write on the wrong side of each fabric shape with a fine pencil to indicate which template was used—especially if it's a reversed piece.

Stripes radiating from the center (traditional setting).

Stripes pointing from outer corners ("star" setting).

Endless Chain Quilt design.

MEASUREMENTS

Quilt size:
76½in (194.5cm) square

Unit size, finished:
6in (15.25cm) square

Block size, finished:
12in (30.5cm) square

REQUIREMENTS

Blocks:
Colorful scraps
Thirty-four pieces, 2½in (6.5cm) x WOF

Cream / neutral
150in (381cm) x WOF

Borders:
59½in (151.25cm) x WOF—*I used the same fabric as the cream / neutral in the blocks*

Backing:
172in (437cm) x WOF

Batting / wadding:
86in (218.5cm) square

Binding:
20in (51cm) x WOF

Everything else:
Fine propelling pencil, to mark the WS of the fabric

Stripe / Stripe R, Center, and Edge / Edge R Templates (see page 190)

FABRIC CUTTING

Blocks:
Note on templates—the SAs (measuring ¼in / 5mm) are included. There are sections of the templates where I think it is best to try to keep the grain line in place. The 90-degree corner/outside edge of the Edge template should be on the grain. On the Center piece, make sure the 90-degree corner is on the grain. The scrappy Stripe pieces do not matter so much as very little of their shape is on the outside edge of the unit.

Colorful scraps
Note—one 2½in (6.5cm) x WOF strip folded in half will yield six shapes, three as the template is printed and three with the template reversed.

- Cut one hundred Stripes using the Stripe Template.
- Cut one hundred Reverse Stripes using the flipped Stripe Template.

Cream / neutral
- Cut sixteen 6½in (16.5cm) x WOF strips. From these, cut one hundred Center pieces using the Center Template. (One 6½in / 16.5cm x WOF strip will yield twelve to fourteen shapes—note that I have worked on the minimum number, so you may have fabric left over depending on how you cut the pieces.)
- Cut seventeen 2⅝in (6.75cm) x WOF strips. From these, cut one hundred Edge pieces and one hundred Edge R pieces using the Edge / Edge R Template. (One 2⅝in / 6.75cm x WOF strip will yield twelve shapes—six as the template is printed and six with the template reversed.)

Borders:
- Cut seven 8½in (21.5cm) x WOF strips. Remove the selvages / selvedges then join the strips into a continuous length by stitching the shorter edges RS together. Press the SAs open.
- Cut two 8½in (21.5cm) x 60½in (153.75cm) strips.
- Cut two 8½in (21.5cm) x 76½in (194.25cm) strips.

Backing:
Cut into two equal lengths. Remove the selvages / selvedges and stitch the two lengths together along the longest edges. Press the SA open.

Binding:
Cut eight 2½in (6.5cm) x WOF strips. Join the short ends with a bias join to make a continuous length (see page 179). Trim the SA to ¼in (5mm) and press open. Fold in half along the length, WS together, and press.

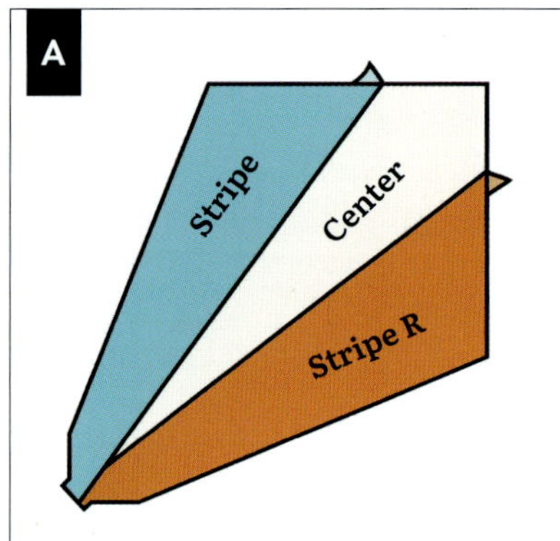

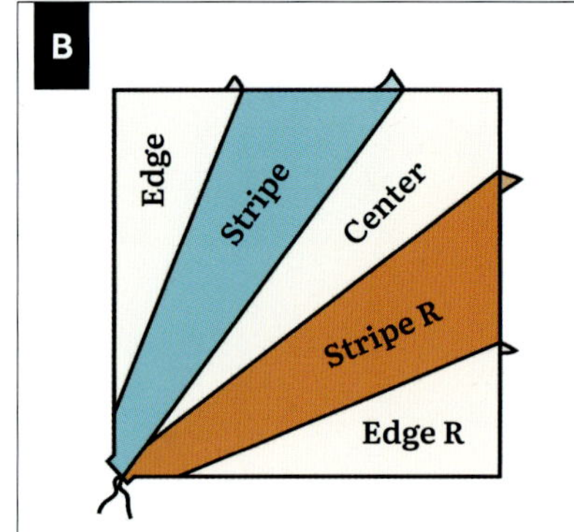

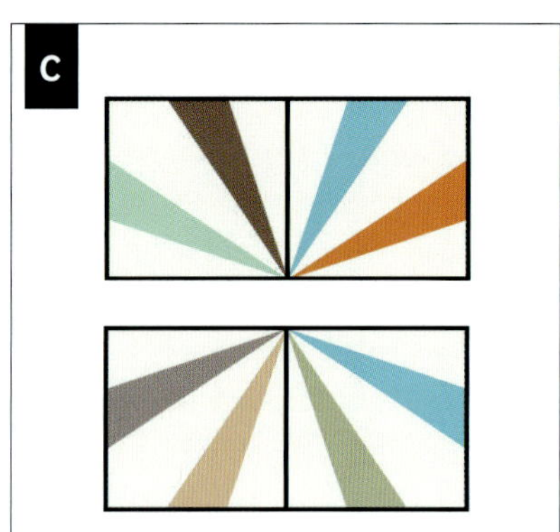

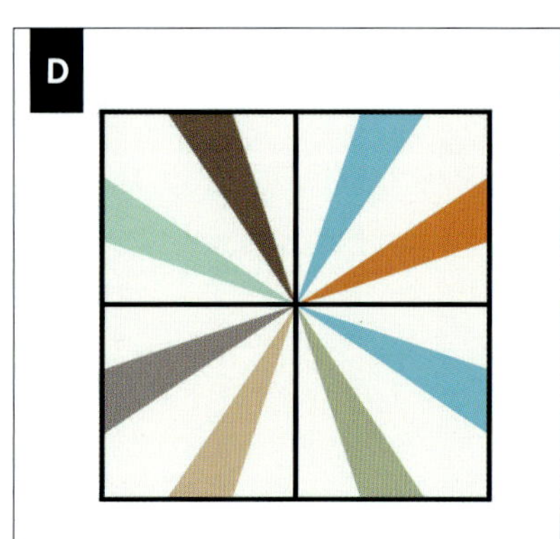

METHOD

Blocks

Step One Start by sewing a Stripe piece and a Stripe R piece to each side of a Center shape, RS together (**A**). Sew one stripe at a time, and press after adding each stripe. Note that the two pieces will be off-set at the top edge. Make sure that the bottom point of the Center shape is ¼in (5mm) from the bottom raw edge where the scraps meet, so the Center shape's point will not be chopped off when you sew the units into a block. Press the SAs of the scrap Stripes away from the Center shape.

Step Two Now sew the Edge and Edge R pieces to the remaining (Stripe) edges of the unit, RS together (**B**). Press the SAs away from the center shape.

Step Three Repeat Steps 1 and 2 to make one hundred units in total.

Step Four Four units sewn together make one block. To sew a block, first stitch the units RS together in pairs, with the scrappy stripes "pointing" toward the center bottom (**C**). Press the SA open; this will help the bulk in the SA sit flatter. (Note: Before sewing, you may wish to pin where the SAs sit on top of each other, to ensure accuracy.)

Step Five Now sew two pairs RS together (**D**). Press the seam open.

Step Six Repeat to sew twenty-five blocks in total.

Assembly and finishing

Step Seven Lay out the blocks into five rows of five blocks, arranging them so that there is a mix and balance of colors across the rows.

Step Eight Stitch the blocks RS together in their rows, pinning at the seam junctions beforehand to ensure accuracy. Press all SAs open.

Step Nine Now sew the rows RS together, again pinning at the seam junctions to nest them neatly. Press the SAs open.

Step Ten Now for the borders (**E**). Sew the two shorter border pieces to the left- and right-hand sides of the quilt, RS together. Press the SAs toward the borders. Sew the remaining longer border pieces to the top and bottom edges of the quilt, RS together, then press the SAs toward the borders.

Step Eleven Prepare your quilt layers: place the backing RS down, center the batting / wadding over the top then center the quilt top over these, RS up. Baste / tack the layers together using your chosen method (see pages 162–165), ready to quilt.

Step Twelve Referring to the quilting ideas on pages 166–169, quilt as desired. The quilt sample was quilted all over with vermicelli machine quilting, but would equally look good with big-stitch quilting (see page 173) or being hand-tied (see pages 176 and 177).

Step Thirteen Once quilted, remove the basting / tacking stitches then trim the edges and square up. Bind the quilt with your chosen method (see pages 180–183), then add a label to finish (see page 185).

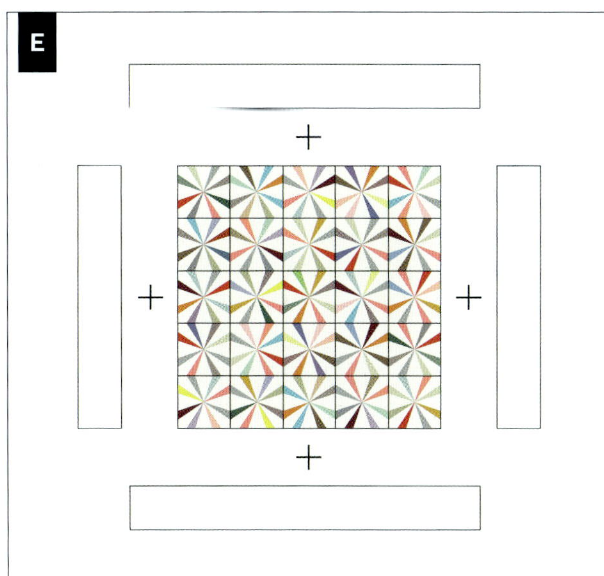

HISTORICAL TECHNIQUE NO. 5

Friendship and Community

Friendship or signature quilts have been popular in the US since the mid-1850s. Family and friends would come together to sew a quilt, each making a block and signing it in ink or thread. The recipient then would have a lasting token from their loved ones to pass down through the generations.

These kinds of quilts were no less popular in the Colonial Revival period: sewing and remembering together (and/or sewing for a cause) engendered a community spirit and companionship that was hard to replicate when stitching solo.

The blocks in friendship or signature quilts are often known as "Album blocks". No specific method is used, so you'll find many block designs going by this name, and they can be made by either piecing or appliquéing. However, the only "requirement" was for the final block to have a large enough solid space on it for the maker to add their signature at the end, and perhaps choosing a block design that is personal to the recipient (particularly with appliqué blocks) to add more meaning.

In the 1930s, when the Depression triggered a growth of migrant and itinerant workers leaving home to find good-paying jobs, friendship quilts were gifted to traveling loved ones; the thought that you could take a quilt with you, reminding you of family and friends while also keeping you physically warm, was not to be overlooked.

Many makers came together to sew quilts, even when the quilt was for personal use, for the sheer enjoyment of stitching with others. "Quilt parties" became popular: if you lived in a rural area, they gave you the opportunity to gather with friends and locals and share in a little gossip; if you had moved to a new town, they presented the chance to chat and socialize with new people. Ironically, many home-making middle-class women felt quite isolated in a city.[1] With labor-saving devices available, these women had more time to fill in a day. The idea of getting together and doing something productive was something to be looked forward to.

Signature quilts are sometimes known as fundraising quilts, as they became a great way to raise money for social and political causes, including the woman's right to vote and promoting temperance.[2] Many women saw quiltmaking as a skill they could use to influence and make a difference, and let their voices be heard. Donors would pay to have their names embroidered on a block; in turn, the quilt makers would raise the vital funds necessary for their cause, and have a finished quilt to promote it further. The donors would benefit from the kudos gained by having their names advertising their support on a quilt.

[1] *Woodard and Greenstein,* Twentieth Century Quilts: 1900–1950, *pp. 8 and 9*

[2] *Woodard and Greenstein,* Twentieth Century Quilts: 1900–1950, *p. 16*

* * *

Opposite:
"Tulip Signature" quilt from the collection of Carolyn Forster; quilt size 78in (198.25cm) wide x 85in (216cm) tall; finished block sizes 15in (38cm).

This is an interesting example of an album quilt, as some of the blocks were cut in half vertically (see the right-hand edge) to accommodate everyone on the front of the quilt.

Above left:
A close up from the "Tulip Signature" quilt opposite. It is fascinating to me to read all the different names embroidered on it, and wonder about the connections of the signatories to each other. If you find quilts like this, and know the area or even family they came from, many people take the time to try to research the connections.

Above right:
"A quilting party in an Alvin, Wisconsin, home" by photographer Russell Lee (1903–1986), May 1937, Farm Security Administration—Office of War Information Photograph Collection (Library of Congress), website link: <https://www.loc.gov/pictures/item/2017763995/>

Above:
Album quilt from the collection of Carolyn Forster; quilt size 78in (198.25cm) wide x 89in (226cm) tall; finished block sizes 15in (38cm).

The block in this quilt is known as "Chimney Sweep" (a Nancy Cabot design, found in the Chicago Tribune *in 1935). I really love the way each person has chosen the fabrics for their respective block; it makes them all very individual.*

Above:
"Friendship Hexagon" quilt, from the collection of Carolyn Forster; quilt size 73in (185.5cm) wide x 92½in (235cm) tall.

The block used here is known as a "Texas Star" (the pattern for which can be found in the Ladies' Art Company publication from 1922), and subsequently as a "Friendship Hexagon" (by Nancy Page in an undated newspaper clipping) then "Hexagon Stars" (also by Nancy Page, this time in Alabama's Birmingham News in 1934).

Friendship Garden Quilt

DESIGNED, HAND-PIECED AND MACHINE-QUILTED BY CAROLYN FORSTER

BACKGROUND

The design for the blocks in this quilt are attributed to the design studio of Laura Wheeler, and first appeared in the *Sioux City Journal* on January 12th, 1940.

This scrappy quilt block is known as Friendship Garden. It's not clear why the name was given by Wheeler's studio—perhaps the makers exchanged fabric scraps to create the blocks? But, as with many quilts given in friendship, there is space in the block design for the makers to sign their names.

Although the block in itself is charming, the lovely thing about its arrangement is that a secondary design appears when multiples of the block are stitched into a quilt: what were once light corners framing a colorful wheel of scraps are now flowers, with the dark fabric of the block corners becoming the circular flower centers.

The center of the block, within the scrappy wheel, has the fabric repeated in the quilt border. This adds some continuity to a scrappy project.

The quilt blocks in the sample opposite and in the instructions are hand-pieced, but once pieced into blocks you could sew them together on the machine along with the borders, if you prefer. Personally, I like to hand-piece some of the quilt and finish with machine stitching: the blocks become lovely slow-stitched projects, and then the assembly and finishing off can be pleasingly fast.

Whether your are hand or machine piecing, remember that the templates for this quilt at the back of the book do not have the seam allowance included; they are the finished size. This means you will be drawing around them on the WS of your fabrics, leaving enough space in between them to add the ¼in (5mm) seam allowance all around by eye (or use one of the alternative methods on page 143 if you are not confident doing this).

To quilt, I've used a utility design consisting of diagonal lines that "point" in one direction.

Gemeine Esche

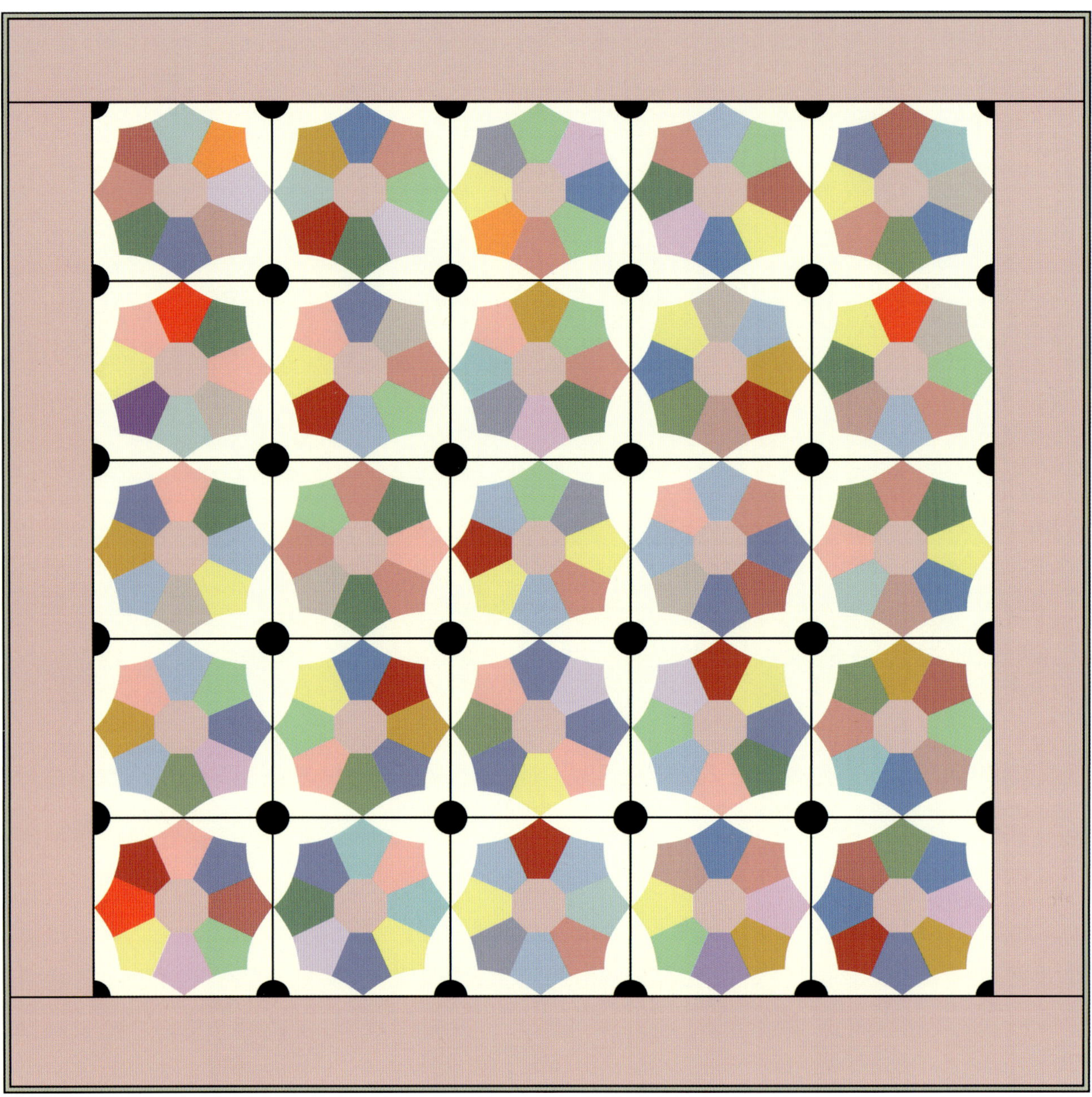

Friendship Garden Quilt design.

MEASUREMENTS

Quilt size:
72½in (184.25cm) square

Block size, finished:
12in (30.5cm) square

REQUIREMENTS

Blocks:

Colorful scraps for the "wheel"
Two hundred 5in (12.75cm) squares

Cream / neutral
56½in (143.5cm) x WOF

Ditsy print centers
12¾in (32.5cm) x WOF

Black prints
5¼in (13.5cm) x WOF each of two black prints (Black Print 1and Black Print 2)

Borders:
45½in (115.5cm) x WOF—*I used the same fabric as the print used for the wheel centers*

Backing:
164in (416.5cm) x WOF

Batting / wadding:
82in (208.25cm) square

Binding:
20in (51cm) x WOF

Notions:
28wt cotton thread for hand piecing, in a shade that blends

Size 10 Sharps needle, for hand piecing

Fine propelling pencil, to mark the WS of the fabric

Patchwork or appliqué pins

Everything else:
Templates A, B, BR, C, and D (see page 191)

FABRIC CUTTING

Blocks:
Note on templates—the SAs (measuring ¼in / 5mm) are NOT included, and will need to be added before cutting out the shapes.

Colorful scraps for the "wheel"
- Cut two hundred shapes using Template A.

Cream / neutral
- Cut two hundred shapes using Template B.
- Cut two hundred shapes using Template BR.

Ditsy print centers
- Cut twenty-five shapes using Template C.

Black prints
- Cut fifty of each print using Template D. You need one hundred black-print D shapes in total.

Borders:
- Cut seven 6½in (16.5cm) x WOF strips. Remove the selvages / selvedges then join the strips into a continuous length by stitching the shorter edges RS together. Press the SAs open.
- Cut two 6½in (16.5cm) x 60½in (153.75cm) strips.
- Cut two 6½in (16.5cm) x 72½in (184.25cm) strips.

Backing:
Cut into two equal lengths. Remove the selvages / selvedges and stitch the two lengths together along the longest edges. Press the SA open.

Binding:
Cut eight 2½in (6.5cm) x WOF strips. Join the short ends with a bias join to make a continuous length (see page 179). Trim the SA to ¼in (5mm) and press open. Fold in half along the length, WS together, and press.

METHOD

Blocks

WHEEL AND CENTER

Step One Start by stitching two A shapes RS together along one long edge: place the patches so RS are facing, matching up the start and finish of the seam and the drawn lines, then pin along the seam. The pins should be perpendicular to the edges of the patches, and approx. 1in (2.5cm) apart (**A**).

Step Two Thread up the Sharps needle, knot the end then bring the needle up at the very start of the drawn line. Work a small backstitch then sew small running stitches up the next pin. Remove the pin, make a backstitch, then sew small running stitches up to the next pin; repeat along the rest of the seam line. To finish, sew two or three backstitches then snip the thread, leaving a tail approx. ½in (1.25cm) long (**B**). There's no need to press the SAs at this stage. See also page 146 for more details on hand-sewing a seam.

Step Three Repeat Steps 1 and 2 to make four scrap-fabric pairs in total.

Step Four Now join stitch the pairs into two sets of four, then sew the two sections into a ring (**C**).

Step Five Now set the C shape into the center of the ring, RS together: working from the wrong side of the block (this will make it easier to handle and stitch), secure the C shape all around with the sharp tips of the pins "pointing" toward it (**D**). If you're concerned about distortion, place pins where the C shape touches the seam junctions of the A shapes.

Step Six Sew the center piece in place in the same way as described in Step 2. When you meet a seam junction, as you work the last backstitch of the seam, slide the thread through to the back, behind the SA, then come up on the other side of the SA on the next piece—you do not sew down the SA (**E**). Continue sewing as before, starting with another backstitch.

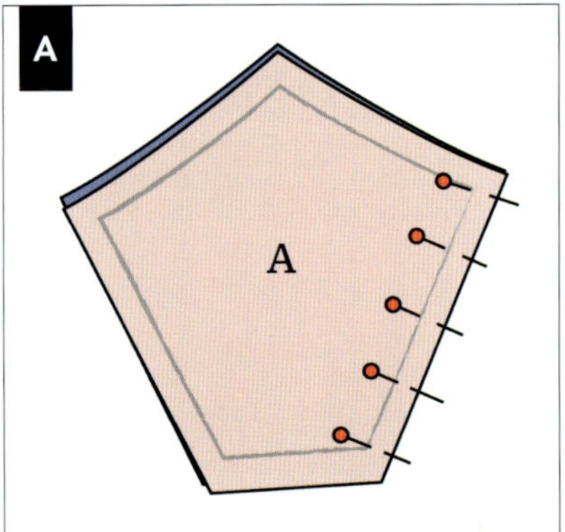

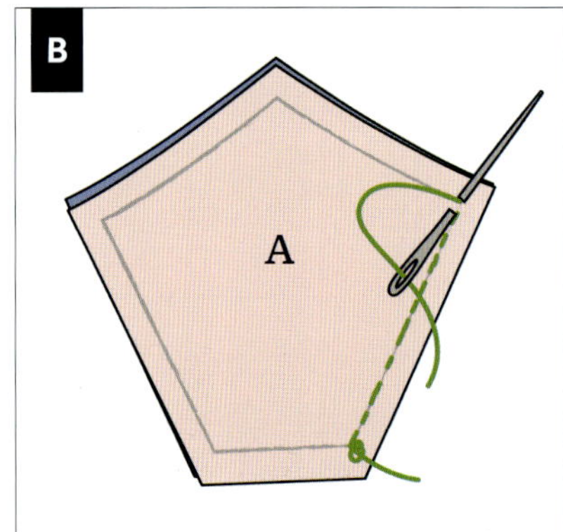

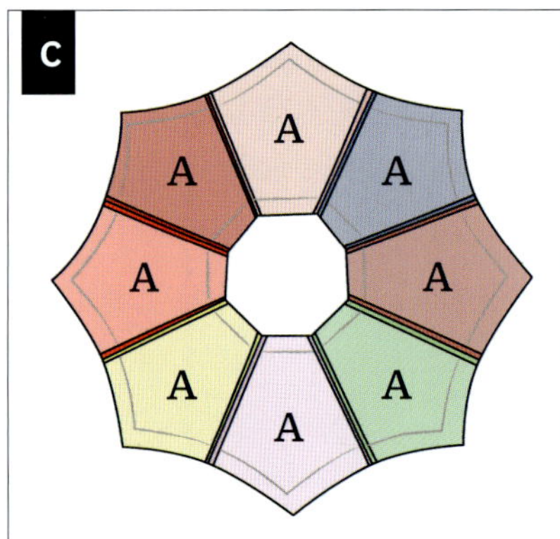

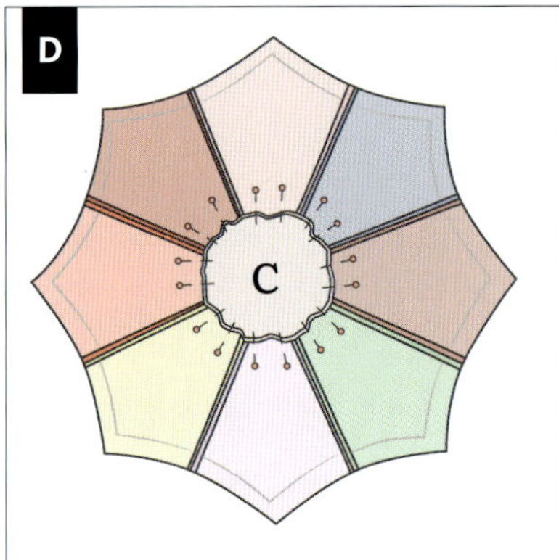

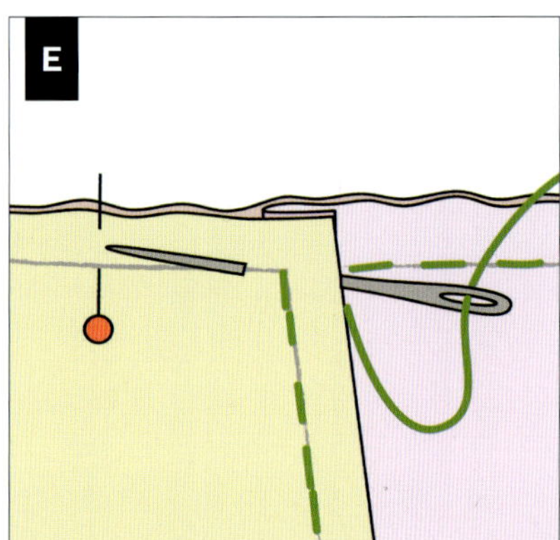

CORNER "FRAMES"

Step Seven Take a B and a BR shape and stitch them RS together along the short straight edge, as per Steps 1 and 2 opposite (**F**). Make four pairs in total.

Step Eight Stitch a D shape into each corner of the four pairs—two with Black Print 1 D shape and two with Black Print 2 D shape. (Note: I find it easier to sew the D shapes at this stage, as it easier to handle a small amount of fabric than the whole block.) Since the corner is quite tight, you may find it useful to snip into the B/BR units before sewing, to help the D shapes fit into the space and to make it easier to stitch in place too (**G**).

Step Nine Position these units around the central A/C wheel, the RS of the B/BR/D corners facing the A/C wheel and with the same-colored D shape are in diagonally opposite corners. Use the balance marks on the B/BR units to match up with the center seam on each curve. Pin in place, with the pins perpendicular to the curve, then sew as per Step 2 and Step 6 (**H**).

Step Ten Once the block is sewn, press the seams, referring to the diagram below (**I**) for direction.

Step Eleven Repeat Steps 1–10 to make 25 blocks in total. Measure and trim the blocks centrally to 12½in (31.75cm) square, if necessary.

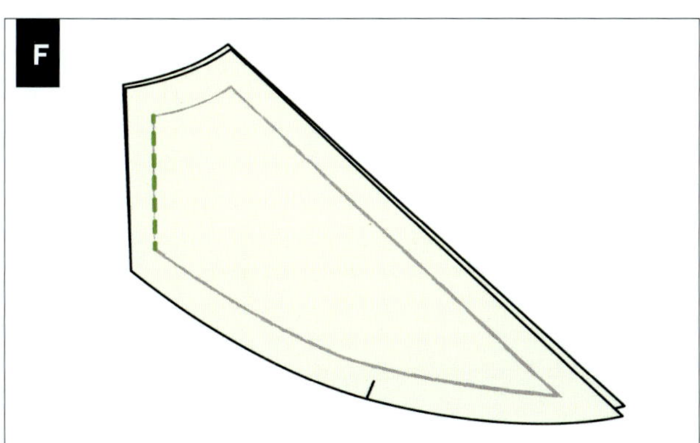

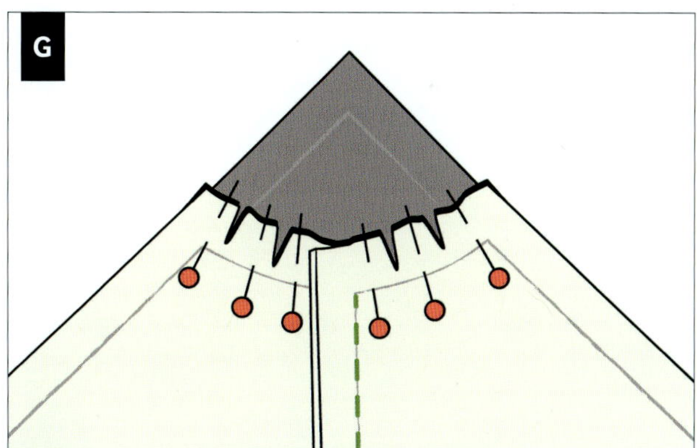

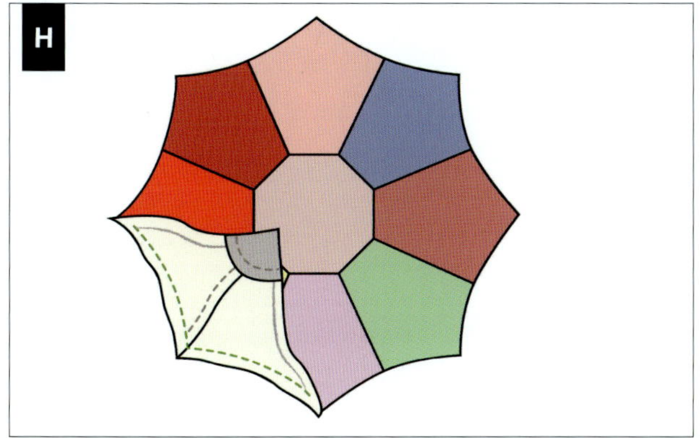

Assembly and finishing

Step Twelve Arrange the blocks in five rows of five blocks, making sure that the Black Print 1 and Black Print 2 corners alternate—see the detail opposite, bottom.

Step Thirteen First stitch the blocks in each row RS together. Press the SAs in one direction for rows 1, 3 and 5, and in the opposite direction for row 2 and 4.

Step Fourteen Now stitch the rows RS together. Press the SAs in one direction.

Step Fifteen Now for the borders. Sew the two shorter border pieces to the left- and right-hand sides of the quilt, RS together. Press the SAs toward the borders. Sew the remaining longer border pieces to the top and bottom edges of the quilt, RS together, then press the SAs toward the borders.

Step Sixteen Prepare your quilt layers: place the backing RS down, center the batting / wadding over the top then center the quilt top over these, RS up. Baste / tack the layers together using your chosen method (see pages 162–165), ready to quilt.

Step Seventeen For the quilting, I've used a utility design of diagonal lines all going in one direction (**J**). The spacing is dictated by the block grid itself and marked with a long rotary cutting ruler and a Hera marker (see page 170). Start by marking the widest spaced lines first, then the lines in between (although these don't necessarily need to be marked in, and can be quilted by eye). Alternatively, you can use the same grid spacing to mark a diagonal cross-hatch quilting design—see pages 166–167 for more details.

Step Eighteen Once quilted, remove the basting / tacking stitches then trim the edges and square up. Bind the quilt with your chosen method (see pages 180–183), then add a label to finish (see page 185).

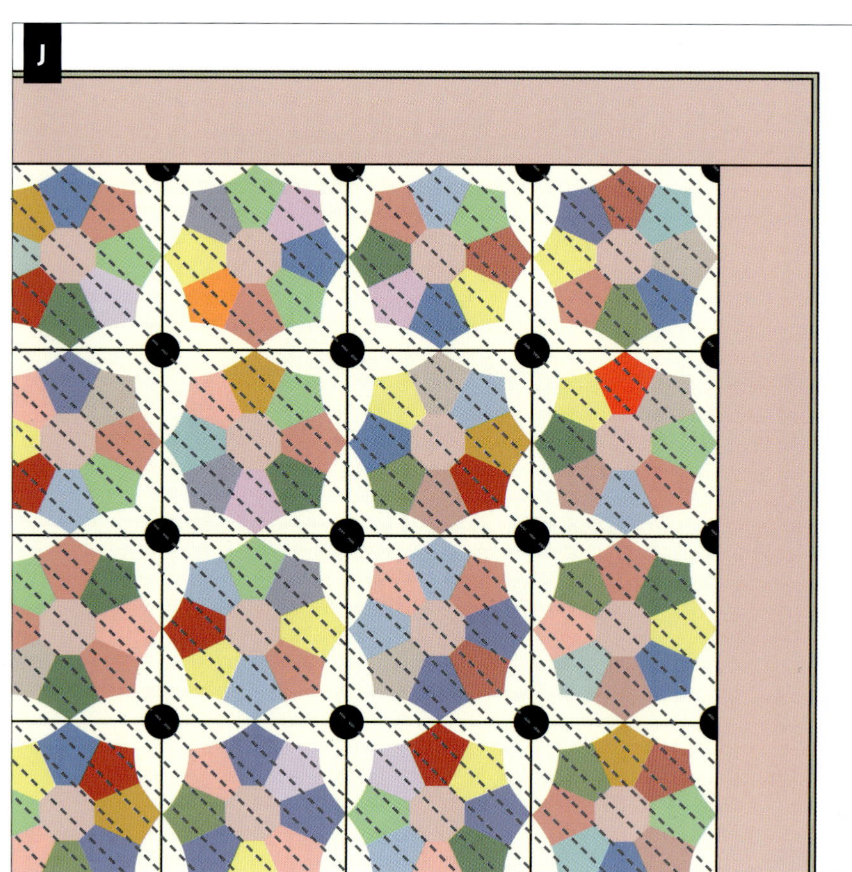

HISTORICAL TECHNIQUE NO. 6

Embroidering Quilts

Quilts during the Colonial Revival era did not just consist of patchwork, they also included embroideries. Designers like Anne Orr and Ruby Short McKim branched into embroidery motifs and patterns for quilts. These stitcheries were more sophisticated than redwork (see pages 116–119 of this book for more information about redwork) and penny squares (ready-to-stitch blocks with the outline to embroider printed on the fabric)†, as they featured more stitches, colors, and details. The designs would often have a common theme—for example, birds or flowers of the States—and sometimes nursery rhymes!

Being inspired to make a quilt like this today creates certain hurdles—the main one being the need to embroider! If detailed embroidery work is not your thing or time is precious, using vintage embroidered linens in a quilt is a great alternative.

Some of us have relatives who still have a few of these packed away in cupboards. However, if you do not have embroidered linens in your family passed down from older relatives, or none in your own home, then many of you will have household table linens, or can find some in thrift / charity / op stores. These include traycloths, napkins, and tablecloths.

Embroidered linens were popular decorative, practical items to buy in the past, but many women stitched the linens themselves. The designs were popular both before and after the Second World War, but it's hard to pin down each individual pattern's origins. Most designs from this period were often floral in nature—bouquets, wreaths, and such like—with numerous colors and different stitches used. Some linens had the outlines printed on them, ready to stitch, or transfers could be purchased and used as many times as you wished. Magazines also printed embroidery patterns, as well as suggestions for the stitches, threads and color combinations.

It may surprise you to learn that vintage embroidery patterns for linens can still be found today. Sometimes you can pick them up in thrift / charity / op stores, or yard / boot sales and house clearances; searching online is the quickest method, with websites such as eBay and Etsy making good starting points.

Using embroidered linens in a quilt not only re-creates the feel of embroidered quilts from the 1930s, but it's a lovely way to keep these decorative linens in use today. To me, making something new from these old linens is a little like what the women in the 1930s were doing with their quilting: looking back at what was nostalgic, using what they had, and giving it a new lease of life.

† *Wilene Smith, "Quilt History Tidbits No. 30: Penny Squares and Picture Quilts", Quilt Index, September 8, 2010, website link: <https://quiltindex.org/view/view/?type=publications&kid=34-136-76>*

* * *

Opposite:
"Rambling Rose" quilt by unknown maker; Pittsburgh, Pennsylvania; c.1935; 75in (190.5cm) wide x 90in (228.5cm) tall; AM&G: 1995, no. 170.

The quiltmaker has used the appliquéd design on this quilt top to showcase their embroidery skills. They have used different stitches for various elements including buttonhole, stem, and satin stitch. The scalloped edge of the quilt is bound with the same plain blue fabric that has been used to frame the central appliqué motifs on the quilt front. The quilt is lightly batted / wadded, and hand quilting in various patterns fills the white background to the applied designs.

Above:
Embroidered motifs from the collection of Carolyn Forster. These have been re-purposed at some stage into flags/bunting pennants, but the detail and imagery is still clear. They look to be from a pattern range based on kitchen utensils, with a blue bird helping out!

Embroidered Linen Squares Quilt

DESIGNED AND MACHINE-PIECED BY CAROLYN FORSTER; MACHINE-QUILTED BY CHRIS FARRANCE

BACKGROUND

I've been collecting vintage linen tablecloths for some time now. Lovely as they are, admittedly I don't really use them for what they were intended. So that I could make them useful to me, I've begun incorporating them into quilts. By putting them into a quilt, I know that the embroideries can still be both admired and used.

When I collect embroidered linens, I am not too worried about whether they are authentically from the 1900–1940 period. In fact, many of mine are technically are from the late 1940s. But, as we've explored already, designs don't just emerge in a specific period; often they're iterations or developments of patterns created from as far back as the 1800s. If a design is popular, it will be replicated across decades and generations; so, we can't truly or accurately date a pattern.

Here I chose a very simple block design that would frame each embroidery piece that I wanted to feature.

Focus on finding linens where the area with the main embroidery is in good condition. If the rest of the cloth is in a worse state, with wear, stains, or other storage damage, you might not be able to cut the white frame fabric from the cloth as I have done (the size of the linen will also be a factor). To solve this problem, you can substitute a white cotton or linen-cotton mix fabric. If you can use the rest of the cloths, you may have odd bits of embroidery popping into the frames, which I find quite quirky.

If you don't want to use as many print fabrics for the frames of the blocks as I have, then choose a single fabric. To add more interest to a quilt with just a single printed fabric, choose one that has a large-print pattern; this way, when you cut into it, there will always be different pieces to see in the patchwork.

Make sure to wash and press the embroidered linens before working with them. If you find them awkward to handle and sew, stabilizing them with a little spray starch will help.

Embroidered Linen Squares Quilt design.

MEASUREMENTS

Quilt size:
64½in (164cm) square

Block size, finished:
16in (40.75cm) square

REQUIREMENTS

Blocks:

Embroidered central squares
Selection of embroidered linens (for example, teacloths and tablecloths) with a useable area measuring 8½in (21.5cm) square

White frames and cornerstones
Either from the same linen

OR

54in (137cm) x WOF

Print-fabric frames
Sixteen Fat Eighths (22 x 9in / 56 x 23cm), each in different prints and colors

OR

One print and color, 54in (137cm) x WOF

Backing:
144in (365.75cm) x WOF

Batting / wadding:
72in (183cm) square

Binding:
18in (45.75cm) x WOF

Notions:
Optional: 8½in (21.5cm) square ruler

FABRIC CUTTING

Blocks:

Embroidered central squares

- Sixteen 8½in (21.5cm) squares, cut from the main embroidered area.

White frames and cornerstones
Cut from the left-over linen fabric:

- One hundred and twenty-eight 2½in (6.5cm) squares, for the cornerstones.
- Sixty 2½ x 8½in (6.5 x 21.5cm) rectangles, for the frames.

OR from the 54in (137cm) x WOF yardage:

- For the frames, first cut four 8½in (21.5cm) x WOF strips; then, sub-cut into sixty-four 2½in x 8½in (6.5 x 21.5cm) rectangles.
- For the cornerstones, cut eight 2½in (6.5cm) x WOF strips; then, sub-cut into one hundred and twenty-eight 2½in (6.5cm) squares.

Print-fabric frames
From each of the sixteen different prints cut:

- Three 2½in x 22in (6.5 x 56cm) strips. Sub-cut one strip into eight 2½in (6.5cm) squares for the cornerstones; sub-cut the remaining two strips into four 2½in x 8½in (6.5 x 21.5cm) rectangles for the frames.

OR from one print:

- For the frames, first cut four 8½in (21.5cm) x WOF strips; then, sub-cut into sixty-four 2½ x 8½in (6.5 x 21.5cm) rectangles.
- For the cornerstones, first cut eight 2½in (6.5cm) x WOF strips; then, sub-cut into one hundred and twenty-eight 2½in (6.5cm) squares.

Backing:
Cut into two equal lengths. Remove the selvages / selvedges and stitch the two lengths together along the longest edges. Press the SA open.

Binding:
Cut seven 2½in (6.5cm) x WOF strips. Join the short ends with a bias join to make a continuous length (see page 179). Trim the SA to ¼in (5mm) and press open. Fold in half along the length, WS together, and press.

METHOD

Blocks

Step One If you have multiple print fabrics, begin by pairing up your print fabric with an embroidered central square of choice. As noted on page 86, if you find the vintage linen to be unstable when you stitch it, then use a little spray starch to help stabilize it.

Note: For the next steps, I like to work on one block at a time.

Step Two Stitch a print framing strip to the top and bottom of the embroidered square, RS facing (**A**). Press the SAs toward the printed fabric.

Step Three Stitch a white cornerstone square to either end of a print framing strip, RS facing. Press the SAs toward the printed fabric. Repeat to make two units in total. Then, stitch these units to the remaining two sides of the embroidered central square, RS together (**B**). Press the SAs away from the center.

Step Four Stitch a print cornerstone to either end of a white framing strip, RS facing. Press the SAs toward to the printed fabric. Repeat to make four units in total. Sew two of these units to the left- and right-hand sides of the block, RS together (**C**).

Step Five On the ends of the two remaining units stitch a white cornerstone, RS together, making these frames longer. Press the SAs toward the printed fabric. Then, sew these to the top and bottom edges of the block, RS facing (**D**).

Step Six Repeat Steps 2–5 to make sixteen blocks in total.

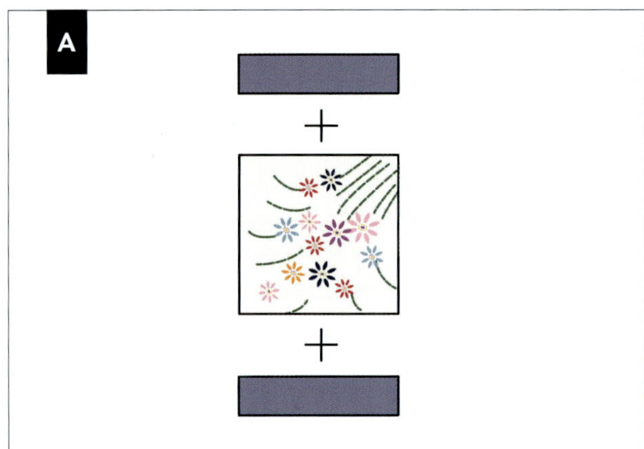

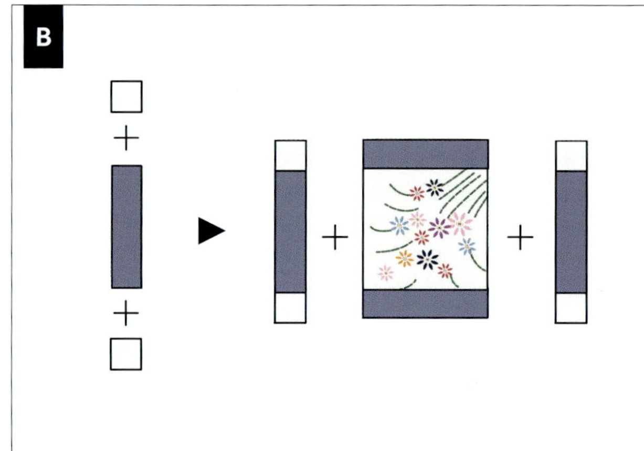

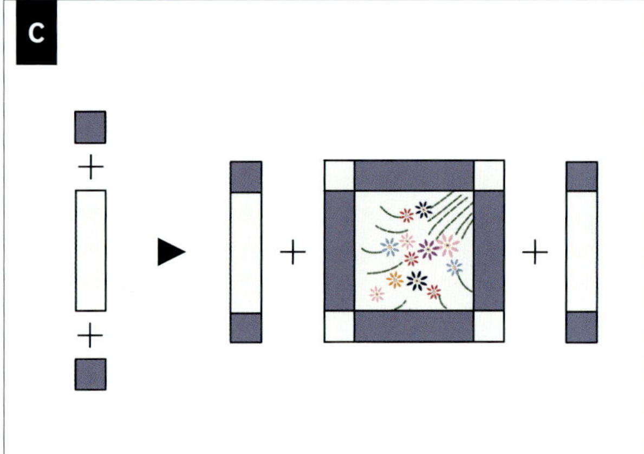

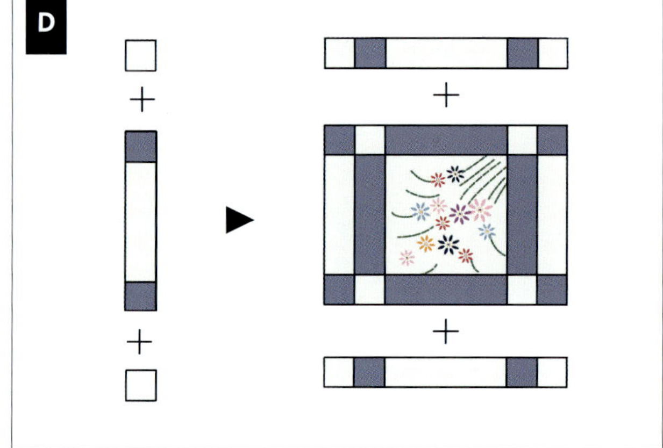

Assembling and finishing

Step Seven Arrange the blocks in four rows of four blocks. Pin the blocks in each row RS together, making sure the seams nest, then stitch in place. Press the SAs in one direction for rows 1 and 3, and in the opposite direction for rows 2 and 4.

Step Eight Pin then sew the four rows RS together. Press the SAs open this time.

Step Nine Prepare your quilt layers: place the backing RS down, center the batting / wadding over the top then center the quilt top over these, RS up. Baste / tack the layers together using your chosen method (see pages 162–165), ready to quilt.

Step Ten For the quilt design, I did 45-degree cross-hatch quilting lines on the sewing machine (see pages 166–167). This could be done easily by hand too, if that's your preference. Alternatively, outline quilting along the seam lines would look great too.

Step Eleven Once quilted, remove the basting / tacking stitches then trim the edges and square up. Bind the quilt with your chosen method (see pages 180–183), then add a label to finish (see page 185).

HISTORICAL TECHNIQUE NO. 7

Black Accents

Something that has always appealed to me about quilts and stitchery of the period is that they were not afraid to use black as an accent—whether it was through the fabric selection or by using black embroidery thread for quilting, embroidery or appliqué.

Although it is something that stands out to me, through my research I've discovered there is little to nothing said about it! It seems to be just what was "done".

You can find lots of examples of 1930s quilts with black stitching (mainly buttonhole stitch), as seen in some of the examples on these pages. The black thread sometimes complements the prints in the quilt but often it is a striking contrast to what's used elsewhere, making a bold statement. For instance, you find several examples of signature and friendship quilts that have been pieced with bright, fresh pastels, but then signed in black embroidery stitches. The "Tulips in a Pot" block, opposite, is a good example of this.

Another way to add some black to the quilt is in the fabrics themselves. Unsurprisingly, especially when combined with vibrant fabrics, black-print fabrics add to the drama in the patchwork. Many of the print fabrics used in conjunction with the black prints fall in the a mid-tone color palette (see page 129) and were of a similar scale; so, by using black-print fabrics, the designs within the blocks gain more definition.

Opposite:
"Polka Dot" quilt from the collection of Carolyn Forster; quilt size 74½in (189.25cm) x 82in (208.25cm) tall; finished block size 5½in (14cm) square.

This is a quilt design by Clara Stone, first published in Practical Needlework in 1906. This is a true scrappy quilt, and even the binding is pieced from many of the fabrics in the quilt. As well the black prints, there are numerous polka dot fabrics, which I like to think are a nod to the name of the quilt design.

Above:
"Nine Patch Quilt" from the collection of Carolyn Forster; quilt size 69in (179.25cm) wide x 83in (211cm) tall; finished block size 4in (10cm) square.

The nine-patch blocks in this quilt are grouped in such a way as to make larger nine-patch blocks. The blocks all include solids, and this black combination stands out in particular. The style of quilting used is utility quilting, and these are simply straight lines that run in rows across the quilt, echoing the seam lines. Very simple but very effective.

Left, middle:
"Tulips in a Pot" appliqué block with a signature, from the collection of Carolyn Forster; 12in (30.5cm) square. The blanket stitch around the appliqué pieces is used to secure them to the background. A regular, finer thread has been used for the blanket stitching around the stems.

Left, bottom:
"Arrowhead" block from the collection of Carolyn Forster; 9½in (24.25cm) square.

This is such a striking combination of fabrics, made all the more so by using the black print as the background fabric for the block.

Split Nine-Patch Quilt

DESIGNED AND MACHINE-PIECED BY CAROLYN FORSTER; MACHINE-QUILTED BY CHRIS FARRANCE

BACKGROUND

I love the accent that the black thread or fabric seems to bring to the patchwork and stitching during this period. Using a solid black fabric seemed like quite a stark contrast in a quilt, but black-and-white prints soften the impact.

For this quilt that features a classic split nine-patch block, I've opted for a black print rather than a solid. I've used a selection of black prints for interest, but one could work just as well. If you use the same print as for the border then you get a nice repetition amongst the rest of the scraps in the quilt.

The split nine-patch block pattern is considered a regional pattern, with examples found mainly in south-east Pennsylvania and New Jersey dating back to 1880. There were quite specific ways of setting the block for quilts that became characteristic to the area.

The block itself has a few more variations, but this placement of fabrics within the block gives a nice clean line running through any design layout that you choose.

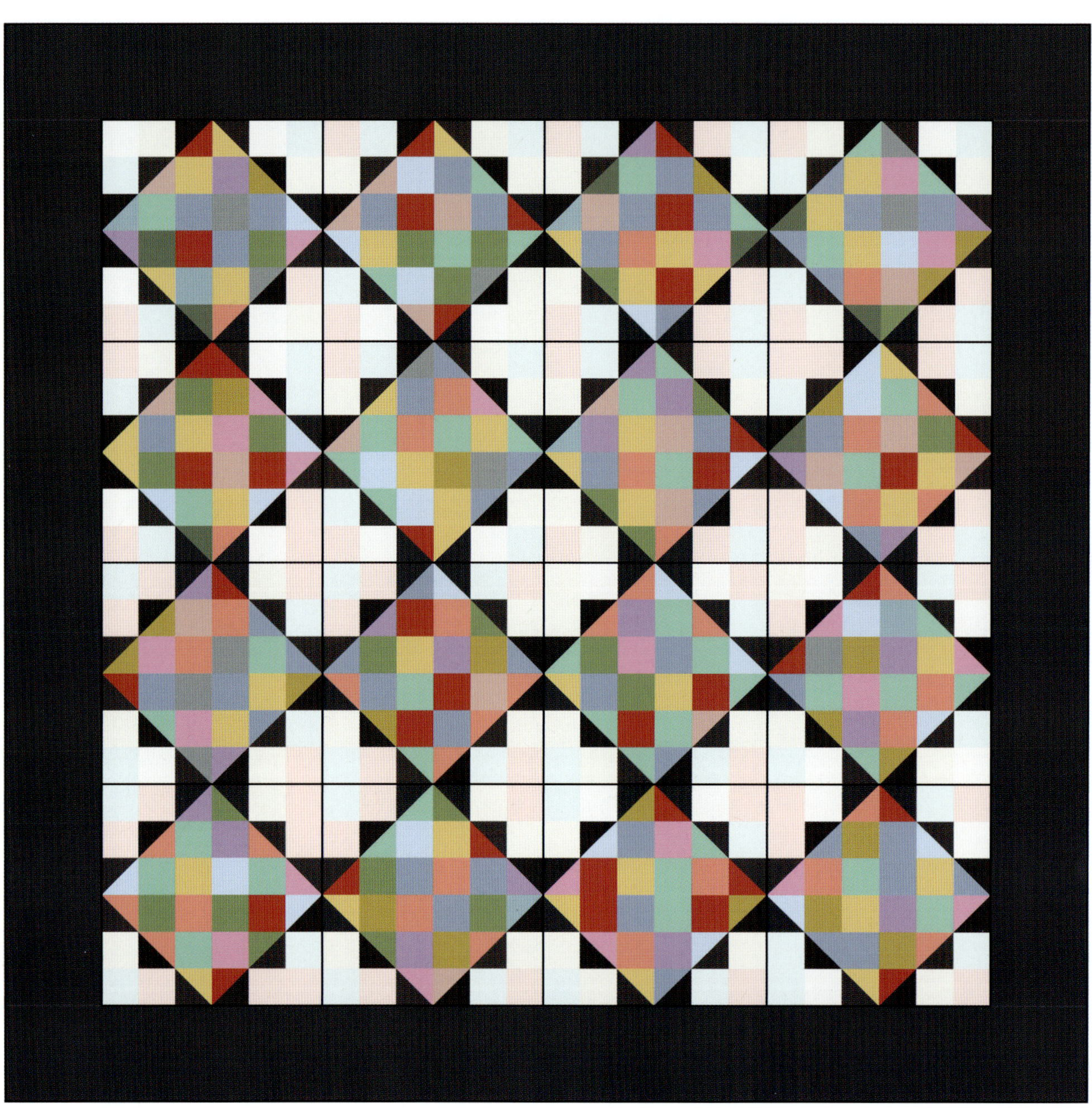

Split Nine-Patch Quilt design.

MEASUREMENTS

Quilt size:
84½in (214.75cm) square

Block size, unfinished:
9in (23cm) square

REQUIREMENTS

Blocks:
Light-colored prints
Eighteen 3½in (9cm) x WOF strips

Darker-colored /contrast prints
- Eighteen 3½in (9cm) x WOF strips
- Ten 3⅞in (10cm) x WOF strips

Black prints
Ten 3⅞in (10cm) x WOF strips

OR

40in (101.75cm) of one black print or solid fabric

Borders:
52in (132cm) x WOF

Backing:
Note—the measurement below will be achieved with two narrow drops of fabric.

180in (457.25cm) x WOF

Batting / wadding:
94in (238.75cm) square

Binding:
Note—for the sample opposite, the print is the same as the one used for the border, for a clean look.

22½in (57.25cm) x WOF

FABRIC CUTTING

Blocks:
Light-colored prints
Sub-cut the strips into one hundred and ninety-two 3½in (9cm) squares.

Darker-colored /contrast prints
With the 3½in (9cm) strips:

- Sub-cut the strips into one hundred and ninety-two 3½in (9cm) squares.

With the 3⅞in (10cm) strips:

- Sub-cut the strips into ninety-six 3⅞in (10cm) squares.

Black prints
If using 3⅞in (10cm) strips:

- Sub-cut the strips into ninety-six 3⅞in (10cm) squares.

If using yardage:

- Cut across the width to make ten 3⅞in (10cm) strips, then sub-cut into ninety-six 3⅞in (10cm) squares.

Borders:
- Cut eight 6½in (16.5cm) x WOF strips. Trim off the selvages / selvedges then join the strips RS together at the shorter ends, RS facing, to create a continuous length. Press the SAs open.
- Cut two 6½ x 72½in (16.5 x 184.25cm) strips.
- Cut two 6½ x 84½in (16.5 x 214.75cm) strips.

Backing:
Cut into two equal lengths. Remove the selvages / selvedges and stitch the two lengths RS together along the longest edges. Press the SA open.

Binding:
Cut nine 2½in (6.5cm) x WOF strips. Join the short ends with a bias join to make a continuous length (see page 179). Trim the SA to ¼in (5mm) and press open. Fold in half along the length, WS together, and press.

METHOD

Blocks

Step One Start by making the HST units. First, pair up the 3⅞in (10cm) squares with RS facing, using one black print and one dark / contrast-colored print for each pair.

Step Two Draw a diagonal line, from one corner to the opposite corner on the WS of the dark / contrast-colored print fabric, so the line is easier to see. Stitch ¼in (5mm) away from the drawn line, on each side (**A**).

Step Three Cut along the drawn line to create two HST units (**B**). Open out the units then press the SAs open; doing this creates less bulk when the units are stitched into blocks later.

Step Four Repeat Steps 2 and 3 to make 192 HST units in total.

Step Five Now arrange nine 3½in (9cm) squares into the block design, as shown in **C**: three light-colored print squares should occupy the top-left section of the block, three black / contrast HST units should sit diagonally in the middle, and three darker-colored / contrast print squares should occupy the bottom-right corner.

Step Six Stitch the squares in each row RS together. Press the SAs in rows 1 and 3 in one direction, and press the SAs in row 2 in the opposite direction; this will help them knit together neatly. Then, sew the rows together one at a time, RS facing (**D**). Press the SAs open this time; as before, this will reduce bulk in the seams at the next stage of construction.

Step Seven Repeat Steps 5 and 6 to make 64 blocks in total.

Step Eight Now arrange four blocks together, rotating the blocks as needed so that the dark / contrast print squares meet in the middle, and the lighter print squares are on the outer corners (**E**). Stitch the blocks RS together in pairs first, matching the seams and pinning as needed. Press the SAs open. Then, pin and stitch the pairs together, RS facing. Press the SAs open.

Step Nine Repeat Step 8 to make 16 large blocks in total.

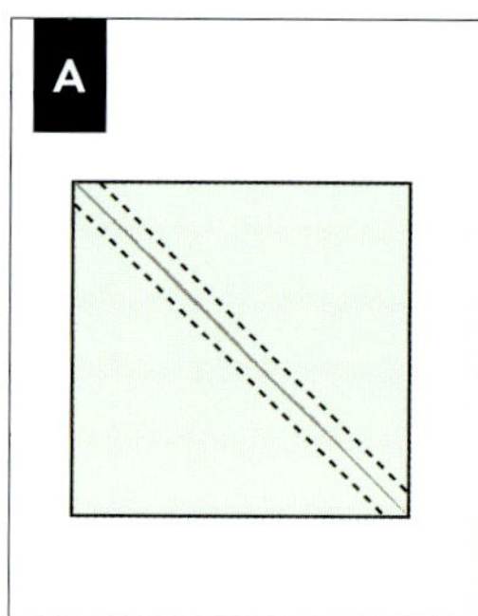

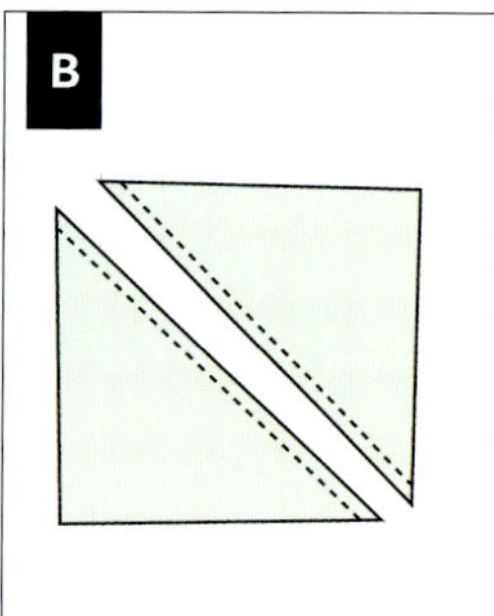

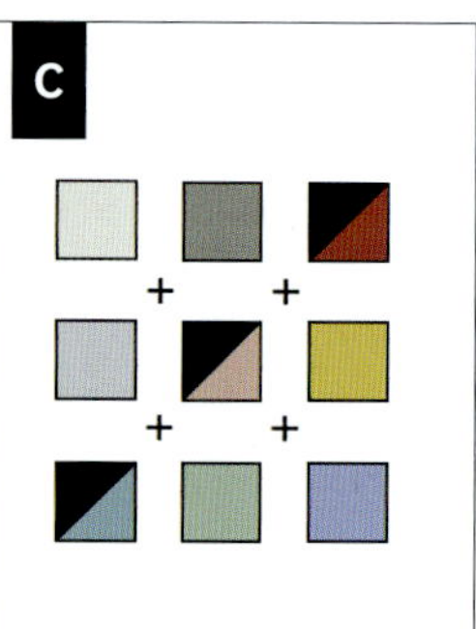

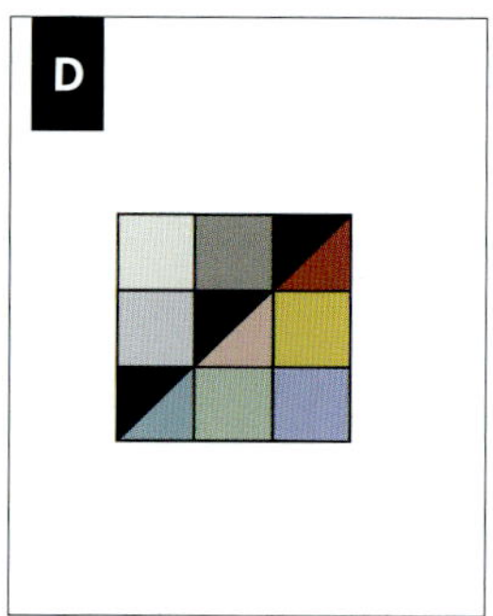

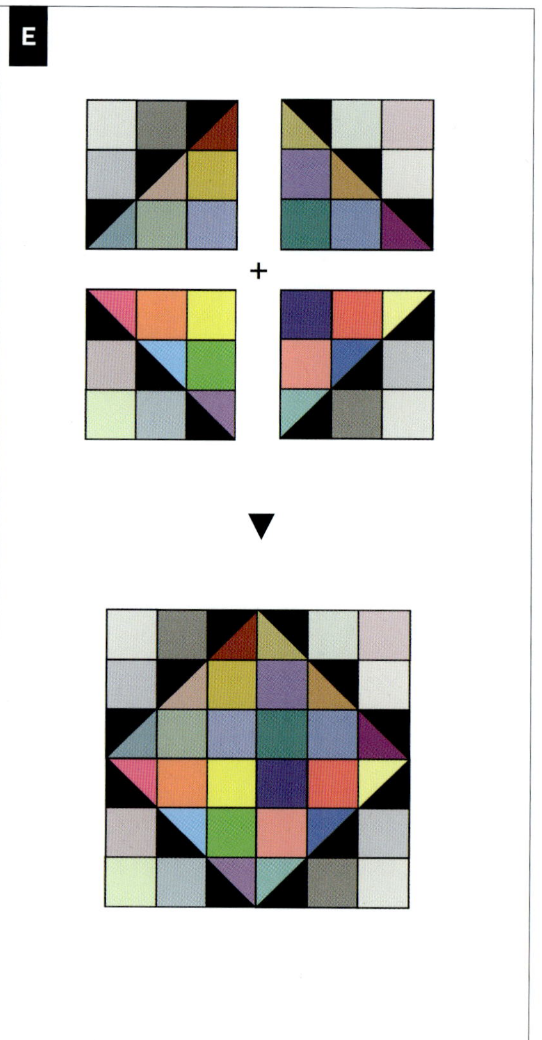

Assembly and finishing

Step Ten Lay out the 16 large blocks in four rows of four blocks. Pin the blocks in each row RS together, making sure the seams nest, then stitch in place. Press the SAs in one direction for rows 1 and 3, and in the opposite direction for rows 2 and 4.

Step Eleven Pin then sew the four rows RS together. Press the SAs open this time.

Step Twelve Now to add the borders. Sew the short border pieces to the left and right-hand edges of the quilt top, RS facing. Press the SAs toward the border pieces.

Step Thirteen Add the longer border pieces in the same way to the top and bottom edges of the quilt top. Again, press the SAs toward the border pieces.

Step Fourteen Prepare your quilt layers: place the backing RS down, center the batting / wadding over the top then center the quilt top over these, RS up. Baste / tack the layers together using your chosen method (see pages 162–165), ready to quilt.

Step Fifteen This quilt was machine quilted with a Baptist Fan design (see pages 168 and 169), a great utility quilting design. Traditionally it was hand quilted—follow the instructions on pages 171–173 for more on hand quilting, if you'd like to do this. Mark then quilt each "fan" one at a time. Start by marking the largest curve of the template (see page 189) in the bottom right-hand corner of the quilt top. Fill in the smaller curves using either the lines on the template or the length of your needle as a gauge. Once marked, quilt the curves. When this first arc is complete, mark the next one: work along the bottom edge of the quilt first, then move up to mark the design on the next "row", which will sit on top of the row you have just quilted. Continue in this way, working from the bottom of the quilt upwards, until the quilt design is complete.

Step Sixteen Once quilted, remove the basting / tacking stitches then trim the edges and square up. Bind the quilt with your chosen method (see pages 180–183), then add a label to finish (see page 185).

HISTORICAL TECHNIQUE NO. 8

Using Feedsacks

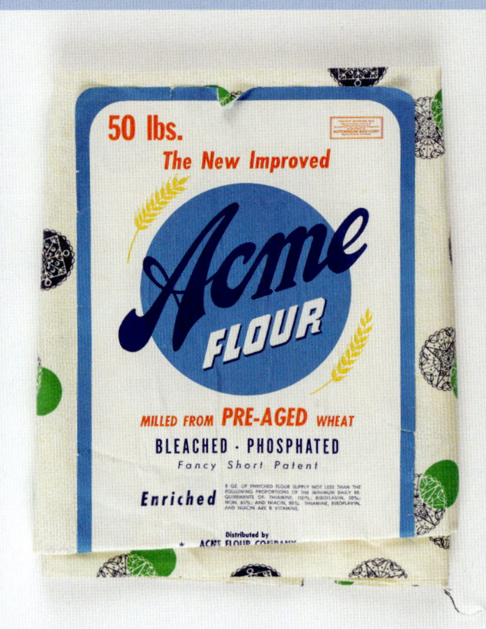

Feedsacks or flour sacks are what many people associate with quilts and their makers during the 1930s. Due to fabric shortages, the rising cost of materials and the economic instability for many, feedsacks were used as a source of fabric by makers well after World War Two.

In the past, it was typical for the American population (particularly those who lived in remote areas) to buy dry, less perishable food in bulk. Manufacturers sold these large quantities of dry food in feedsacks, which would be made either of sturdy paper or fabric. The feedsacks were printed with the manufacturer's details, the contents of the bag, and the weight.

From the early 1900s, when more manufacturers were using soft fabrics like cotton for the feedsacks, women started using the feedsacks to make clothes, quilts, curtains, and more. Thanks to the simple chain stitching on the feedsacks and the different size sacks you could buy, it was easy for makers to take apart and transform their old dry-goods bags into a mix of items. Makers would often go to great pains to get rid of the printing on the fabric, to hide the fact they were using cotton sacks—this included soaking away the logos, or covering them with stitching or trims like ric-rac.

When some manufacturers cottoned on (no pun intended) that the sacks were being used for domestic sewing during the Great Depression, and saw competition from a growing paper-sack industry, they responded not only by improving the quality of the feedsack fabric, but they also printed designs on them too. Furthermore, labels were stamped with washable ink, to make it easier for makers to remove them.

Eventually there were thousands of designs printed onto feedsacks. Brands also became synonymous with their prints and sack sizes: if you liked one print and needed more for curtains or a dress, then you would look for that brand.

Over the years, printed feedsacks have turned into collectors' items, and quilts that have feedsack backings are highly sought after. (If makers struggled to remove the labeling on the sacks, often they used the fabric for the back of the quilt, where it wouldn't be on show.)

I must admit to having a soft spot for quilt fabric with some text on, and this probably comes from a fascination with the feedsacks. With sustainable packaging becoming more popular, and when we can now buy some goods like rice or coffee beans in cotton fabric bags once again, it's more possible for us to emulate our predecessors and repurpose these bags into our quilts and more. The thought of what the bag could be sewn into is often more exciting than the edible contents!

Opposite, top:
From the collection of Carolyn Forster. This cotton feedsack quite clearly states its contents and brand. This blue ink was something that the seamstress would try to remove through washing; or the feedsack could be used for the quilt's backing fabric, or arranged wrong side out on the quilt top.

Opposite, bottom:
From the collection of Carolyn Forster. This feedsack has a printed fabric which would have enticed the buyer to purchase the feedsack. In contrast to the feedsack above it, the label is now made from paper and could have been easily removed, leaving unblemished and sewable fabric.

Above:
Blocks from the collection of Carolyn Forster; both measure 13½in (34.25cm) square.

These two blocks feature a design first noted by Clara Stone in Practical Needlework in 1906, *which she called* "Grandma's Star". *It rapidly gained favor, and over many years went by many different names. It appeared in the following publications with these names: "Fifty Four Forty or Flight"* (Ruth Finley, 1929); "Garden Patch" (Grandma Dexter's New Appliqué and Patchwork Designs, 1932, *36b*); *"54 40 or Flight"* (Aunt Martha series, The Quilt Fair Comes to You, 1933); *"Railroad"* (Aunt Martha series, The Quilt Fair Comes to You, 1933); *"Texas" (January 9, 1934,* Nancy Page, Port Arthur News); *"Garden Walk"* (Kansas City Star, *April 26, 1939); "Nine Patch Star"* (Kansas City Star, *January 4, 1956); "Old Fashioned Pinwheel"* (Kansas City Star, *February 12, 1958).*

From this list of names for only one block design, one can see how the name changes can impact the accurate dating of a quilt!

Both blocks feature feedsack prints, used for the cream/neutral background; however, the left-hand block's print is much for subtle than the one on the right, presumably because the feedsack fabric has been used wrong side out.

Five-Patch Star Quilt

DESIGNED AND HAND-PIECED BY CAROLYN FORSTER; MACHINE-QUILTED BY TRUDI WOOD

BACKGROUND

The blocks in this quilt are inspired by those in a pattern by Laura Wheeler called "Noon and Night", which was printed in *Kansas City Star* in February 1934. I saw a version initially in an interiors magazine, where there were vintage quilts styled in a dormitory bedroom. After some research, I realized I had a version of the quilt in a book by Jan Halgrimson; her version, which used a Five Point Star, enabled me to adapt the design in the way I wanted.

The change I made was a non-directional layout and fabric choice, to keep the use of the red fabric to the small outside-edge triangles. However, use your fabrics in any way you like if you wish, as the fun scrappy design means you can play around with it.

The background fabric I've used—off-white, with printed lettering—is a tribute to the use of printed flour sacks in many 1930s quilts. If the maker unsuccessfully bleached their feedsack fabric, often they'd use it for the quilt backing; however, sometimes you can see examples of quilts where lettering is used on the quilt top. When looking for your own printed lettering fabric, try to find ones with fonts and styles that wouldn't look too out of place next to a genuine 1930s quilt.

The sashing continues the scrappy feel of the whole quilt block, but using a soft green solid for the cornerstones adds calm, unifying spots throughout. As a nod to the period's frugality and the scrap-using mission of the quilt, I recommend using what you have for these cornerstones; if you don't have enough of one fabric, only buy what you need to complete the quilt.

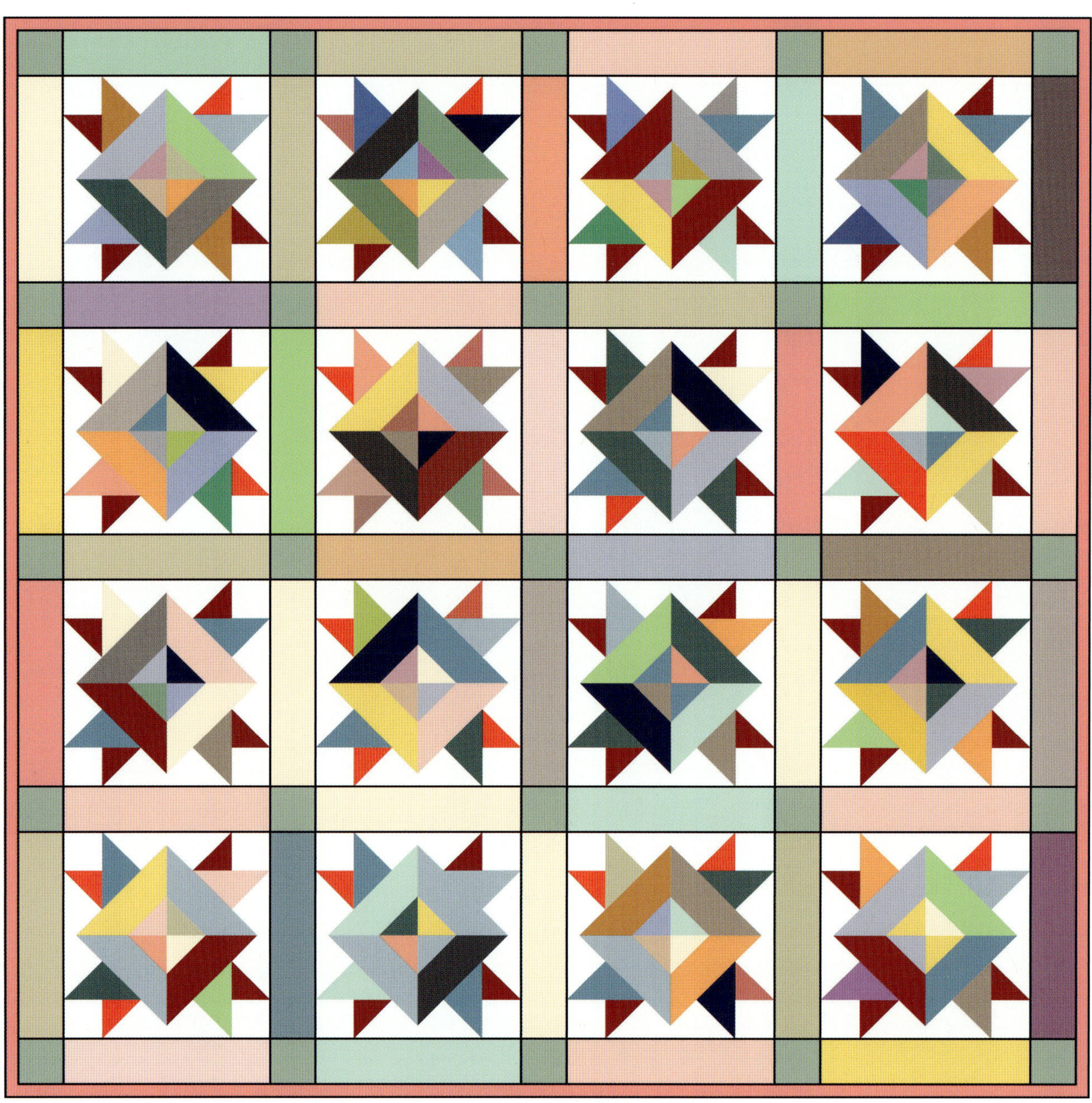

Five-Patch Star Quilt design.

MEASUREMENTS

Quilt size:
63½in (161.25cm) square

Block size, finished:
12in (30.5cm)

REQUIREMENTS

Blocks:
Background (Templates B, C and CR)
51in (129.75cm) x WOF

Stars—red triangles (Template A)
21in (53.5cm) x WOF of one fabric

OR

Six 3½in (9cm) x WOF strips in different fabrics

OR

Thirty-two scraps, minimum 3½in (9cm) square

Stars—small triangles in the block center (Template A)
As for the red triangles, but from assorted scrap prints

Stars—trapezium shapes (Template D)
Sixty-four scraps, minimum 7¾ x 2½in (19.75 x 6.5cm) in size

OR

Eleven 2½in (6.5cm) x WOF strips in different fabrics

Stars—large outer triangles (Template E)
Sixteen squares, minimum 6½in (16.5cm) square in size, in different fabrics

Sashing:
Forty 3½ x 12½in (9 x 31.75cm) strips, some or all in different fabrics

OR

50in (127cm) x WOF of one fabric

Cornerstones / posts:
10½in (26.75cm) x WOF

OR

Three 3½in (9cm) x WOF strips

Backing:
148in (376cm) x WOF

Batting / wadding:
74in (188cm) square

Binding:
17½in (44.5cm) x WOF

Notions:
Size 10 Sharps needle

28wt cotton thread, in a shade that blends

Fine propelling pencil, to mark the WS of the fabric

Patchwork or appliqué pins

Everything else:
Templates A, B, C/CR, D and E (see page 192)

FABRIC CUTTING

Blocks:
Note on templates—the SAs (measuring ¼in / 5mm) are NOT included, and will need to be added before cutting out the shapes. I've designed the templates this way, as these are hand-pieced.

Background (Templates B and C/CR)

- From the yardage cut six 2⅞–3in (7.5–7.75cm) x WOF strips. From the strips cut sixty-four shapes using Template C and sixty-four CR shapes using the flipped template. Each strip should yield twelve shapes.
- From the same yardage cut five 3in (7.75cm) x WOF strips. From the strips cut sixty-four shapes using Template B. Each strip should yield thirteen shapes.

Stars—red triangles (Template A)
From the yardage cut six 3½in (9cm) x WOF strips. From the strips cut sixty-four triangles using Template A. Each strip should yield twenty-two triangles.

OR

From the six 3½in (9cm) x WOF strips cut sixty-four triangles using Template A. Each strip should yield twenty-two triangles.

OR

From the thirty-two scraps cut sixty-four triangles 3½in (9cm) using Template A.

Stars—small triangles in the block center (Template A)
As for the red triangles, but from assorted scrap prints.

Stars—trapezium shapes (Template D)
Cut sixty-four shapes using Template D.

OR

From the strips cut sixty-four shapes using Template D. Each strip will yield six shapes.

Stars—large outer triangles (Template E)
Cut sixty-four triangles using Template E. Each square will yield four triangles.

Sashing:
Use strips as is.

OR

From the yardage cut four 3½in (9cm) x WOF strips, then sub-cut into forty 3½ x 12½in (9 x 31.75cm) strips.

Cornerstones / posts:
Cut into 3½in (9cm) x WOF strips, if needed, and then sub-cut the strips into twenty-five 3½in (9cm) squares in total.

Backing:
Cut into two equal lengths. Remove the selvages / selvedges and stitch the two lengths RS together along the longest edges. Press the SA open.

Binding:
Sub-cut into seven 2½in (6.5cm) x WOF strips. Join the short ends with a bias join to make a continuous length (see page 179). Trim the SA to ¼in (5mm) and press open. Fold in half along the length, WS together, and press.

METHOD

Block

You will see that each block has four segments that are the same (see **F**). You could work on sewing all the segments first before constructing the blocks, or make one block at a time; the choice is yours. The blocks are stitched by hand; see pages 144–151 for more details on how to hand-piece.

Step One Stitch one B piece to one red A piece (**A**).

Step Two Stitch this A/B unit to an E piece (**B**).

Step Three Sew the C and CR pieces to either side of this unit (**C**).

Step Four Now sew one D piece to a non-red, scrappy A piece (**D**).

Step Five Sew both units together to complete one segment (**E**). Press the SAs in the direction of the arrows in the **E** diagram—single arrowheads indicate one direction; double arrowheads indicate the SA must be pressed open.

Step Six Repeat Steps 1–5 to make four segments in total; this will make one block.

Step Seven If you wish, at this stage you can sew the segments together by hand or machine. Sew two segments RS together, rotating the blocks as necessary so the small red triangles "point" outwards at the outer corners. Sew two more segments together in the same way. Sew the two pairs RS together, again ensuring the small red triangles sit in the outer corners (**F**). Press the SAs in the directions indicated by the arrows in diagram **F**.

Step Eight Repeat Steps 1–7 to make 16 blocks in total. Once complete, square up all the blocks centrally so they measure 12½in (31.75cm) square.

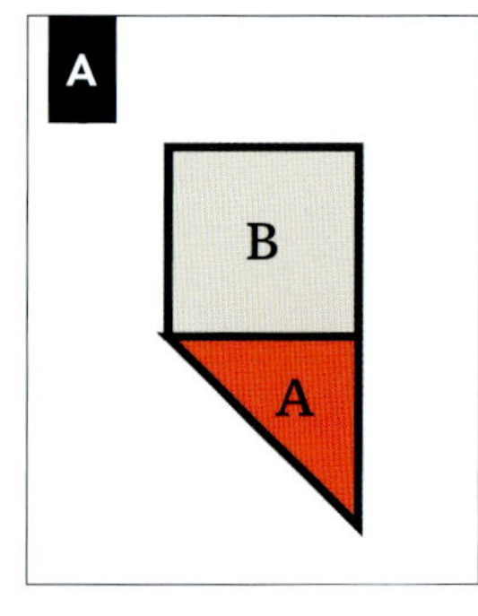

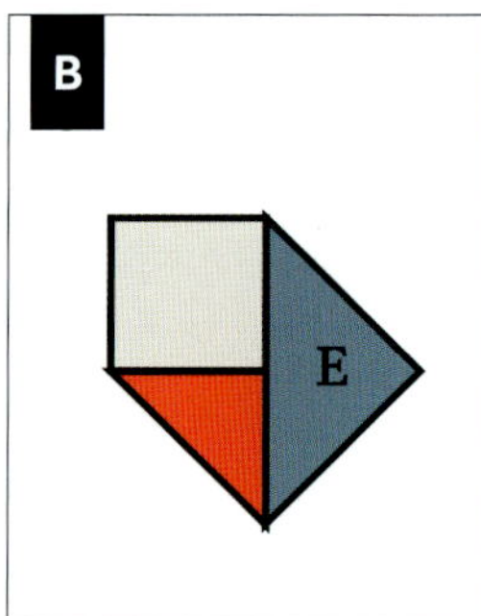

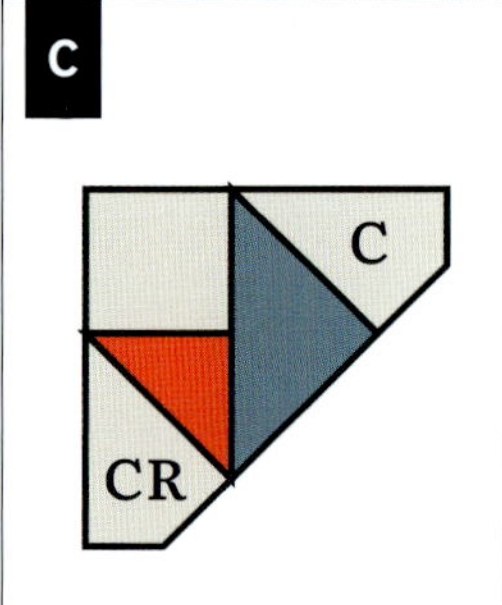

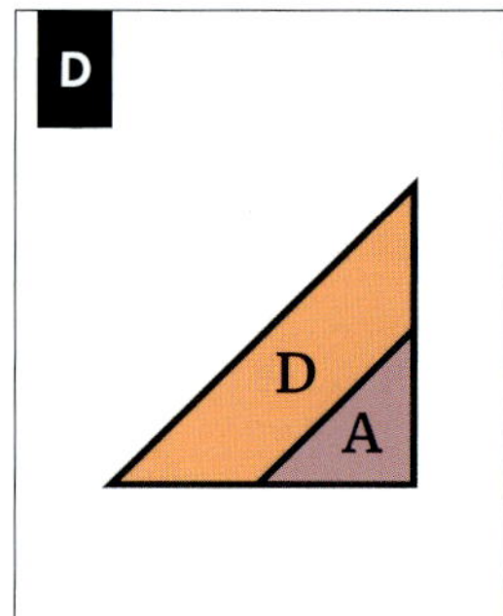

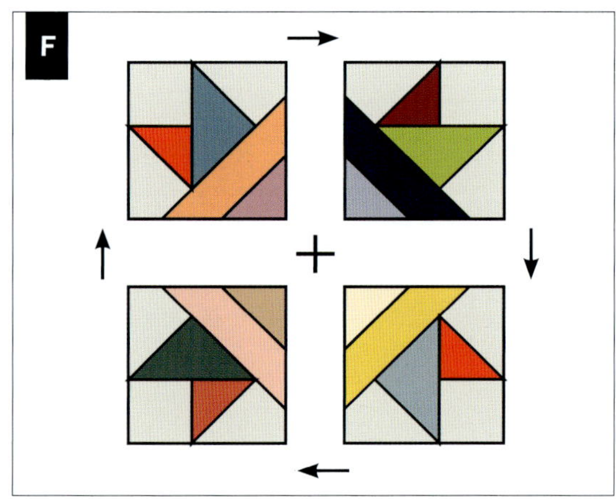

Assembly and finishing

Step Nine Lay out the blocks in four rows of four blocks. Between each block, and on the sides of the outer blocks, place a vertical sashing strip. Stitch the row RS together (see pages 156 and 157 for guidance on stitching the sashing), then press the SAs toward the sashing.

Step Ten Repeat Step 9 to sew the blocks and vertical sashing together in the remaining three rows.

Step Eleven Now for the horizontal sashing and cornerstones. Referring to the quilt diagram on page 104, lay out the cornerstones and horizontal sashing pieces in the following order: cornerstone, sashing, cornerstone, sashing, cornerstone, sashing, cornerstone, sashing, cornerstone. Stitch the pieces RS together, one by one, along the shorter ends (see pages 156 and 157 for guidance on stitching the sashing and cornerstones). Repeat to make five sashing / cornerstone rows in total. Press the SAs toward the sashing.

Step Twelve Between the rows with vertical sashing, above the top row and below the bottom row, lay out these sashing / cornerstone rows. Sew them RS together in turn, then press the SAs toward the horizontal sashing rows.

Step Thirteen Prepare your quilt layers: place the backing RS down, center the batting / wadding over the top then center the quilt top over these, RS up. Baste / tack the layers together using your chosen method (see pages 162–165), ready to quilt.

Step Fourteen This quilt was machine-quilted with a Baptist Fan design (see page 168 and 169). If you'd like to quilt by hand, take a look at the guidance on pages 171–173. Mark then quilt each "fan" one at a time. Start by marking the largest curve of the template (see page 189) in the bottom right-hand corner of the quilt top. Fill in the smaller curves using either the lines on the template or the length of your needle as a gauge. Once marked, quilt the curves. When this first arc is complete, mark the next one: work along the bottom edge of the quilt first, then move up to mark the design on the next "row", which will sit on top of the row you have just quilted. Continue in this way, working from the bottom of the quilt upwards, until the Baptist Fan quilt design is complete.

Step Fifteen Once quilted, remove the basting / tacking stitches then trim the edges and square up. Bind the quilt with your chosen method (see pages 180–183), then add a label to finish (see page 185).

HISTORICAL TECHNIQUE NO. 9

Using Small Scraps

One of the things that appeals to me about the quilts from the period is the sheer number of fabrics used in many of them. Often they are small pieces of fabric, but sometimes you can find several tiny scraps of fabric stitched together into a single patch that's then used in a block. When we see scrappy quilts from this period, particularly ones with really tiny pieces, it's easy to assume it was so makers could use up left-over fabrics. And it's likely many were. However, we should question whether this was wholly the case, and if there were other reasons for making scrappy quilts in the 1930s.

In the late 1800s, there was a craze, if you like, for using as many tiny pieces as you could in a quilt. One lady, Martha Haggard, recorded on the back of her quilt she made in 1897 that she had used 62,948 separate pieces.[1] Then later, during the Twenties and Thirties, you start to see newspaper articles about record-breaking quilts. Quilts were reported to be made with 10,000 pieces, then 21,840 pieces! Albert Small of Ottawa, Illinois stitched 63,467 hexagons in a quilt, but the top number recorder seems to be a Grace Snyder, who stitched 87,789 triangle pieces in 1948![2] Although quilts were not officially sewn competitively back then, there was obviously an underlying spirit of competition needing a release. Roderick Kirakofe, talks about this phenomenon in his book, *The American Quilt*, in greater detail.

Whether small pieces can be considered frugal is sometimes questioned too. They do use a disproportionate amount of seam allowance compared to larger pieces, so could be seen as wasteful—however, this is based on our idea of a ¼in (5mm) seam allowance. Lots of antique blocks that I have, including the Double Wedding Ring block (which features a great number of tiny scrap pieces), use a much smaller SA; so, there was likely less fabric waste.

I also wonder if using such tiny pieces was being frugal in another sense?

Many of the patterns in the newspapers and magazines in the Twenties and Thirties encouraged readers to cut and clip, to save in a scrapbook and trace off the pattern pieces. Others, however, required you to send a small amount of money in order to obtain the pattern pieces. If the latter was beyond your means, then the next best thing was to trace from the newspaper. But, obviously these newspaper patterns didn't print the full-size pieces. So, if you traced off the newspaper you got a smaller pattern.

Whatever the reason for the numbers of fabrics or the size of the pieces, it does give us plenty of fodder for speculation and research, all adding to the enduring fascination of these quilts for me!

[1] Kiracofe, The American Quilt, A History of Cloth and Comfort 1750–1950, pp. 192 and 193

[2] Kiracofe, The American Quilt, A History of Cloth and Comfort 1750–1950, p. 192 and 193

* * *

Opposite:
"Double Wedding Ring" quilt from the collection of Carolyn Forster; quilt size 70½in (179cm) wide x 88in (223.5cm) tall.

This design was popularized in the 1930s by Ruby Short McKim. The small pieces allowed for scrap bags to be raided or fabrics swapped with friends.

Top left:
Close-up of the "Double Wedding Ring" quilt opposite. This close up shows the selection of fabrics the maker used. Only small pieces were needed for these blocks, the segments measuring 1½ x 2½in (3.75 x 6.5cm) when cut.

Top right:
Fabric pieces and part-made "Double Wedding Ring" segments, from the collection of Carolyn Forster.

The scrap pieces measure just ¾in (2cm) wide x 1½in (3.75cm) long, and they've all been cut in preparation for stitching into 8in (20.25cm) long segments for a block. The seam allowance used is only ⅛in (2–3mm). When pieces like this are found there is lots of speculation as to what the maker was intending. Could it be a doll quilt? Or are the patches this small because that was the size of the pieces in the newspaper pattern in which they were printed? Or was it part of the fad for very small patches in quilts? This one would certainly have been a challenge to sew, and perhaps is why it was never finished.

Scrap Doll Quilt

DESIGNED, MACHINE-PIECED AND MACHINE-QUILTED BY CAROLYN FORSTER

BACKGROUND

This one-patch doll quilt (and its little-sister coaster, a bonus project in this section) is a tribute to the fabric collector!

As noted on the previous pages, although we can find small pieces of fabric in examples of Twenties and Thirties quilts, they may not indicate a frugal quiltmaker—in fact, due to the SAs, quilts like this can "waste" as much fabric as a regular quilt.

However, what quilts like these do show off are how many different fabrics you have! There are 144 scrappy squares in this mini quilt, so why not see if you can use 144 different prints in your own design?

I'll tell you now before you start looking: there are many repeated fabrics in mine!

As with quilters in the 1930s, we are always on the lookout for a notion or tool to help our stitching along. In this case, I find the printed gridded interfacing a fun and useful product. We are using the grid of 1in (2.5cm) squares for this project (which will come into their own in the coaster project). Simply lay your squares of fabric over the iron-on side (which is slightly shiny) then, when you are happy, iron them in place. Since the scraps are stuck in place, it will make stitching the patches together not only more accurate but much easier too.

MEASUREMENTS

Quilt size:
18in (45.75cm) square

Patch size:
2in (5cm) square cut;
1½in (3.75cm) square finished

REQUIREMENTS

Squares:
Note—it's OK to repeat fabrics if you don't have lots of scraps!

One hundred and forty-four different scraps, minimum 2in (5cm) square in size

Foundation:
Fusible interfacing with a printed quilt grid with whole 1in (2.5cm) squares, 24in (61cm) square piece

Note—I've used Quilter's Grid by Vlieseline®; you could also use Quilter's Grid 820 by Pellon®

Backing:
20in (50.75cm) square

OR

Large Fat Quarter (20 x 22in / 50.75 x 56cm)

Batting / wadding:
20in (50.75cm) square

Binding:
Note—I've used a darker, almost black fabric to help frame the quilt

5in (13cm) x WOF

FABRIC CUTTING

Binding:
Cut two 2½in (6.5cm) x WOF strips. Join the short ends with a bias join to make a continuous length (see page 179). Trim the SA to ¼in (5mm) and press open. Fold in half along the length, WS together, and press.

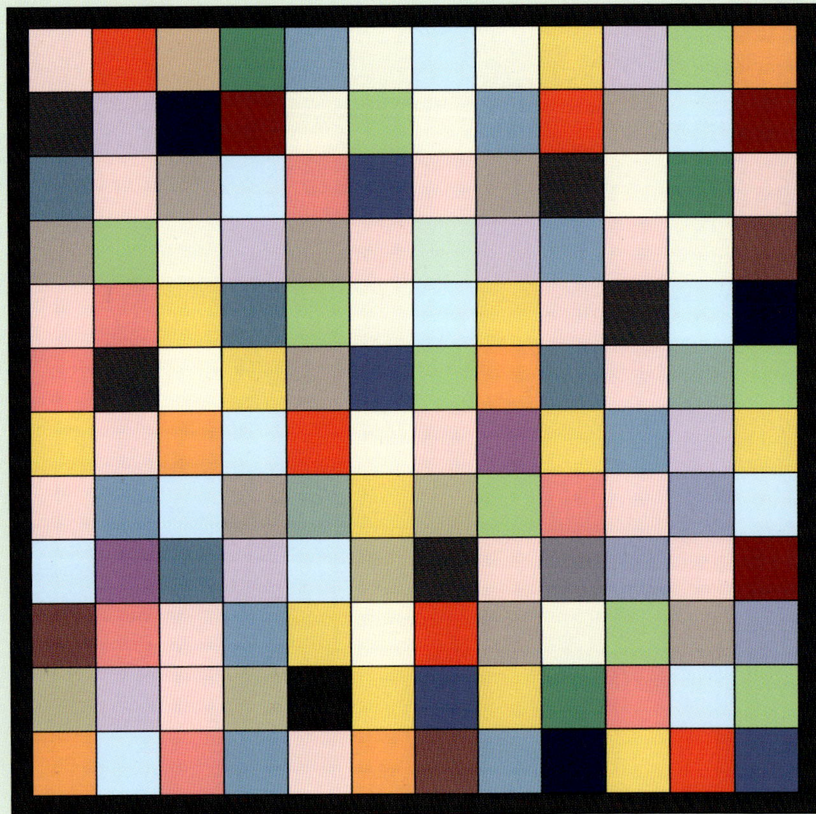

Scrap Doll Quilt design.

METHOD

Quilt top

Step One Lay out the your quilter's grid with the sticky side up. I find it helpful to do this on my rotary cutting mat, so I can line up the printed grid with the grid lines on my mat. With the fabrics RS up, cover four 1in (2.5cm) squares on the grid with one of your 2in (5cm) fabric squares—so a 2in (5cm) square area.

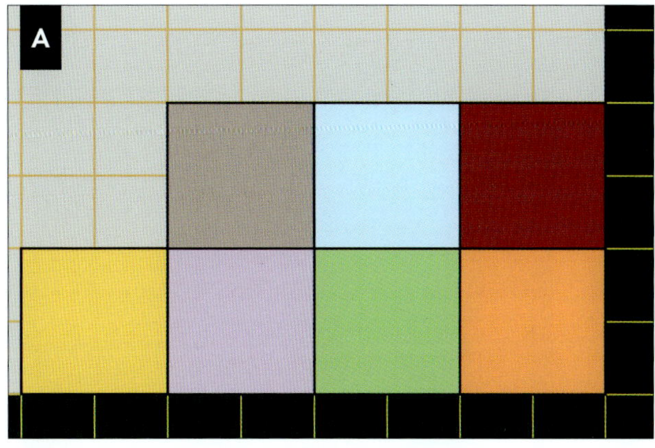

Step Two Repeat to cover the grid with all 144 fabric squares (**A**)—this will be 12 squares across and 12 squares up on the printed grid.

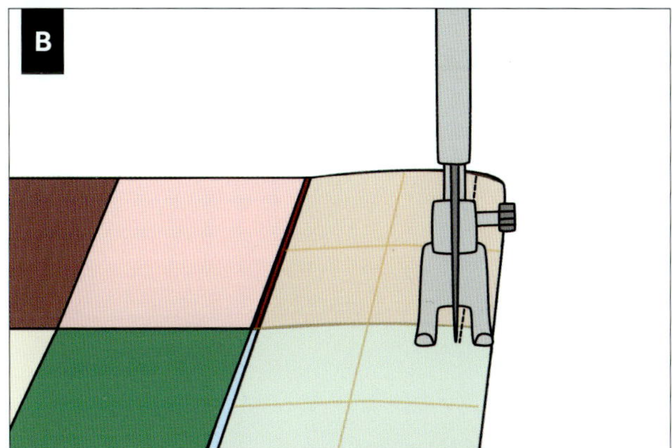

Step Three Carefully slide the quilter's grid with the squares onto your ironing board (or gently slide an ironing mat under the grid and remove the cutting mat). Press all the squares in place with an iron; this will fuse the fabric squares to the grid.

Step Four Now start to sew the squares together. Fold the first row RS together along the grid line where the first and second rows of the squares butt against each other. Using a ¼in (5mm) SA but a slightly smaller stitch length (around 2.00), stitch along the grid line from beginning to end (**B**). Using a smaller than usual stitch length will add more security to the seam, as we'll be cutting through the grid later on.

Step Five Repeat for the remaining rows, until all the horizontal grid lines where the fabric squares butt together are stitched.

Step Six Now, using sharp pointed scissors, and folding each row RS together as you work, cut along the horizontal grid line between every set of rows—you shouldn't be touching the stitching (**C**). Press all the SAs open once they have been snipped.

Step Seven Repeat Steps 4–6, this time along the vertical grid lines where the edges of the squares butt each other (**D**).

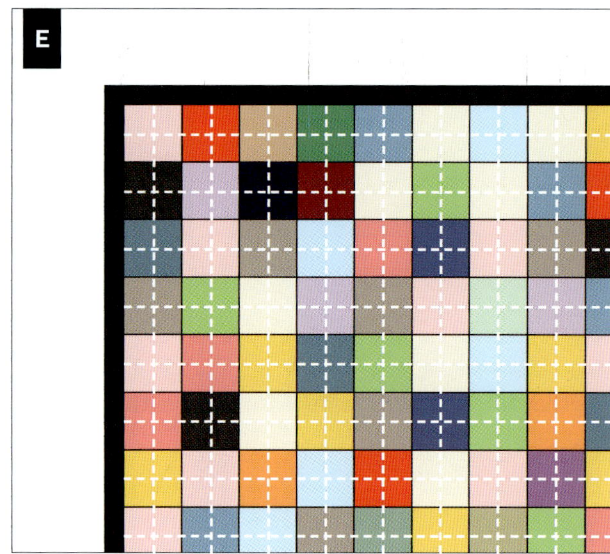

Assembly and finishing

Step Eight Prepare your quilt layers: place the backing RS down, center the batting / wadding over the top then center the quilt top over these, RS up. Baste / tack the layers together using your chosen method (see pages 162–165), ready to quilt.

Step Nine For the quilting, I machine quilted down the center of the squares in continuous lines (**E**). You could big-stitch quilt by hand if you prefer—see page 173 for more details.

Step Ten Once quilted, remove the basting / tacking stitches then trim the edges and square up. Bind the quilt with your chosen method (see pages 180–183), then add a label to finish (see page 185).

Below:
Scrap Doll Quilt (left), Tiny Scrap Quilt (right).

TINY SCRAP QUILT: COASTER

MEASUREMENTS

Quilt size:
6½in (16.5cm) square

Patch size:
1in (2.5cm) square cut; ½in (1.25cm) finished

REQUIREMENTS

Squares:
Note—it's OK to repeat fabrics if you don't have lots of scraps!

One hundred and forty-four different scraps, minimum 1in (2.5cm) square in size

Foundation:
Fusible interfacing with a printed quilt grid with whole 1in (2.5cm) squares, 12in (30.5cm) square piece

Note—I've used Quilter's Grid by Vlieseline®; you could also use Quilter's Grid 820 by Pellon®

Backing:
8in (20.5cm) square

Batting / wadding:
8in (20.5cm) square

Binding:
Note—I've used a darker, almost black fabric to help frame the coaster

2½in (5cm) x WOF. Fold in half along the length, WS together, and press.

Method

Repeat Steps 1–10 as for the Scrap Doll Quilt on pages 113 and 114, but this time in Step 1 each fabric square will only cover one square of the grid. I bound the coaster using the "Hacked mitered binding" method on page 182.

HISTORICAL TECHNIQUE NO. 10

Redwork Embroidery

In the 1920s and 1930s, a new kind of quilting was coming to prominence. Quilt patterns, once traced and shared with only family and friends, were being distributed on a national scale through newspapers and magazines.

Some were based on older designs, but some were entirely new, and attributed to specific designers—an entirely new phenomenon. These named designers were mostly real people, but occasionally the newspaper or magazine created a quilter persona for marketing purposes.[1] Faux byline names included Hetty Winthrop, Alice Brooks, Grandmother Clark, and Nancy Page—all solid American names, and demonstrating the passion for Colonial Revival in quiltmaking during this time.

The designer of prominence and a real person was Ruby Short McKim. She was a trained designer from the Parsons School of Design in New York, and started out creating her first embroidery quilt design for her local newspaper, the *Kansas City Star*, while she was still teaching. Her business grew into a needle-art business that then thrived during the Twenties and Thirties. By 1928 she had more than 10 nationally syndicated quilt pattern series in newspapers and magazines.[2]

[1] Barbara Brackman, "Who was Nancy Page?", Quilter's Newsletter, No. 235, September 1991, pp. 22–29

[2] Jill Sutton Filo, "Ruby Short McKim", American Patchwork and Quilting magazine, February 1998 issue (article based on "Ruby Short McKim: The Formative Years", published in Uncoverings 1996: Research Papers of the American Quilt Study Group, Vol. 17)

* * *

Opposite:
Redwork quilt from the collection of Marion Drake; quilt size 60in (152.5cm) wide x 49in (124.5cm) tall.

These 6in (15.25cm) square blocks that make up the quilt top contain a variety of motifs, but mainly err towards family life, childhood and nature. It is finely hand quilted with "tram lines" of stitching all going in one diagonal direction, from top right to bottom left.

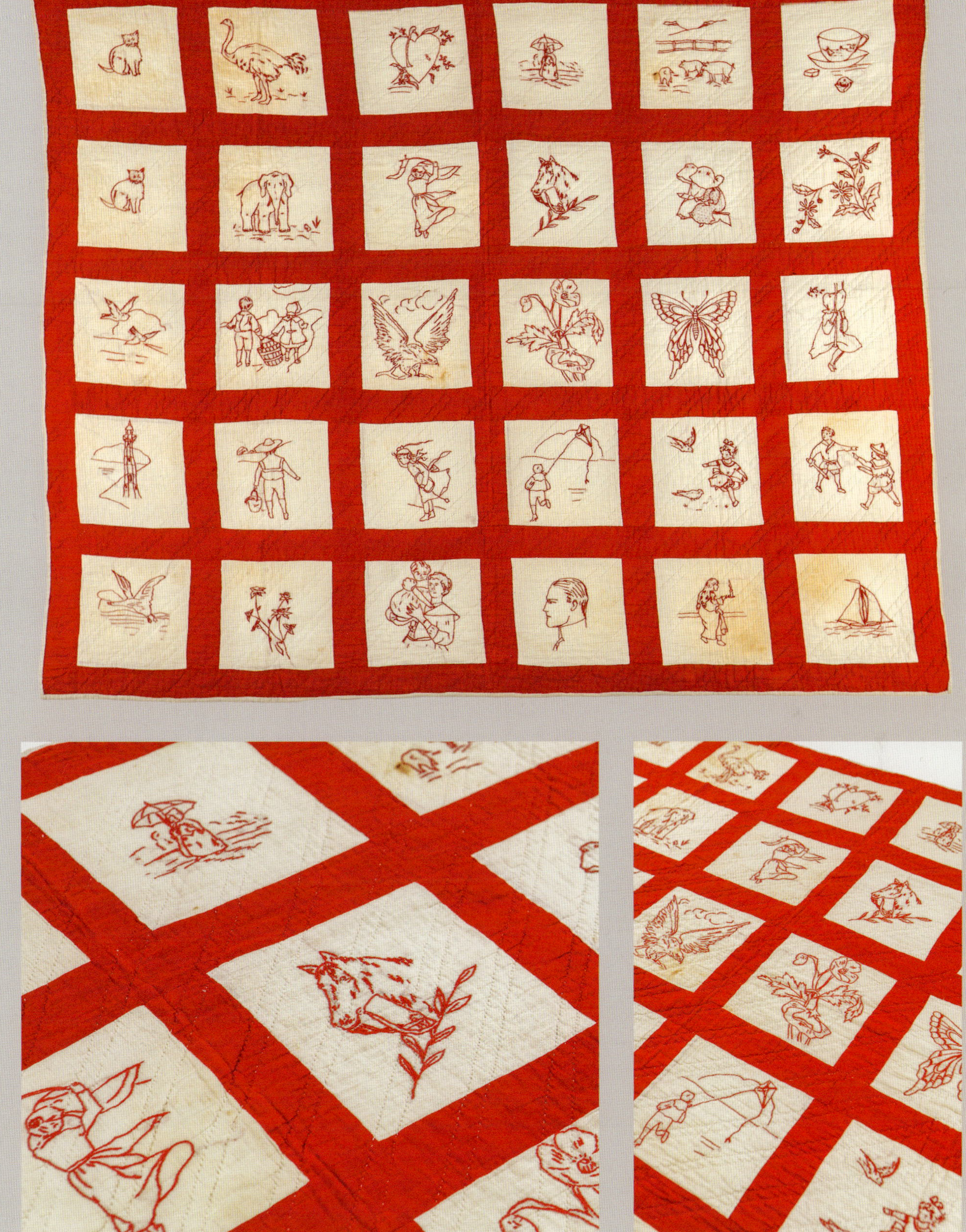

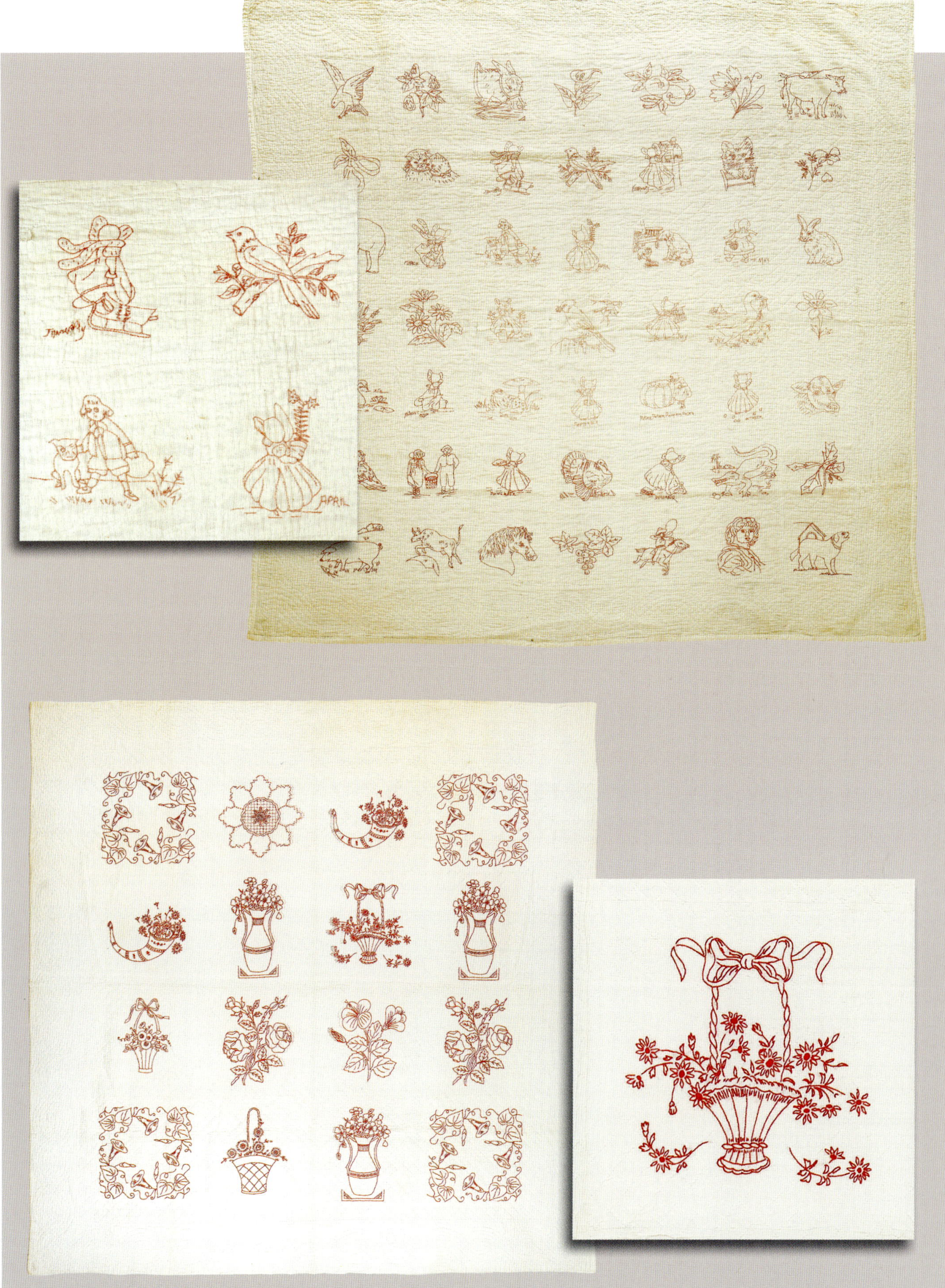

Top left:
Redwork quilt by Aurel Belle Dickey; USA; c. early 20th century; 70in (178cm) wide x 68in (173cm) tall; AM&G: 2012, no. 1.

Aurel Dicky has decorated 49 white cotton squares with embroidered designs in pink thread. It is likely that the thread was originally red and has faded over time. Pictures include animals, birds, and plants. The months of the year are represented by "Sunbonnet Sue" figures in different poses. Dickey has quilted the layers together using parallel lines of stitches 1in (2.5cm) apart. She has filled the wide border with a quilted cable pattern.

Bottom left:
Redwork quilt from the collection of Marion Drake; quilt size 82in (208.25cm) square.

The 16in (40.5cm) square blocks have been stitched with some repeated motifs. One of the blocks is even embroidered with cross stitch. Some of the motifs may have been originally designed to feature multiple colored threads, such as the basket of flowers, based on other examples of Thirties quilts with similar motifs.

In 1931 Ruby Short McKim established McKim Studios with her husband and published her book, *101 Patchwork Patterns*—which is still in print today. She had kits and designs for sale through a catalogue, *Designs Worth Doing*, all of which appealed to the modern quiltmaker. You could buy anything from a 25c pattern to a $10 sateen First Lady quilt kit. The designs offered were a mixture of older traditional patchwork designs re-imagined in the new fabric colors and combinations of the day, appliqué designs, often floral and even embroidery designs. Blocks could be bought ready-cut or marked for appliqué.

One way to celebrate McKim's appliqué designs is to stitch them as redwork—McKim designed a number of redwork quilts over her career, and some of the designs from her *101 Patchwork Patterns* are the basis for the designs on the quilt coming up.

Redwork or "penny square panels" were a popular form of stitchery at the time. Originating in Germany and brought over to America by settlers in the 1860s, this type of stitching was still popular in the 1930s. The designs were called "redwork" as they were commonly stitched in one color, a turkey-red thread. They are sometimes called "penny squares" as the printed or marked panels cost a penny and the thread also cost a penny. The designs ranged from nursery rhymes to birds, state flowers, and buildings, and the incentive was to collect the whole the set.

Redwork Cot Quilt

DESIGNED, MACHINE-PIECED, EMBROIDERED AND MACHINE-QUILTED BY CAROLYN FORSTER

BACKGROUND

I'm mixing up what I consider the "best of all worlds" here with a little quilt based on some popular designer appliqué patterns of the time, but stitching them instead in red with stem stitch for some redwork. The patterns are quick to stitch, and I can see why the Penny Squares—or the patterns printed onto feedsacks—were so popular for embroidery in the Thirties.

I've chosen a small size for this quilt (baby-quilt size), as I was interested in reflecting the new popularity of designing quilts specifically for babies and children in the early 20th century. Previously, quilts for babies had often been normal-size patchwork blocks, but with fewer stitched together to make a quilt small enough to be suitable for use in a crib.

The new designers and the companies creating baby and children's quilt designs often featured appliqué or redwork motifs in the patterns. Like adult-sized quilts, they ranged from simple to more elaborate designs, and it was typical for them to depict scenes in nursery rhymes or storybooks. The popular quilt designer from this time, Ruby Short McKim, designed several quilts for children in a mix of large and small sizes, and her "Rhymeland Quilt" is a good example of a children's quilt she designed with redwork embroidery.

With my little quilt here, I have taken inspiration from some of the appliqué designs from McKim's *101 Patchwork Patterns*. They are worked in stem stitch, which was commonly used for redwork in the Twenties and Thirties, but I've used a variegated thread instead of the usual solid, as I think this adds a nice touch as the color changes subtly over the design. I've sneaked in a design from a vintage appliqué quilt in my collection too (see below right), which is unnamed but very typical of the period.

When looking at appliqué designs, it is very easy to see how to translate them into an embroidery design. So, if you are looking through old quilts for ideas, you can always adapt the design and add it as an embroidery motif in your own quilt.

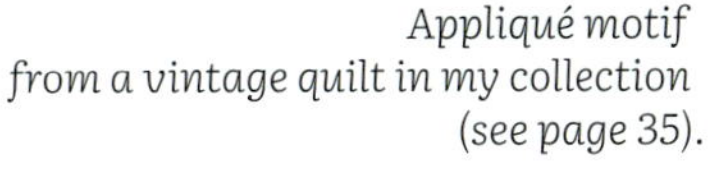

Appliqué motif from a vintage quilt in my collection (see page 35).

Redwork Cot Quilt design.

MEASUREMENTS

Quilt size:
31½ x 41½in (80 x 105.5cm)

Block sizes, unfinished:
9in (23cm) square

REQUIREMENTS

Quilt top:
White
Cotton-linen blend, 20in (50.75cm) x WOF

Note—I've used Essex linen, as I like to use this for embroidery, but you can use a plain or textured quilting cotton instead if you wish

Red
Quilting cotton with a linen texture, 39in (99cm) x WOF

Note—I've used Makower 1473/R, Linen Texture Red, but you could use a solid red quilting cotton if you don't want the texture

Batting / wadding:
41 x 51in (104.25 x 129.5cm)

Backing:
51in (129.5cm) x WOF

Binding:
10in (25.5cm) x WOF

Note—I've used the same fabric as selected for the quilt top

Notions:
28wt white cotton thread, for hand quilting

Four to five skeins of red stranded embroidery cotton floss—*I've used Anchor 01206, which is a variegated red*

Size 6 Embroidery needle OR size 24 Chenille needle, for both embroidering and hand quilting

Fine propelling fabric pencil and bold pen for marking the design

Everything else:
Templates A, B, C, D, E, and F (see pages 193–197)

Optional: lightbox, if you have one

FABRIC CUTTING

Quilt top:
White
Cut two 10in (25.5cm) x WOF strips, then sub-cut into six 10in (25.5cm) squares.

Red
For the sashing:

- Cut two 1½in (3.75cm) x WOF strips. Sub-cut one strip into three 1½ x 9½in (3.75 x 24.25cm) strips for the vertical sashings; sub-cut the remaining strip into two 1½ x 19½in (3.75 x 49.5cm) strips for the horizontal sashings.

For the borders:

- Cut your sashing and binding strips first and then, from the remaining red fabric, cut two strips 6½in (16.5cm) wide x 29½in (75cm) high and two strips 6½in (16.5cm) wide x 31½in (80cm) high.

Backing:
Cut into one 41 x 51in (104.25 x 129.5cm) piece.

Binding:
Cut four 2½in (6.5cm) x WOF strips. Join the short ends with a bias join to make a continuous length (see page 179). Trim the SA to ¼in (5mm) and press open. Fold in half along the length, WS together,

METHOD

Embroidered blocks

Step One Trace off the templates onto copy paper. For the templates that need mirroring (Templates A, B, C and D), trace the half of the design printed in the book onto copy paper with a bold pen, fold the paper in half (making sure the drawn side is facing out), hold it up to a window or place it on a lightbox (the drawn side facing down), then use your original drawing to trace over the lines again on the other sides of the paper. Ensure the alignment crosses on the templates are added.

Step Two Fold each white square into four then unfold to create crease marks; these will help you center the embroidery designs in the next step.

Step Three Place a white fabric square RS up over the tracing of Template A, lining up the intersection of the fold lines with the alignment cross on the template. With the help of a window or a lightbox, trace the template onto the fabric with the fine pencil (**A**).

Step Four Repeat Step 3 to trace off Templates B–F. Where necessary, refer to the positioning diagrams on pages 195–197 to ensure the design sits in the correct place on the fabric square.

Step Five Using three strands of the stranded embroidery cotton floss, embroider over all the pattern lines with stem stitch (**B**). To start, thread the needle with the floss, tie a knot on the end then take the needle through the work from back to front. When you run out of thread or finish the outline, ensure there is an approx. 3–4in (7.75–10cm) tail, take the needle to the back of the work, weave through the back of the stitches then cut the thread. Make these stem stitches as small as a backstitch for a smoother design. Use an embroidery hoop if you wish; I simply held the fabric in my hand for my own embroideries.

Step Six Once all the squares are stitched, square up the fabric squares to 9½in (24.25cm) square.

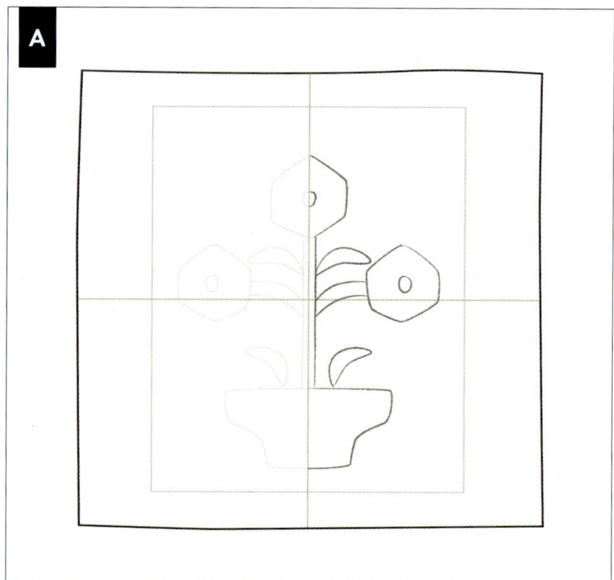

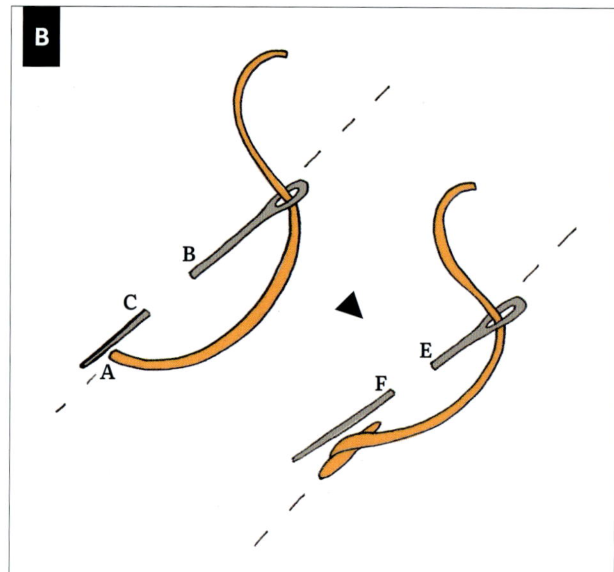

Assembly and finishing

Step Seven Using the diagram on page 122 to help you with placement, arrange the blocks into three rows of two. Between each pair of blocks, position a vertical sashing strip. Sew the first block in the row and the vertical sashing strips RS together, then sew the remaining block to the other long edge of the sashing strip, RS together. Repeat for all rows. Press the SAs toward the sashing strips.

Step Eight Position a horizontal sashing strip between each row, then sew the rows and sashing strips RS together in turn. Press the SAs toward the sashing strip.

Step Nine To add the borders, stitch the longer border strips to the left- and right-hand sides of the quilt, RS together. Press the SAs toward the borders.

Step Ten Sew the shorter border pieces to the top and bottom edges of the quilt in the same way. Again, press the SAs toward the borders.

Step Eleven Prepare your quilt layers: place the backing RS down, center the batting / wadding over the top then center the quilt top over these, RS up. Baste / tack the layers together using your chosen method (see pages 162–165), ready to quilt.

Step Twelve For the quilting, I marked then hand quilted a 45-degree cross-hatch grid over the entire quilt, spacing the lines 1½in (approx. 4cm) apart.

Step Thirteen Once quilted, remove the basting / tacking stitches then trim the edges and square up. Bind the quilt with your chosen method (see pages 180–183), then add a label to finish (see page 185).

Patchwork and Quilting Basics

In this final section, you'll find all the information on the key materials, equipment, and techniques needed to make the quilts in the book. If you're a beginner quilter, I recommend reading through this chapter carefully before stitching the quilts.

THE
BIG BOOK
OF
NEEDLECRAFT

ORIGINAL
ORGANIC
NATURAL

Choosing fabrics

One thing that I keep in mind when choosing fabrics with a Thirties-inspired palette is that I am not trying to reproduce a quilt from this time; I'm just dipping into the period's color pool of fabrics.

One reason that I enjoy using a Thirties color palette is the ease in using it. It is often of a mid-tone shade—if you look at a group of Thirties fabrics in grayscale (take a picture on your cellphone, then convert the photo in your phone's picture editor to black and white), you'll often see that they all merge together. Since nothing is fighting, there are no big decisions to make when selecting fabrics, and you don't have to worry that your choices won't work out.

Another reason I like to use Thirties-inspired fabrics is because, generally, the scale of the print in Thirties fabrics is the same, and is neither too big nor too overpowering. This means that, even if you start adding checks, stripes, shirtings, or woven chambrays to the mix, everything still falls neatly into place.

Use all the clues in the fabrics of the old quilts to springboard your imagination and your choices to create a quilt as fresh and vibrant as those from this innovative period.

Vintage fabrics

Perhaps the most costly and time-consuming way to source fabrics for your quilt is to buy actual fabrics from the period. Start by looking for vintage fabric and quilt sellers either online or in person. I'm based in the UK, and often purchase vintage fabrics when traveling in the US.

Vintage fabrics tend to be more costly, by virtue of their age and rarity; for this reason, perhaps invest in one print that you love then base other, less expensive fabrics around that.

One of the most iconic fabrics from this time is the feedsack. We talk more about this on pages 28, 100 and 101, but if you are looking to buy these fabrics today then do your research. Study old quilts, read the books, look on the internet—the more you look at the prints and quilts, the more likely it is you will recognize an old print when you see it. The quality of cotton will also be an identifying factor, as will either the holes where the bag was stitched up, or the fact that it is still stitched up. Feedsacks come in many different sizes, so don't be confused into thinking what you're looking at is not authentic, just because it's not the usual size.

This leads nicely on to my next point: do your research before buying your vintage fabrics, so that you are happy with what you are being sold. Although many specialist vintage textile sellers are genuine and can perfectly date their fabric collections, you do come across some sellers who think, "This looks old, so it must be!" Because there are modern reproduction fabric lines around it is easy to get confused between what is old and what just looks old.

Reproduction fabrics

Buying and using these will instantly give you the look of the quilts from the Colonial Revival period. Many fabric manufacturers now produce ranges inspired by or based on prints from the 1930s. You can make your quilt entirely from reproduction fabrics, but personally I think that using them as a starting point then adding fabrics from your stash is a good approach; this way, you're only investing in a few fabrics then making use of what you already own.

Prints

If you're selecting modern prints to use for your Thirties quilts—whether brand-new or from your existing stash, start with prints that have that "fresh" look of vintage 1930s quilts. By this, I mean brights and pastel shades. Ensuring they're in a similar color palette, mixing these with your reproduction or vintage fabrics will help them mingle, and give your quilt the vibrancy that would have been experienced by the quilters in the Thirties.

Checks and stripes

These are the classics and very much timeless fabrics in our quiltmaking. They have always featured in quilts, and will continue to be found in our patches. You can use them with abandon in your quilt: there will always be a place for these in quilts, but they sit particularly well in the 1930s palette.

Plains and solids

Vintage examples of solids are hard to come by, but the large, modern selection that's available to buy today makes it easy to choose one that fits into our 1930s scheme.

If using completely solid fabrics seems a bit too much of a contrast for your particular group of fabrics, look at modern prints that have a subtle texture to them. Also consider woven chambrays and cotton shirtings; these are often found in old quilts as they were leftovers from dressmaking.

Backgrounds

Classic background fabrics—consisting of bright whites or light creams—are designed to show off the patchwork and stitching. Historically, background fabrics were used to eke out scraps from costly yardage as, typically being made from muslin / calico, they were cheaper to buy.

Using cheaper, neutral fabrics for the backgrounds is an approach we can still take today. If you want to be a bit more authentic and give a nod to the past, the washed calico bags used to put our shopping in, or that cotton tote bag that has seen better days, could be repurposed into background fabric. Giving old cottons a new lease of life in a quilt is not only sustainable, but follows in the footsteps of the needlewomen before us that were doing what needs must.

If you wish to source new fabric, there is a great variety of "low volume" fabrics (i.e. white fabric with a gentle print or texture on it) available to buy online or in brick-and-mortar stores. In particular, I like prints with text and words— it reminds me of the early feedsacks that were printed with the contents and brand names, before they were (or were not) bleached out.

Backing fabric

When choosing what fabric to use for your backing, I recommend selecting one that is a similar weight to those used on the front of the quilt. Note that if you choose a plain fabric, your quilting stitches will be more visible on the back of your quilt.

You will need

THREADS

There are many makes and types on the market but the list below details the threads I use most frequently in my sewing. Note that, as the numbers get smaller, the thread gets thicker.

- **Basting / tacking thread:** As its name suggests, this is a specialist thread for hand basting / tacking that can be broken easily but holds the layers of a quilt together securely enough for quilting. It tends to be cheaper than regular sewing thread.
- **50wt:** This is the most familiar weight of thread, and is often used on the sewing machine for piecing patches. It can also be used for machine quilting and adding texture, but its weight means it's not too visible.
- **40wt:** Slightly thicker than 50wt, 40wt can be used for patchwork piecing but it also works well for machine quilting. It is my preference for hand finishing the binding on a quilt.
- **28wt:** I use this for hand piecing patches and for fine hand quilting, as I like the thickness of the thread—it seems to fill the hole the needle makes in the fabric.
- **12wt:** This is the thickest general thread I use, and it works well for anywhere you want a strong bold stitch (like big-stitch quilting), even on the machine.
- **Coton perle and coton à broder:** These are embroidery threads and they come in different weights. I use 12wt coton perle for big-stitch quilting; 8wt coton perle is great for tying quilts; coton à broder in 16wt is good for both.

When buying thread, typically I buy the biggest spool possible, and in neutral, toning colors. This way you save money in the long run: large spools are often more economical, and neutral colors can be used in lots more sewing projects too. You will also be using less plastic, as it takes less to create a large spool than lots of small ones. If you need a smaller amount of thread for portable stitching, then wind a bobbin from the large thread cone and take that with you.

If you have old threads that were thrifted or handed on to you, then use them by all means. If you can read the spool label, look for the weight and fiber content. Test the thread for strength too, as it can deteriorate over time. This will also help when considering fiber content: man-made fibers will stretch before snapping, and natural ones have less give. Pull the thread between your hands; if it snaps easily, don't use it for seams—keep it for basting / tacking, as it doesn't matter if the thread breaks for temporary stitches.

You can thrift thread from certain fabrics and clothes that often use strong thread, like jeans and cotton or paper sacks, by carefully unpicking the seams. The chain-link stitching for these, if undone correctly, can be saved for tying quilts or wound around an old empty spool. I've saved the cords threaded through the top of a pair of curtains; these are great for tying quilts, which has been a common practice in quiltmaking since at least the 1930s.

BATTING / WADDING

Purchased

If you wish to buy batting / wadding for the projects in this book, you can. That said, I'd recommend looking for brands that use recycled resources and follow sustainable practices. These might include fibers from rapidly growing plants/fiber sources, like bamboo, or recycled fibers.

Recycled

Have a look at what you have left over from finished projects—chances are you will have spare batting / wadding. If you tend to use one particular type or brand, pieces can easily be joined together to form a bigger piece.

Methods to join pieces include:

- **Sewing-machine zigzag stitch (A)**. Butt the edges of the batting / wadding then sew over the "line" where the edges meet with zigzag stitch. Make sure your stitch is wide enough to cover the edges, and that the stitch is not too short: you do not want a hard line of dense stitching holding the batting / wadding together, as it can affect the drape of the quilt.
- **Hand stitching with baseball/suture stitch (B)**. Bring the needle up on one side of the batting / wadding, ¼in (5mm) or so away from the central gap. Bring the needle up on the other side, a little further along than your previous stitch so they're slightly offset. Repeat this motion of coming up alternately left and right; the stitch will evenly pull the edges of the batting / wadding together. Finish off with a few backstitches in the batting / wadding to secure.

If you don't want to use batting / wadding, then there are plenty of alternative fillings for your quilt. What you use will often depend on how the quilt will be quilted.

- **Wool blankets**. Old wool blankets add a lovely weight to a quilt, and great insulation too. Depending on the thickness of the quilt sandwich, you can quilt as usual or simply hand tie (see pages 176 and 177).
- **Old quilts**. Controversial as this might sound, filling your quilt with a much older one was once not an uncommon practice. When a quilt became too thin or worn, or out of favor or fashion, in the past it could be recycled as the batting / wadding in a new quilt. It might not be to everyone's liking, but some think it's better to use a quilt in this way than to let it sit forgotten in a cupboard.
- **Flannel sheets**. If you want to use light-weight batting / wadding, old brushed cotton or flannel sheets work well. Often they are large enough for a quilt, and once quilted give the quilt a lovely texture without adding too much insulation.

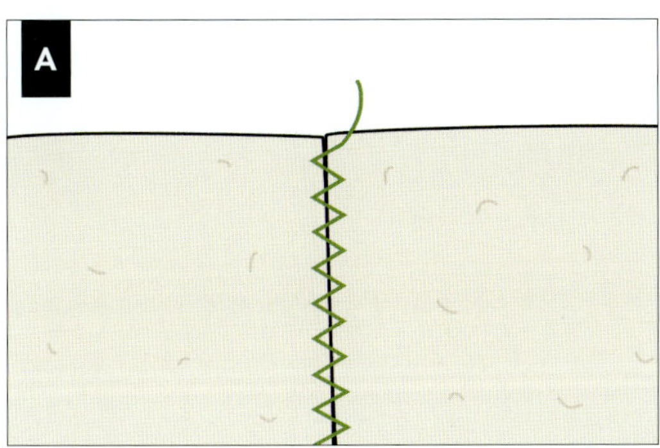

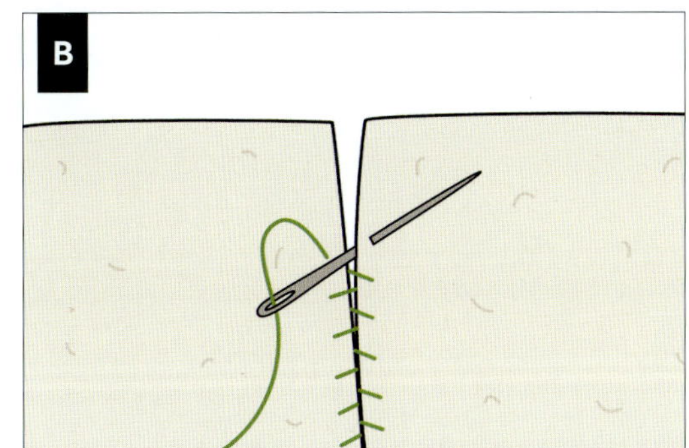

NEEDLES

Buy good-quality needles. They will last longer than cheaper versions and be a pleasure to sew with. The more stitching you do, the more you will realize that the different needles work best for specific jobs.

- **For hand-piecing and hand-finishing binding**, sizes 10 and 11 Sharps needles are my go-to.
- **For big-stitch hand quilting** I use a size 6 Betweens (quilting), Embroidery, Chenille or Sashiko needle.
- **For fine hand quilting**, size 10 Betweens or Embroidery needles are my preference.
- When it comes to **machine needles**, sizes 70/10 to 90/14 are ideal for general piecing and sewing patchwork; you'll also need quilting and topstitch needles for those specific jobs.

PINS AND QUILT SAFETY PINS

Patchwork pins are fine and are great for piecing; **short appliqué pins** are great for piecing as well as appliqué. For safety-pin basting / tacking, I use special **quilt safety pins** that are 1in (2.5cm) long; if you can get the ones with plastic covers, it will make the process easier on your hands. Using a teaspoon (or a grapefruit spoon) to help close the safety pins makes it easier on your hands.

SEWING MACHINE

You do not need a fancy sewing machine—as long as it does a straight stitch you can quilt and sew as you please. You'll find lots of hints and tips in the instruction manual that comes with your machine, as well as troubleshooting pages.

Many machines can stitch through multiple layers without you needing to adjust the foot pressure on the top of the machine; others need a walking foot attached. A large extension table is particularly useful when working with your machine. It will allow you to keep your work flat and gives you a better surface area in order to handle and control what you are working on. If your machine does not come with one, it is worth the investment, and it can be easily removed and folded away when not in use.

Housekeeping on your machine is very important when you are regularly stitching through multiple layers including batting / wadding. This sort of stitching generates a lot of lint, and this is often hidden under the foot plate and around the bobbin casing. If you can, give the area a little dust with a fine brush each time you change the bobbin. At other times, take the machine apart in the bobbin area following your instruction manual, and give it a proper clean. This will increase the working life of the machine and make your quilting a much better experience.

You will find certain feet useful:

- A **¼in (5mm) piecing foot with no guide** is good for piecing patchwork shapes.
- A **walking (dual- / even-feed) foot** is ideal for stitching through multiple layers of fabric and binding the quilt.

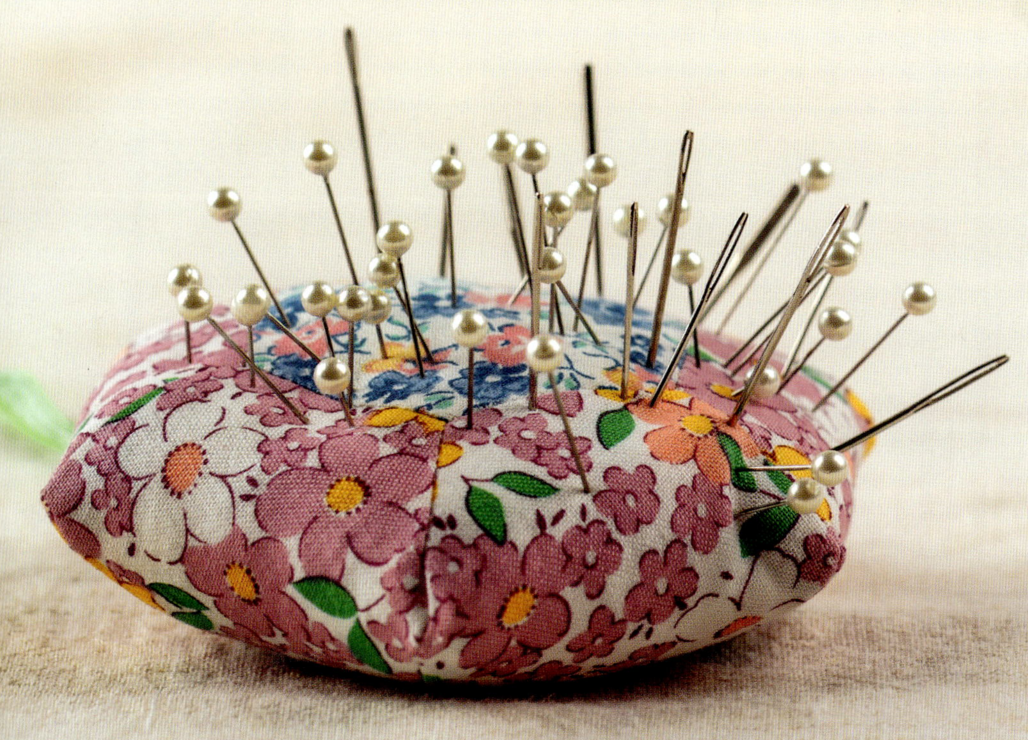

CUTTING TOOLS

Scissors

Use a large pair of long-bladed scissors for cutting the fabrics. I have a specialist pair of quilting scissors that is ideal for this purpose. You will also want small scissors with fine points, which make snipping threads easy and give you more control over the blades.

Seam ripper

Use this tool to undo sewing mistakes quickly and easily. I also use the point to help guide in the fabric under the machine foot, close to the needle, which helps to protect my fingers.

Rulers

Various specialist acrylic rulers are available that work with a rotary cutter and self-healing cutting mat to cut the fabric easily and quickly in layers where necessary. There are many different sizes and the most common one (and the one I recommend investing in) is a 6½ x 24½in (16 x 60cm), which is often sold in a starter set with a mat and rotary cutter. Buy a brand with markings that you find easy to read, and that line up with the grid on your cutting mat.

A square ruler is also useful, and it makes sense to buy a larger square if you can, as it includes all the smaller sizes too. A 16½in (42cm) square is a great one for this. Since I often work with 12½in (31.75cm) square unfinished blocks in my quiltmaking, I use a12½in (31.75cm) square ruler the most.

Rotary cutter

Looking much like a pizza wheel, a rotary cutter cuts through up to about eight layers of fabric at a time. Keep the blade sharp and free of nicks, and cut through as many or as few layers as you are comfortable with. The most useful size rotary cutter is one that holds a 45mm blade. Look for makes that have in-built safety features: some have a blade that automatically retracts when not in use; others have a blade lock that will stop you from cutting yourself if you accidentally nudge it with your hand.

Self-healing cutting mat

This is a purpose-made mat, available from craft stores, on which to cut your fabric using the rulers and cutters. It is marked into a grid that you can use to help you measure and cut the fabric in straight lines. Buy the largest size you can afford, as the larger the cutting mat, the less you will need to fold your fabric.

OTHER KEY EQUIPMENT

Quilter's tape measure

This type of tape measure is longer than a normal tape measure, and is so useful for measuring quilt sides. It's usually 120in (300cm) long.

Iron

Your patchwork will need pressing, so a good hot iron is useful. You can use a steam iron, but be careful not to distort the seams when pressing. A seam roller can be used for quick pressing, but for me there's no replacing an iron.

Fabric markers

Hera markers, tailor's chalk, chalk wheels and pens (such as a Chaco Liner) and soap slivers are all things that have been around for many generations, and there is a reason for this. They are not only economical but mark accurately too. Think about trying these tried-and-true tools before buying disposable plastic pens and markers than not only leave chemicals on the fabric, but can be tricky to remove too.

Template materials

If the shape you need to cut out is one you will use a lot, then it is worth investing in **plastic sheets**. Mark the outline with a fine permanent marking pen then cut it out with sharp household scissors. The plastic will keep its shape through multiple uses. Some template plastic sheets have a graph printed on them. You might find these useful for certain shapes—such as squares, rectangles and triangles—as you can use the grid to help measure and cut out the desired shapes. If you're struggling to see your drawn lines, placing masking tape on the back of the sheet, behind the drawn lines, will make them easier to see before cutting out.

If the shape is only being used a handful of times, then photocopying it (or tracing it off), gluing it to a firm piece of **card** (like a cereal packet) then cutting it out will be fine. A card shape like this will deteriorate over time, with the edges getting softer and less accurate, but for a few uses it is all you need.

Whether you choose to write directly onto the template or on a sticker attached to it, remember to add details about each template shape (such as its name and the grain line) with a **sharp propelling pencil or a suitable pen**, so you remember what it's for (and which way up it should be) later!

Hand-piecing tools

Use **paper-cutting scissors** for cutting out your templates. They should be comfortable to handle and have a sharp blade. If you have some old fabric-cutting scissors that have become dull or nicked, repurpose these for cutting templates.

In addition to the rulers listed on page 135, I like to use a **Perfect Piecer by Jinny Beyer** (great for lining up angled templates and shapes; **Marti Michell's Deluxe Corner Trimmer and Hand Piecing Aid** offers a similar purpose), **Omnigrid Marking Trio** rulers (useful for marking and checking ¼in / 5mm seams) and a **quilter's quarter** (useful for adding ¼in / 5mm seam allowance to templates).

To add a seam allowance around the templates, onto the fabric, I use a **Magic Seam Marker® by Sew Easy**; this is a metal disc with a hole in the center to insert your pencil tip, and allows you to "roll" the disc around the template—see page 143 for more information .

Quilting tools

For hand-quilting large quilts (i.e. anything larger than a pillow cover) I like to use a **quilting hoop**. The hoops acts like a third hand, holding the quilt for you while you use both hands for the hand stitching. The most common and useful size is a 14in (35.5cm) diameter hoop, 1in (2.5cm) deep. Never try to quilt with an embroidery hoop; these are too shallow, and your quilt will pop out of the hoop.

A **teaspoon or grapefruit spoon** is good to have on hand if I need help easing a needle or pin through the quilt layers.

Use **painter's / masking tape** to mark quilt lines temporarily; it's also handy for securing your quilt to a surface when basting / tacking.

Thimbles and finger protection

For quilting and some hand sewing, you will find it easier on your hands if you can protect your fingers with thimbles. It takes many of us a while to get used to these, and there are many products in the shops to help. Trying anything to protect your fingers is a good thing, but it can be expensive. Bear in mind that the goal is always to make your sewing practice more comfortable and, ultimately, if you can get used to using a durable metal thimble, like the ones our great grandmothers used, so much the better.

Techniques

BEFORE YOU BEGIN

- All seam allowances ("SAs") are ¼in (5mm) unless otherwise stated.
- All fabric cut from the bolt is cut across the full width of the fabric ("WOF"), unless stated otherwise.
- All fabric quantities are based on a 40in (101.5cm) useable width of fabric, bolt, or yardage.
- "RS" means the right side of the fabric; "WS" means the wrong side of the fabric; "HST" means Half Square Triangle; "QST" means "Quarter Square Triangle".
- When machine stitching, set your straight-stitch length to 11 or 2.0 to 2.5, depending on how your machine is calibrated. It needs to be small enough to hold the fabrics together, but large enough to unpick easily, if the need arises.
- Press with a hot iron and a pressing pad or ironing board. Whether you use steam or not is up to you; some people think it distorts the work, but this hasn't been my experience.
- When **pressing seams in one direction**, I will press from the front. **When seams need to be pressed open**, flip your work and press from the WS, using the point of the iron to open the seam as you press. Take care to position the work and the seam you want to press correctly; you will then find you can press in one stroke.
- **Pressing seams for hand-pieced quilts** is not the same as for those that are machine pieced. Unlike machine-piecing, which requires you to press the seams as you sew, and to press in certain directions, with hand piecing you press only when you've finished making the block. The seams also tend to fall naturally in a certain direction, so you can simply press in the angle the block dictates.
- **When using a rotary cutter**, always push it away from you to make the cut; never pull it towards you.

CUTTING FABRIC

Preparing the fabric for cutting

If your fabric is brand-new, begin by prewashing it. This preshrinks the fabric (so there are no shrunken surprises later), prevents color-bleeding, and washes out chemicals from the manufacturing process, making the fabric softer. I do not recommend prewashing pre-cuts smaller than a Fat Eighth, as they are at risk of fraying.

Most natural fibers—like cotton fabrics, which I recommend using for this book's projects—will shrink between 5%–10% on their first wash. Once you've given the fabric an initial wash (with a color-catcher to stop any color bleeding from spreading), it shouldn't shrink again.

If you are upcycling fabric or using older fabric, I'd recommend a gentle wash to remove any dirt it may have collected over time.

Allow your fabric to dry completely, or dry it in a tumble dryer, then iron it, ready for the next stage.

Trimming the fabric for cutting

Even if you are using pre-cut fabric, such as Fat Quarters, I recommend checking and trimming your fabric as instructed below before cutting out any shapes. This is because, once the fabric is washed, dried and pressed, there is often a misalignment of the raw edge when you line up the selvages / selvedges. This uneven edge needs to be trimmed off.

Note that all the steps on these pages assume you are right-handed and work from left to right; if you are left-handed, work from right to left.

Step One Fold the fabric in half lengthwise then hold it up with the two selvages / selvedges together to see if the fabric is twisted. If it is, shift the fabric in your hands until it's straightened out. (When the fabric is on the grain, there should be no shifting when you pull down on it.) This will often mean that the cut edges are now not even, but these will be trimmed off next.

Step Two Lay the folded fabric on the cutting mat, with the selvage / selvedge on a horizontal line closest to you and the fold along the top. Align the ruler with one of the vertical lines on the cutting mat and trim off the uneven fabric along the cross grain (the edge that is parallel to the cut edge of the fabric bolt), about ¾in (2cm) in from the side. Hold the ruler in place throughout the cutting process, and push the cutter away from you. Keeping the cutter pressed firmly against the ruler as you go will help create a straight, even edge.

Trimming the uneven fabric edges.

Cutting for your quilt top

When it comes to cutting out shapes for your quilt top—its patchwork, any framing strips, sashing and posts, and border strips—you will need to make sure to cut them out with the SA already included. This is so that, when you sew all the pieces together, they create the desired finished size.

If you'd like to learn how to design your own quilt, generally the principle is to start off knowing what size you'd like the finished shape to be (i.e. its size once it's sewn into the quilt, from seam to seam); you then add an extra amount to ensure that there's a ¼in (5mm) SA added to each side of the shape once cut out.

CUTTING STRIPS

These are for your borders, coping strips, sashing, posts, squares, and rectangles. Except where you may have used pre-cuts, you will cut your strips from yardage across the usable width of fabric (WOF). Therefore, the length of your strip will be dictated by your width of fabric.

Step One If it's an uncut length of fabric, first trim as on page 139.

Step Two Next, match the long edge with a vertical line on the cutting mat, and the selvage / selvedge edge on a horizontal line. Place the ruler so that it lies at the desired width from the vertical fabric edge, and is aligned with a vertical line all the way down. Holding the ruler firmly in place, cut through the fabric with the rotary cutter, from bottom to top.

Step Three First strip cut. Remove the ruler and put the fabric strip to one side. Replace the ruler and continue, cutting as many strips as you need.

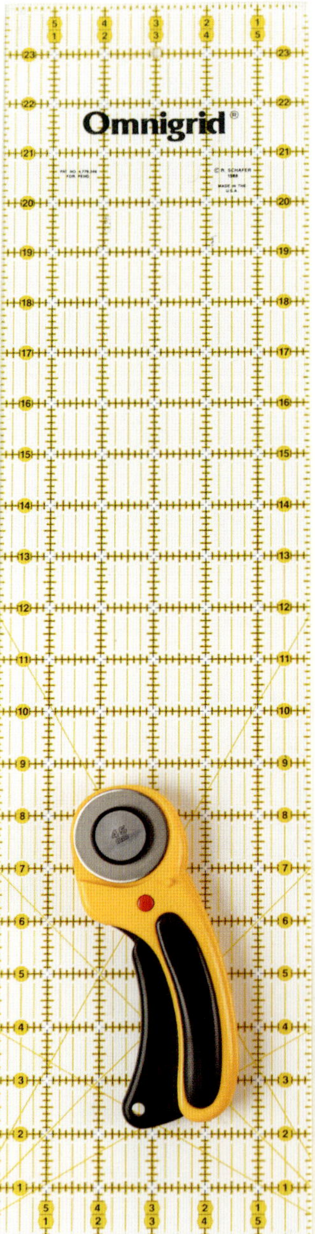

Squares in the Split Nine-Patch Quilt (see page 94).

CUTTING SQUARES AND RECTANGLES

Step One Cut a strip as per the instructions opposite.

Step Two Rotate the strip so it lies horizontally on the mat, and so the selvage / selvedge edge aligns with a vertical line on the mat and the bottom lengthwise edge matches a horizontal line. Trim off any selvages / selvedges.

Step Three With the ruler, measure along where you want to cut. At your chosen measurement, make sure your ruler is aligned with a vertical line on the mat all the way down. Holding the ruler in place, cut through the fabric with the rotary cutter, from bottom to top. Remove the ruler and put the fabric shape to one side.

Step Four Replace the ruler and continue, cutting as many squares (**A**) or rectangles (**B**) as needed for your project.

CUTTING HALF SQUARE TRIANGLES

Squares cut in half only once create what is known as Half Square Triangles (HSTs). They will have two straight sides on the straight grain, and one on the bias.

Step One Cut out your square from a strip of fabric (see pages 140 and 141). Move your square on the cutting mat until a 45-degree diagonal line runs through the middle of it, and its edges align with horizontal and vertical lines. Lay your ruler halfway over the square at a 45-degree angle, matching it to the 45-degree angle on the cutting mat (**A**).

Step Two Holding the ruler firmly in place, cut through the square with the rotary cutter, from the bottom corner to the top corner (i.e. away from you). Two HSTs made (**B**).

CUTTING QUARTER SQUARE TRIANGLES

Squares cut into four quarters on the diagonal create Quarter Square Triangles (QSTs). Each of these triangles will have only one side cut on the straight grain; the other two sides are cut on the bias.

Step One Cut out your square from a strip of fabric (see pages 140 and 141), then cut your square into two HSTs—see the steps above.

Step Two Arrange your HSTs on the mat, so that the bias edges align with a horizontal line on the cutting mat, and each one's corner at the 90-degree angle aligns with a vertical line. Holding the ruler firmly in place, cut through the middle of one HST with the rotary cutter, from bottom to top. Two QSTs made (**A**).

Step Three Cut through the second HST in the same way to make four QSTs in total (**B**).

USING TEMPLATES

For shapes in quilts that don't have easily cut angles or curves, you will need to use a template. All the templates needed to make the quilts in this book are printed 100% to scale at the back, on pages 186–197.

For machine-pieced shapes, all the templates include the seam allowance (SA). When stitching shapes together on the sewing machine, you will stitch a specified distance from the raw edges—usually ¼in (5mm).

However, typically for hand-pieced shapes (like the ones in the this book), a SA is not included in the template. This means the template is the actual finished size of the patchwork piece (patch). The reason: when you transfer and cut out the templates from your chosen material, you can decide whether they will include the SA (this is the standard ¼in / 5mm), or whether to keep them at the finished size of the actual patch and add the SA when you cut them from the fabric.

If you need help deciding whether to include the SAs or not, here is some general guidance.

- **Adding a SA when cutting out:** This method is useful if you're working with curved shapes or ones with unusual angles. It's also a speedy way to add a sewing line to your fabric too, to follow later.
  The process involves drawing around your templates as they are, onto the WS of your fabric, then adding the SA when cutting out (**A**). I tend to eyeball the SA at the cutting stage; if you're less confident doing this, always cut out a larger SA than needed; you can always trim down a too-large SA, but you can't add one back in! Remember to leave a good amount of space on the fabric between shapes, if you're cutting multiple pieces from the same fabric, to allow you to add the SA.
- **Adding a SA before cutting out:** This is a great method to use if you'd like to be economical with your fabric (as you'll be able to place shapes closely together on the fabric), and if you'd like to cut out multiple shapes quickly.
  For this approach, you add the SA around the template, then cut out the shape afterwards. For shapes with straight edges, you can use a ruler to add the SA; for curvy or unusual shapes, I like to use the Magic Seam Marker®, which is ¼in (5mm) across its radius (**B**). Once your template is cut out and on the fabric, insert your pencil through the hole in the marker, then run this along the edge of the template.
  If you'd like a stitching line to follow when sewing, you'll need to add this in. With your pencil and the Marking Trio rulers or Quilters Quarter, draw in the seam line using solid or dashed lines (**C**). Once you're used to knowing what a ¼in (5mm) SA looks like, this drawing process is optional and you can simply eyeball it when it comes to the sewing stage.

A

B

C

HAND PIECING

Starting to sew

CUTTING THE THREAD

Cut the thread to the length of your arm: hold the end of the thread between your thumb and index finger, and unwind the spool with your other hand until it hits your shoulder. This is the length to cut. This length results in fewer knots, better tension and consistent stitches, but also encourages the most ergonomic, rhythmic sewing action, as you pull the thread from the pivot point of your elbow.

THREADING A NEEDLE

When threading a needle, I always find it easier to hold the thread and put the needle over it (**A**), rather than trying to poke the thread through the needle's eye. If you find threading the needle difficult, invest in a needle threader, or easy-thread needles.

STARTING AND ENDING A STITCH

I've found the following technique the most secure way for starting and ending a stitch when piecing.

Step One Tie a knot at one end of a length of thread as long as your arm Thread the free end onto the sewing needle.

Step Two You will start to stitch with a knot and a backstitch (**B**); when you finish stitching, end with two or three backstitches (see Steps 5 and 6 on page 146).

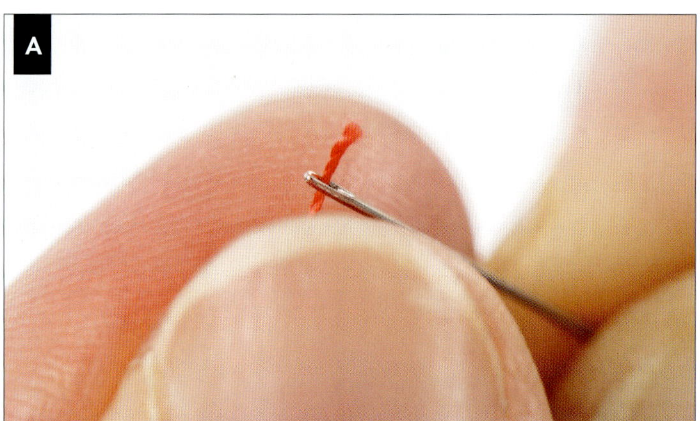

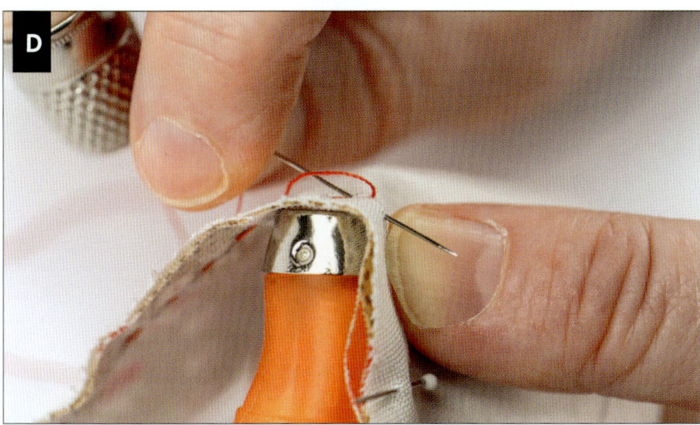

A note on pressing

Unlike machine-pieced quilts, where you press after sewing each seam, and in a specific direction, with hand piecing you press only when you've finished stitching the whole block. You'll find the seams for hand-pieced blocks tend to fall naturally in a certain direction, so you can simply press the angles as they fall.

WHAT STITCH TO USE?

Running stitch and backstitch are used for sewing all the pieces together. The running stitches need to be relatively small and firm, so that if you pull the seam open, you shouldn't see daylight through the gaps. Every 1in (2.5cm) or so of your running-stitch seam, make a backstitch; this helps to secure the seam a little more.

Often I'm asked how many running stitches I work in a seam. I stitch roughly nine running stitches every 1in (2.5cm), which means five on the top and four on the back. This can vary depending on the fabric and where I am stitching, so don't take it as something to aim for!

For speed, you can gather up two, three, or four running stitches on the needle and then pull the needle through (**C**).

HOLDING THE THREAD AND FABRIC

Think about how you put the needle through the fabric. I find it easier to have the fabric taut over the edge of the ridged thimble on my underneath hand, and then use this finger to push the fabric onto the needle (**D**). This way, the needle is kept flat and almost stationary. The middle finger of my top hand (wearing the round thimble) is then basically being pushed against until I pull the needle through. It is a bit like gathering the fabric up on the needle.

Hand sewing a single seam

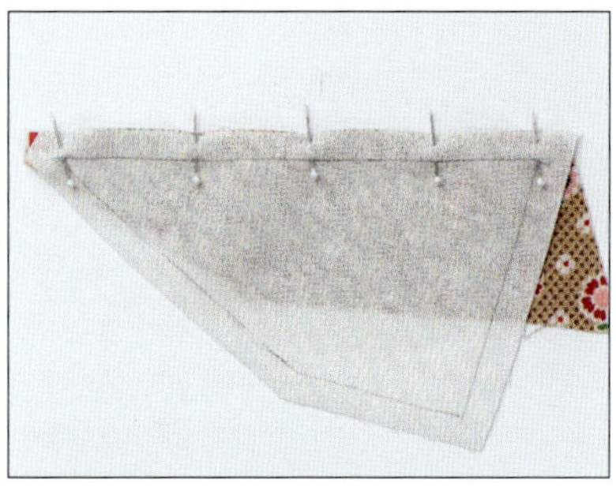

Step One Pin the two patches RS together at the start and finish of the stitching line, and in between as necessary. Remember to pin along the sewing line and into the seam allowance. I tend to pin the seam line in 1in (2.5cm) increments.

Step Two To check what the seam will look like before you stitch it, I recommend flipping up one patch so the RS of both pieces are facing up. It may not be so important on a straight seam like this, but on seams with curves or multiple patches it will help you see how accurate you are before you begin stitching.

Step Three Thread the needle with a length of thread that tones well with the fabric and knot the end (I've deliberately used a contrasting thread for these steps). Remove the first pin and insert the needle on the corner to make the first stitch, then work a backstitch. Note: I'm right-handed, so am sewing from right to left. If you are left-handed, you will be sewing from left to right.

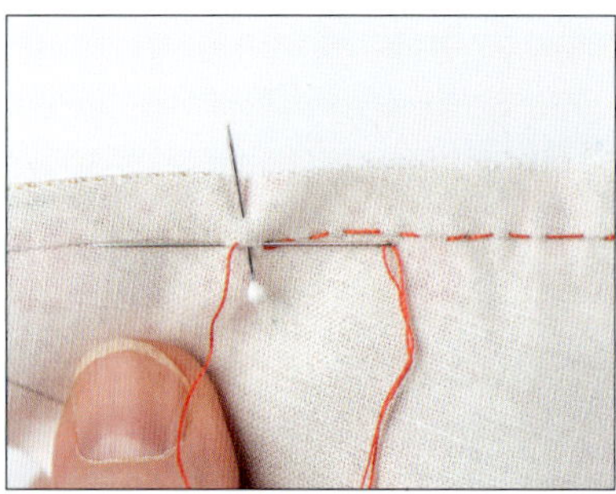

Step Four Continue making small running stitches up to the first pin. Backstitch at the pin, then remove the pin. Sew to the end of the seam in the same way, backstitching at every pin. These backstitches will stop the thread gathering up if it gets pulled and will give your seam a nice, even tension.

Step Five When you reach the end of the seam, bring the needle up from the back where the last pin sits. Remove the pin then make a backstitch.

Step Six Make two more backstitches back along your seam (so in reverse). Snip the thread, leaving a tail of about 1in (2.5cm) in length. This will give you some thread assurance if the seam gets pulled—if the thread is cut very close to the stitches, it could start to unravel.

Hand sewing a seam with a junction

When stitching two units together, there will likely be a junction along the joining edge (i.e. where two SAs meet). It makes it easier not to sew down the SA, in case you want to press it in a certain direction later. The pressing of the SA is something that is done when the work is finished. So, the answer is simply to skip the SAs and not sew them down.

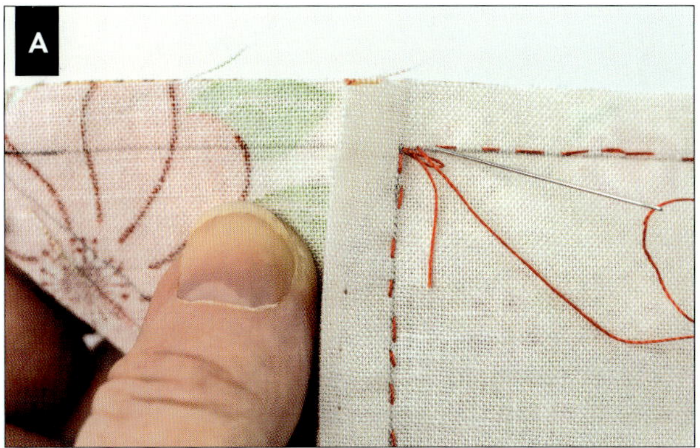

Step One In this example, the unit is made up of three patches—two that have already been joined, and another behind the two patches. Pin your pieces as shown opposite, RS together on the seam line and into the SA.

Step Two Start stitching as usual from the corner and progress toward the upright SA junction. Make sure the upright SA is pushed away from the seam you are sewing so that you do not accidentally sew it down (if you're right-handed it'll be toward the left; if you are left-handed, it will be toward to right).

Step Three When you get close to the end of the seam on the first patch, make sure that you come up at the end of the first patch seam line, ready to make a new stitch (**A**).

Step Four Make a backstitch (see diagram **A**) then take the needle down and underneath the SA (**B**).

Step Five Come up on the other side of the upright SA, ahead of the junction. Now move the upright SA toward the seam line you have just sewn. Make a backstitch at the beginning of the second patch seam line (**C**), which will start your next seam. By making this backstitch after skipping the seam, you will lock the stitches in place to stop them gaping at this point.

Step Six Continue on to the end of the seam as described in the steps opposite.

Hand sewing a seam with matching junctions

When joining two units that have SAs meeting in the middle, just like a single junction the best way to deal with this is to skip the SAs and not sew either of them down. The method below shows how to do this, and will still leave you with a nice, precise join.

Step One Pin the pair of patch units RS together along the seam line and into the SA as before (see page 146). If you are right-handed, make sure that, as you approach the two seams from the right, you push them both away to the left before pinning at the end of the seam. (If you are left-handed then push to the right.) Sew along the seam, up to the junction, following the "Hand sewing a single seam" instructions on page 146 (**A**).

Step Two As you approach the seam junction, at the end of your first patch seam line, make sure that the needle will go down at the end, as though it is going into the back of the work. As you go down at the corner, push the needle through the junction at a diagonal angle, keeping the SA on the front to the left and the one on the back to the right (**B**).

Step Three Take the needle up ahead of the corner on the back of the work, ready for a backstitch (**C**). Once the backstitch is complete and pulled tight, the junction will knit neatly together.

Step Four Continue along and finish as usual.

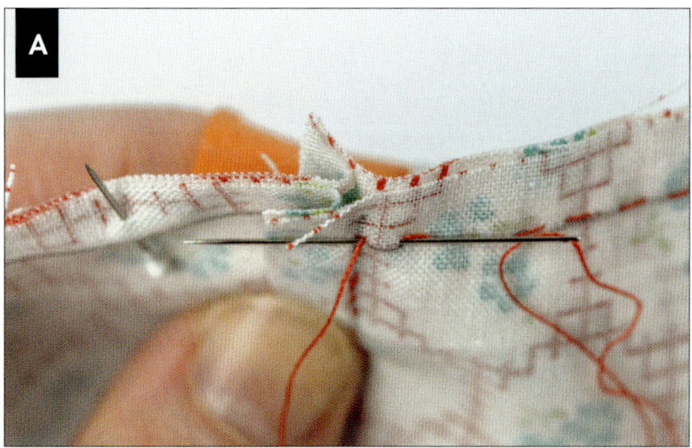

Setting in and Y-seams by hand

For units and blocks that cannot be successfully assembled with continuous straight seams, when you have to sew around a corner, you'll need to "set in" the patch. This is often necessary when three or more patches (that may have angles other than 90 degrees) meet at one point. The seams often form a Y-shape, hence the name.

Step One First sew the patches with the straight edges RS together, as per page 146. For my unit (which is for Grandmother's Prize Quilt on page 56), these are straight edges of the two wider trapezoid patches (see the arrows numbered 1 and 2 in **A**), and the straight edges of the narrow trapezoid shapes (see the arrow numbered 3 in **A**). Once the straight edges are sewn, pin the next Y-seam patch to your joined patches (here, the top diamond-shaped patch), RS together (**A**).

Step Two Start stitching from one outer SA towards the end of the inner SA, as detailed in the steps on page 146 (see the black arrow). At the junction, begin to make a backstitch (**B**).

Step Three At the end of the backstitch, take the needle behind the SA then through to the next patch, as per page 147. Note how the SA facing you is pushed toward the newly stitched seam, once the needle is in the next patch. Make a backstitch (**C**).

Step Four Continue making small running stitches up to the first pin see the black arrow in **C**). Backstitch at the pin, then remove the pin. Sew to the end of the seam in the same way. The backstitches will stop the thread gathering up if it gets pulled and will give your seam a nice, even tension.

Hand sewing a seam with converging junctions

Sewing units and blocks that have several seams coming together at a junction may sound daunting, but it's easier than it sounds. By stitching your patches in pairs, and then stitching the pairs into quarters then halves of the block, you'll see the approach is similar to sewing a seam with matching junctions (see page 148).

Step One Here, I am sewing together a unit for the Grandmother's Prize Quilt (see page 56) where six patches meet in the middle—a result of sewing two sections together. To join the two sections, begin by placing them RS together, matching the junctions. Start stitching from one outer SA to the center as per the steps on page 146 (see the arrow in **A**). When you reach the end of the seam line and are close to the junction where all the patches meet, begin to make a backstitch (**A**).

Step Two At the end of the backstitch, take the needle diagonally behind the SA—into the "gap" between all the SAs—then out to the left of the SA of the unstitched patch (**B**). Finish the backstitch, folding the SAs to the right.

Step Three Continue to sew up the left-hand side as per page 146.

Hand sewing round shapes and curved seams

With some preparation and considered sewing, curved seams and round pieces are much easier to sew than many quilters believe—especially if you are hand sewing your patches together. I like to use the pinning method described here, as I find this creates the neatest finish. For this example, I'll be joining patches for the Friendship Garden Quilt on page 76.

Step One I like to work by pinning the concave curve to the convex curve (**A**). I find this works best for me as I can see the excess fabric that I'm easing round the curve and can hold it in place with pins. With RS facing, begin by pinning the curved edges of the patches with three pins—one in the center and one at each end of the seam. If you are pinning your curved shape to joined patches, I recommend pinning at each seam junction to avoid distortion. Make sure that the edges of the patches align.

Step Two Once you're happy with how the fabric is lying with the three pins, add more pins in between (**B**)—the number will vary depending on the size of your unit or block.

Step Three Simply sew the curved seam following the technique on page 146. As we have more pins and they are sitting closer to each other, I like to backstitch every ½in (1.25cm).

MACHINE PIECING

Most of the quilts in this book are machine-pieced and machine sewn. Unless stated otherwise, as for hand piecing you will use a ¼in (5mm) seam allowance (SA) to stitch all the units and blocks together.

Basics

When sewing patchwork on the sewing machine, typically you will be sewing from one raw edge of the fabric to the other. There is no need to reverse stitch or make a securing stitch at each end of a seam; you just run off the end of the fabric, and either cut away the thread, leaving an approximate ½in (1.25cm) tail; chain piece (see opposite); or use a thread saver (also see opposite). The subsequent seam stitching in the rest of your block will secure the thread and the seams.

The stitch length you use will vary, depending on your machine. Some will have it programmed in, with others you will need to judge for yourself. Try out lengths on some samples first. Generally, on modern machines, the stitch length would be around 2.0, 2.2 to 2.4. However, I cannot emphasize enough how much you need to experiment with this on your own machine.

The easiest way to achieve the correct width for the SA is by running the paired pieces to be sewn together under a ¼in piecing foot, with the raw edges aligned with the edge of the foot. The stitching (or seam) will then be exactly ¼in (5mm) away from the raw edge, assuming you have cut out your fabric accurately.

Maintaining the SA

If your units and blocks are not accurately sewn together—especially if they have several seams—there can be consequences later when it comes to sewing the blocks together and turning them into a quilt.

In a block that has very few seams, if you are ⅛in (3mm) too big or small with your SA, this will only alter the size of the overall block by a small amount. However, with blocks that have multiple seams (like the blocks in the Ric-Rac Baskets Quilt; see page 36), the result is amplified—⅛in (3mm) off in three seams is ¾in (2cm) off the desired block size. It's amazing how such a tiny amount can add up, and affect the next part of the block's construction.

If a block has not come together as well as you would hope, check the following:

- **Did you cut out your pieces accurately?** If not, don't panic: put the block aside and go on to the next one you had decided to make.
- **Did you sew the seams accurately?** If not, you have two options: you can put it aside, as above, or unpick the seams and start again. If you put the block aside, you can then decide if you want to remake it or roll with the imperfection.

Everyone is different in how they work and the standards that they set for themselves. Neither way is wrong; this is what will make your quilt truly your own.

Chain piecing

This is a quick way to join pieces of fabric together in pairs and will also help reduce wasted thread. You will feed paired pieces of fabric under the machine foot, one after another, continuously sewing but leaving a gap of about ½in (1.25cm) between them. The paired pieces of fabric are then held together by the line of thread, hence the term "chain piecing".

Step One Arrange all your fabric pieces together in pairs, with right sides facing. Place the first pair under the machine foot and stitch the seam with a ¼in (5mm) seam allowance. Continue stitching until the paired patches come out from the back of the foot. When you reach the end, continue stitching for about ½in (1.25cm) to create a small chain of stitches, then feed the next pair under the foot and continue until they are all joined.

Step Two Simply separate your fabric pairs by cutting the threads joining them together.

Thread savers

When sections of work can't be chain pieced, thread savers—folded pieces of scrap fabric used as "bridges" between pieces of fabric—can speed up sewing and reduce thread wastage. For those of you who have problems with the threads "eating themselves" when you start sewing, this method mitigates that too.

When you come to the end of sewing your patch, block, binding or other pieces of fabric, and there is no more to stitch at this point, take a piece of left-over fabric that's about 2½ x 2in (6.5 x 5cm)—often I use a piece cut from left-over binding—then fold it in half so it measures 1¼ x 2in (3.25 x 5cm). Place the folded edge in front of the machine foot as you finish stitching your patch then, as the patch comes out the machine foot, insert your thread saver. This is so the machine "thinks" it's still sewing.

As you sew into the next, unstitched fabric piece, and when you're done with the thread saver, just snip the threads close to the thread saver. Pop it back under your foot when you finish up your final patch, so no thread is wasted!

PRESSING

When you are machine sewing your blocks, it is essential that you press after each sewing stage, ready for the next seam; this will give you a nice, crisp finish. (As noted on page 138, with hand piecing you only press after the whole block is made.)

Occasionally you might want to finger-press or use a seam roller, but this should always be the exception rather than the rule. At the end of the day, there is no replacing a hot iron.

Pressing is about distributing the bulk in the seams so that the work lies as flat as it can. Occasionally, you will need to press the seam allowance "open"; this means pressing the seam allowance for each patch toward its own wrong side. I don't do this often; only if there will be another seam added later, and I need to reduce the bulk in that area early on.

Most of the time, you will press the seam allowances in one direction; this creates a more secure seam, and it means (if pressed accurately) that the seam junctions don't need to be pinned—they will "knit" together automatically.

- **When pressing seams in one direction:** press from the front. Place the work on the ironing board right side up then and use your fingers to position the seam allowances in the correct direction underneath. You then only press once, which saves time and energy!
- **When seams need to be pressed open:** flip your work and press from the wrong side, using the point of the iron to open the seam as you press.

Tips for good pressing

- **Use a hot iron:** assuming you're using a cotton or linen fabric, you should have the iron set to these fabrics (three-dots symbol). If the iron's not hot enough, the seams will pop up instead of staying flat. Be careful if you decide to use the steam function in conjunction with pressing; if you over-steam, it's possible to distort or stretch the seams.
- **Press from the front where possible:** this eliminates the need to press everything twice, which can lead to fabric distortion, and saves time too! Just take care to position the work and seam you want to press correctly; you should then be able to press in one stroke.

FRAMES

Adding frames around your blocks not only increases the size of the blocks but also allows you to add another design element to them. New fabrics can be introduced for more interest, or you can cut your frames from a fabric used elsewhere in the quilt top, unifying blocks if there are lots of different colors at play.

The frames are made up of four strips—two long and two short. I tend to position the shorter strips on the left- and right-hand sides of the block; the longer strips then are stitched to its top and bottom edges. If you have a directional print, you may need to adjust the positioning of your strips.

Step One Fold and finger-press the mid-point of one short framing strip; repeat with one side of your block, where you want the short framing strip to be.

Step Two Pin the short framing strip to the block, RS together: start by pinning the mid-points indicated by the finger-pressed creases, then pin the ends of the strip to the ends of the block.

Step Three Now pin the quarter points. You can eyeball this, although it's just a case of making sure the strips fit. If any easing is needed, it is done evenly over the side of the block. If you'd like to add more pinning points you can, but do have confidence and don't waste time adding too many pins.

Step Four With the block underneath, stitch the strip to the side of the block, removing the pins as you work.

Step Five Press the SAs toward the framing strip.

Step Six Repeat Steps 1–5 with the other short framing strip, on the opposite side to the previous strip.

Step Seven Repeat Steps 1–6 with the long framing strips, this time attaching them to the short ends of the previous framing strips as well as the block sides.

SASHING AND CORNERSTONES

Sashings are strips of fabric that can be sewn between the blocks to spread them out, and create a quilt design that looks like a divided grid of blocks. They can run both horizontally and vertically, and can be used with or without cornerstones, also known as "posts". (Cornerstones are the squares of fabric that sit at the junctions where the ends of sashing strips meet.)

Sashing and posts create the opportunity to add new fabrics or use up oddments (if you like a scrappy quilt), and can also help in the construction of the quilt top too by giving us more seam junctions to help match up.

Sashing with cornerstones

Before you stitch the sashing and cornerstones, you will need to lay out your blocks. To ensure your blocks stay in the correct order, it's often worth labeling the rows (I just clip a numbered piece of paper to the left side of the first block on each row) then take a picture of the overall arrangement so you can refer to it if needed.

Step One Lay out the blocks in a row in your preferred setting (i.e. your desired arrangement).

Step Two Stitch the first vertical sashing strip to the right-hand side of your first block, RS together (**A**). Finger-press the SA toward the sashing. (Note that the position of the sashing strips will vary from quilt to quilt. For the Five-Patch Star quilt in this book you will also need to add a sashing strip to the left-hand side of your first block in every row and to the right-hand side of the last block in each row too, so check your design before adding the sashing.)

Step Three Lay the next block over the sashed block, RS together and with its left-hand raw edge matching the right-hand raw edge of the recently added sashing strip. Sew along this edge (**B**). Press the SA toward the sashing as before.

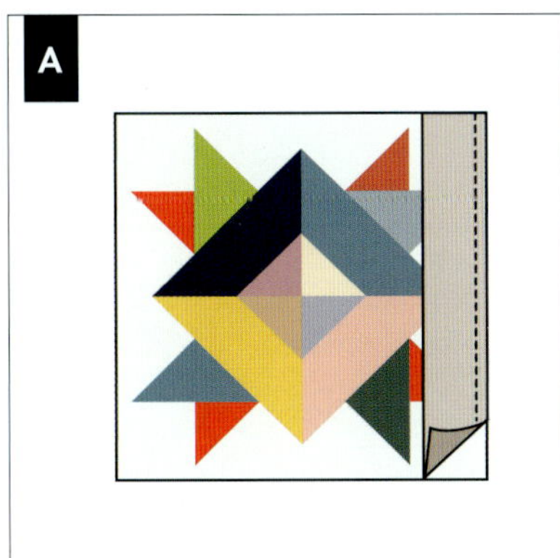

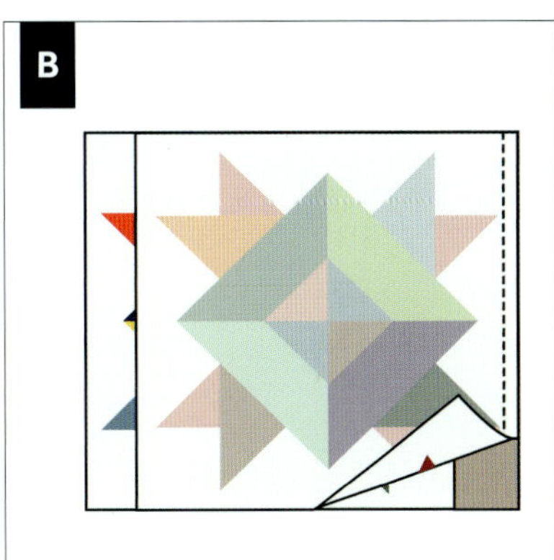

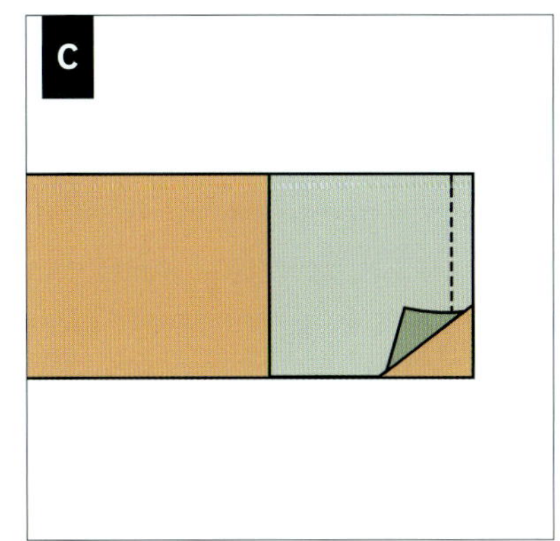

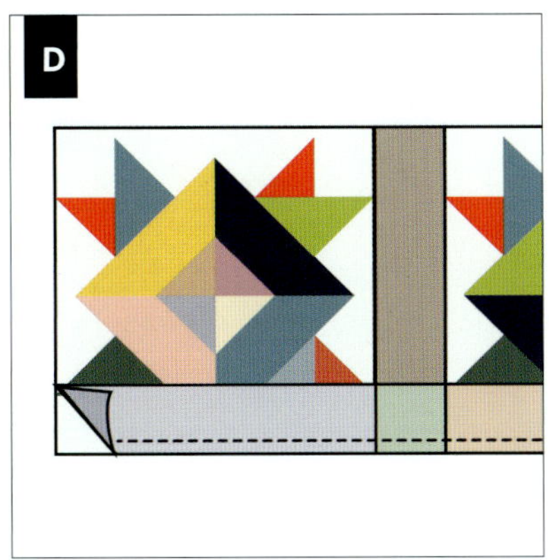

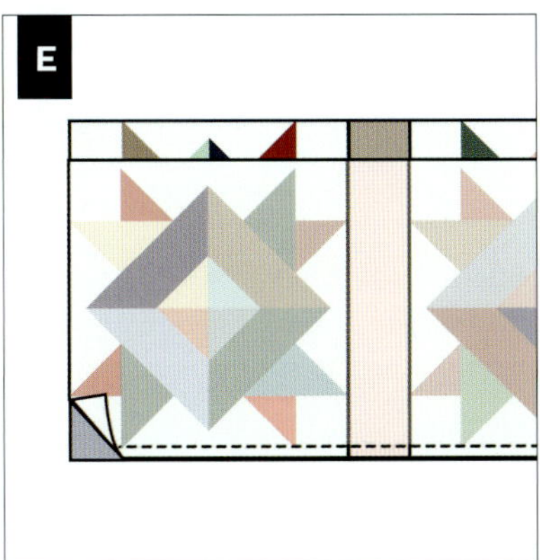

Step Four To add the remaining blocks and sashing strips in the same row, repeat the same process until you have added the final block of the row. Only stitch a sashing strip to the right-hand edge of the final block in the row, if it's included in the design. Join the blocks and vertical sashing strips of the remaining rows in the same way.

Step Five Now to stitch the rows of horizontal sashing, which include the cornerstones. Take one horizontal sashing strip then lay a cornerstone over the right-hand end, RS together and matching the raw edges. Stitch (**C**) then press the SA toward the sashing.

Step Six Lay a sashing strip over the right-hand end of your joined cornerstone, RS together and matching the raw edges. Stitch, then press the SA toward the sashing.

Step Seven Repeat Steps 6 and 7 until all the sashing and cornerstones for a row have been stitched into one long strip.

Step Eight Lay the long sashing-and-cornerstones strip over a row of blocks with vertical sashing, RS together and the raw edges matching. Pin, matching the seam junctions of the sashing and cornerstones with the junctions of the sashing and blocks. Stitch the strip in place (**D**), then press the SA toward the strip. (For the Five-Patch Star quilt you will need to attach a long sashing-and-cornerstones strip both above and below the first row of blocks but for other designs the sashing may only go below the first row, as shown in the illustration.)

Step Nine Lay the next row of blocks with vertical sashing over the newly added strip, RS together, matching the seam junctions and with the edges aligned. Sew in place (**E**), then press the SA toward the strip.

Step Ten Repeat Steps 6–10 to join the rest of the strips and blocks.

Sashing with no cornerstones

When there are no cornerstones, you'll need to make the horizontal sashing strips longer than the vertical sashing strips, or vice versa, to account for the "missing" junction square.

Like the sashing with cornerstones, it's a good idea to lay out all your blocks and sashing pieces first, before stitching, to ensure you're happy with the placement.

The steps on this page show the process of adding longer horizontal sashing strips to blocks; for longer vertical sashing, just rotate the diagrams by 90 degrees!

Remember that if you're using a directional fabric, this would need to be taken into consideration when cutting out and stitching the sashings in place.

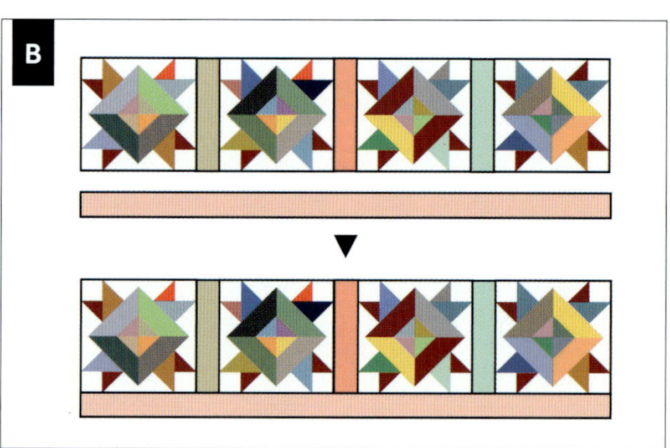

Step One Follow the instructions in Steps 1–4 on pages 156 and 157 to add the vertical sashing strips to each row of blocks (**A**).

Step Two Now to add the horizontal sashing pieces. With RS together, center and pin your long horizontal sashing strip to the bottom of your first row of blocks with vertical sashing, aligning the raw edges (**B**). Place pins at each quarter, and add more if necessary. Stitch in place. Press the SA toward the sashing.

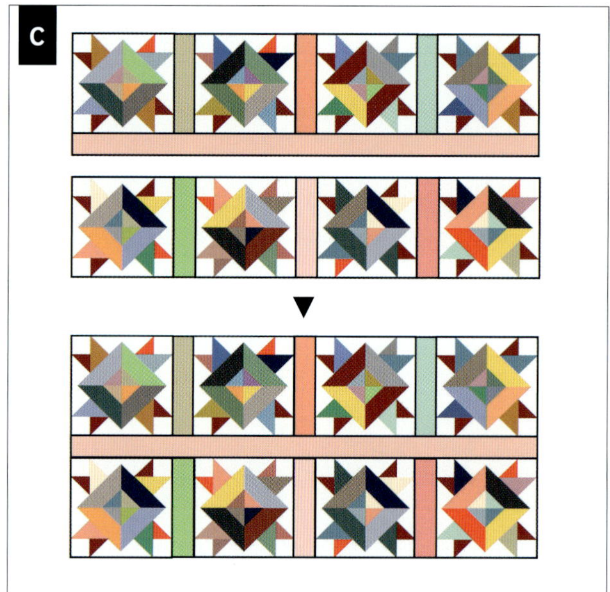

Step Three With RS together, lay the next row of blocks with vertical sashing over your recently added horizontal sashing, aligning the raw edges. The vertical sashing strips should align on either side of the horizontal sashing strip. Pin then sew as before (**C**).

Step Four Repeat Steps 2 and 3 until the quilt top is complete.

QUILTING

Once you've stitched your blocks together to make your quilt top, and you've pressed the whole top, you can begin to quilt. As when piecing, you can choose to quilt entirely by hand or by machine; each have their pros and cons, but at the end of the day it's all about personal preference. Machine quilting is no doubt faster and more accurate if you are already sitting at a sewing machine or using a long-arm quilter, but there's a charm to hand quilting that can't be achieved on a sewing machine, and for me, quilting by hand makes me feel closer to the quilters before us who didn't have the same choices. However, whether you want to quilt by hand or machine is entirely up to you and your quilt.

Preparing the backing fabric

Your backing fabric will need to be wider and longer than the patchwork top. Generally, I add roughly 10in (25.5cm) to the overall size of a quilt for the backing. If your yardage isn't wide enough (as often will be the case), you will need to buy enough fabric to join together. (You can buy special wide-width fabrics for backing fabric; this means you won't need to join your fabrics, saving you from having seams on the back of the quilt.)

From the diagrams, below, you can see that the backing fabric can be pieced and seamed vertically (**A**) or horizontally (**B**). Or you can cut one of the lengths of backing fabric in half lengthwise and join it to either side of the wider piece (**C**); some people prefer this method so that when you fold the quilt the seams do not come under so much stress.

If you choose fabric that will need joining, follow these three basic points:

- Remove the selvages / selvedges from the sides of the fabric (see page 139).
- Sew the seam using a ¼in or ⅜in (5mm or 1cm) SA.
- Press the SAs open; this will reduce the bulky areas you need to quilt through.

Once the backing fabric is ready, press before layering it in a quilt sandwich (see page 160).

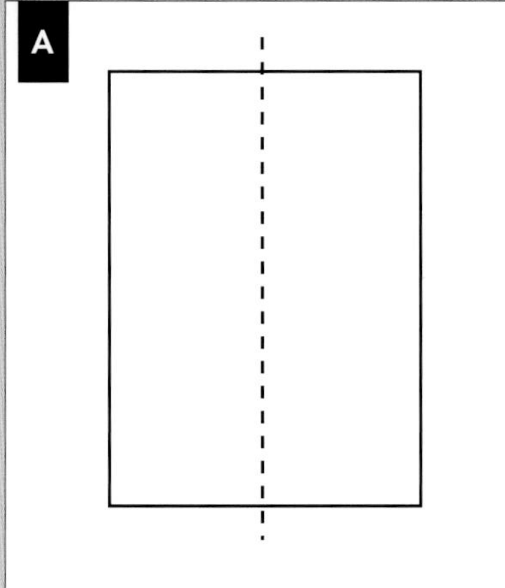

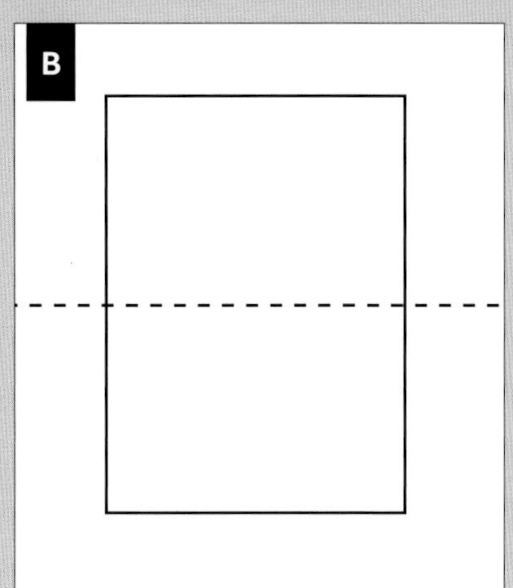

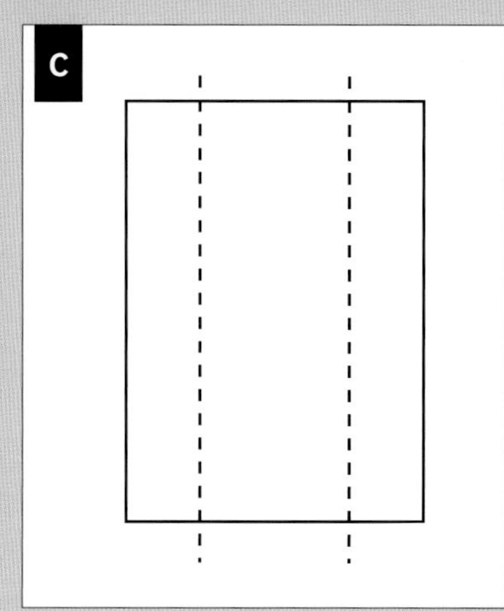

Holding the layers together

The layers that make up a quilt—backing fabric, batting / wadding and quilt top— are known as a "quilt sandwich".

There are different ways to hold your quilt sandwich together before quilting, detailed on the following pages. Which one you choose will depend mostly on how you'll be quilting your quilt.

Generally, for all methods of basting / tacking, the securing method should form a grid (see opposite). This grid is often dictated by the patches in the quilt. There should not usually be a gap bigger than 6in (15cm) between the basting / tacking lines—about the size of your spread hand. If the patchwork does not have a grid to follow, again use your hand span as a guide.

If you're planning to use a quilting hoop then safety-pin basting / tacking (see page 163) might not be the best choice. This is because the pins tend to get in the way of the hoop and need moving every time you reposition the hoop. If you are happy to keep doing this, then go ahead! It bothers some people but not others, but it is worth being aware of this before you start.

When you lap quilt, you do not have the additional stability that a hoop gives, so a little denser basting / tacking will help to stop the layers shifting. For lap quilting, think about basting / tacking perhaps every 4in (10cm) rather than 6in (15cm). Use your closed fist as a gauge between tacking/basting lines, rather than a spread hand.

Basting / tacking tips

- **Use a clear, flat floor to lay the quilt flat.** If you don't have the space, you can use community and church halls—just make sure to book the space when you know the cleaner has just been! This saves you having to move your own furniture around to make room for the quilt on the floor.
- For any basting / tacking done on the floor, consider using a **kneeling mat or knee pads** to cushion your knees.
- Using **a carpeted floor will stop the quilt moving too much**. The edges can also be secured with masking tape.
- **Use large tables if kneeling on the floor is not an option**. Community and church halls often have these, if you don't have one at home.
- If space, time or health prevent you from basting / tacking, don't be afraid to **use a long-arm quilting company**. Many long-arm quilters offer a basting / tacking service, which lets you sit down and enjoy the quilting. This thread-basted / tacked method offers all the advantages of manageability and no added weight, but with someone else having done the work.

Basting / tacking system

I find it easier to work to a grid system when basting / tacking. Since I always use the same system, I don't have to think or plan—just baste / tack! Below is the way I hand baste / tack my quilts when they are on the floor. It smooths out any wrinkles or puffs that may arise.

Step One Press the backing fabric and lay it on the floor WS upwards. Pat it flat. Secure to the floor with tabs of masking tape at the corners and the mid-points on all four sides. Do NOT stretch the fabric: you'll find it will pucker when the basting / tacking stitches are in and the masking tape comes off.

Step Two Lay the batting / wadding on top of the backing fabric. If it helps, fold the batting / wadding into four and line up the outside edge with the corner of the backing fabric then unfold a quarter at a time. Pat it flat.

Step Three Press the patchwork top for the last time, then center it on top of the batting / wadding, RS up. Again, fold into quarters if this helps. Pat flat. Add some tabs of masking tape at the corners.

Step Four Pin the three layers together in the center, at the corners and the mid-point on each side. This is just to keep things in place while you baste / tack.

Step Five If you are hand basting / tacking, begin with a knot and a backstitch to secure your thread. Start by basting / tacking the diagonals (**A**). If necessary, use a teaspoon to bring the needle up out of the quilt for ease, or use your thimble to protect your fingers. Finish with a backstitch. You never need to have your hand under the quilt; you are working from the top all of the time. This way you do not disturb the layers.

Step Six Baste / tack across the middle in both directions (**B**). Remove the pins as you come across them.

Step Seven Using your hand span as a guide, baste / tack in rows from the center, working toward the outside edge (**C**). When this section is full, move round to the next (**D**). There are four sections to fill in this way, always starting from the middle and working toward the outside edge (**E** and **F**).

Step Eight When complete, baste / tack ¼in (5mm) away from the outside edge of the quilt sandwich. This will eventually be removed, and will stop the edges getting tatty or stretched before the quilt is quilted.

Step Nine Remove the masking tape, and pick up the quilt (and yourself) from the floor! If you like, you can now fold over the extra batting / wadding and backing fabric and baste / tack it abutting the edge of the quilt.

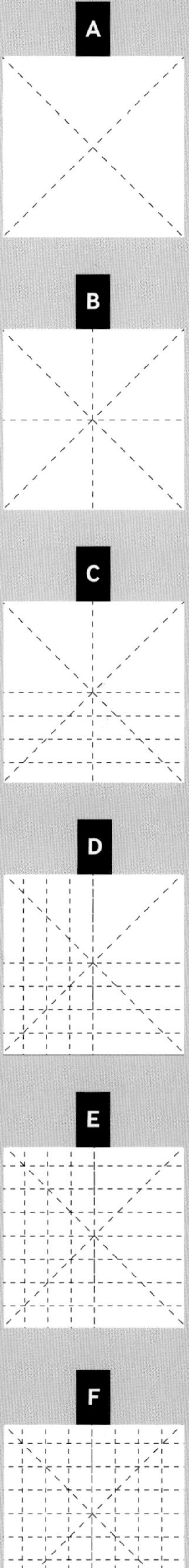

Hand basting / tacking

Hand basting / tacking a quilt gives you the best control over the layers of the quilt and does not add any extra weight or bulk. Baste / tack the quilt in rows that are 6in (15cm) apart. You could use specialist basting / tacking thread for ease; however, think about using old threads that prove too weak to use for general stitching: basting / tacking thread is generally a thread that is easily breakable between your fingers, so any weak threads will be well used here.

REGULAR BASTING / TACKING

Start with a knot and a backstitch, then work running stitch from right to left on the quilt (left to right if you are left-handed). The stitches should be about ½in (1.25cm) long and evenly spaced (see the diagram below; the dashed lines indicate the thread and stitches below the fabric). Finish with a backstitch to keep the thread secure.

TAILOR BASTING / TACKING

Some people find the action of basting / tacking uncomfortable, as the needle is held horizontally to your body. If this is the case for you, try basting / tacking diagonally, known as tailor basting / tacking: the needle is held so it points toward your body, which can feel a more natural position.

To tailor tack, thread the needle and knot the end. Work the stitch from right to left (left to right if you are left-handed). Create rows of ½–1in (1.25–2.5cm) long diagonal stitches, depending on the length of the needle (see the diagram below; the dashed lines indicate the thread and stitches below the fabric). Finish with a backstitch.

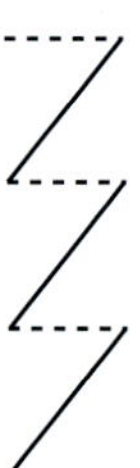

Using a spoon

As the needle and your hands are always on the top of the quilt, your fingers can get sore as the needle or safety pin pushes up against them. Using a teaspoon or a grapefruit spoon helps ease the needle or safety pin up through the layers, and makes the process quicker. As you take the needle or safety pin through the layers, simply push the needle or pin point up against the edge of a teaspoon or grapefruit spoon.

Safety-pin basting / tacking

For large quilts you'll need a lot of safety pins, and buying multiple packs of these can be a large outlay to start with. I'd recommend building up your safety-pin supply gradually over time. I started off just safety-pin basting / tacking small quilts, as I had a limited number of pins; as I purchased more over time I was able to use them on bigger quilts. Slowly accumulating is not only better for your pocket, it also ensures that you like that way of working. There is nothing worse than buying a huge amount of pins and then finding that the method is not for you. If you discover you enjoy this method, you will see how handy pin basting / tacking can be, as you can use the pins over and over again. Some people find the pins with pin covers easier on the hands—they give you something bigger to get hold of, and "magically" the open pins do not stick together in clumps when stored.

Safety pins with covers.

- Lay out the quilt sandwich, but do not pin (see Steps 1–3 of basting / tacking system, on page 161). Starting from the center of the quilt, and from the top / RS, use the safety pins to hold the layers together. Insert each pin and bring it back up through all three layers. This is where a teaspoon will ease the fingers as you bring the point of the pin up against its edge and clip the pin closed (see the second image opposite).
- The pins should be placed neither too closely nor too far from each other. Use your clenched fist as a gauge for pin placement—about 4in (10cm) apart.
- When the quilt is covered with pins, baste / tack around the edge as described in Step 8 on page 161.

REQUIREMENTS

One table at a comfortable height. The table does not have to be as big as the quilt—you can use a large dining table, a table-tennis table or a wallpaper pasting table. I use a 24 x 31in (61 x 79cm) collapsible picnic table that folds away, for easy storage. Unless it's an old table you're not worried about, I recommend covering it with a thick cloth or a cutting mat, so it doesn't get marked by pins or clamps.

Chair, ideally one that allows you to adjust its height to suit.

Painter's / masking tape and marking pen.

Spring clamps or bulldog clips.

Table-top basting / tacking

Learning to baste / tack on a table top will save you crawling around on the floor, and often having to clear the space in the first place. It will mean that you can sit and work in relative comfort without the worry of sore knees, or putting a room out of use while you use the floor space.

Step One Measure and mark the halfway points on each side of the table by sticking painter's / masking tape down and drawing in the halfway marks on top. Mark the center of the table top in the same way, this time marking a cross shape (**A**).

Step Two Press the backing fabric and fold it into quarters, WS together. Place it on the table in one quarter section—the right side of the fabric will be facing you and, as you unfold it, the wrong side will be uppermost (**B**).

Step Three Unfold the backing fabric. Line up the edges with the points on the sides of the table so as to keep it straight. Use spring clamps or bulldog clips to secure the fabric to the edges of the table (**C**). If the quilt is smaller than the table, the edges that don't overhang can be taped into place. There is no need to stretch the fabric—it just needs to lie flat, and this is done by gently patting the fabric and securing in place with a clamp at each corner. If the fabric is stretched, when the clamps are undone, the fabric will release and make ripples.

Step Four Now fold the batting / wadding in the same way as before and place on top of the backing fabric (**D**). Smooth the batting / wadding by patting it gently into place, without stretching it. Replace the clips already in position to hold both layers in place.

Step Five Press, fold into quarters (this time RS together) then unfold the quilt top in a similar way to the backing and batting / wadding. The quilt top should end up RS up (**E**). Pat the fabric smooth and use the clamps or clips to hold the three layers together.

Step Six Baste / tack the area that is being held on the table with your chosen method (see pages 162 or 163). Work only from the front of the quilt. If you find it hard to push the needle or the pin heads up from beneath the quilt, use a teaspoon (**F**).

Step Seven Once the area has been basted / tacked, remove the clamps or clips. Carefully shift the layers toward or away from you so the next unbasted / untacked area is on the table top (**G**).

Step Eight Secure the edge of the quilt that has been basted / tacked with clamps or clips, then lift up the quilt top and make sure the rest of the backing and batting / wadding are still flat (**H**). Reposition the quilt top.

Step Nine Repeat the process of basting / tacking then shifting until the entire quilt is basted / tacked. You will likely need to move the quilt between three to nine times. When the quilt is completely basted / tacked, finish by basting / tacking all around the outside edge with a ¼in (5mm) SA.

C

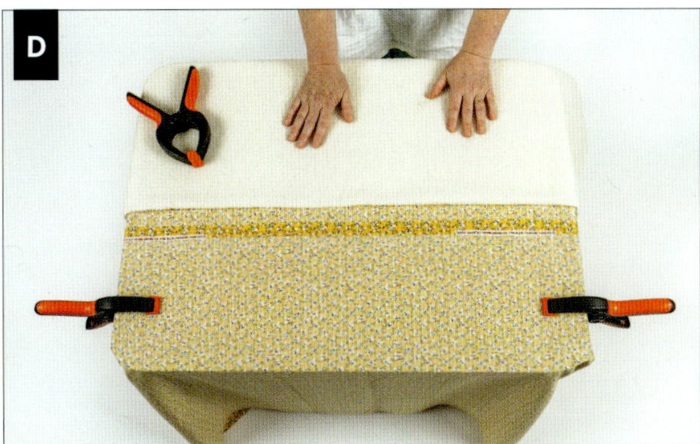
D

G

H

Quilt designs

Up to and during the 1930s, quilts were still being quilted as they had been done in the past: either at home alone or around a frame with other women, where they could meet and chat while stitching. The type of quilting was something that got the job done. Tying was the fastest method (see pages 176 and 177 for more information), and there are examples of quilts where cotton strings from the feedsacks have been used for tying—a very frugal option.

With the increased ownership of sewing machines, more quilts were machine-quilted, although these quilts tended to feature basic straight lines and grids. Like quilters today, sometimes they justed wanted the quilt to be finished! The influence of quilt designers and kits also made its mark: quilters who used quilt designs from kits or patterns just followed what was recommended in the instructions, without the need to come up with a design themselves. This led to many women challenging and improving their skills.

Generally, you need to look at the quilt as a whole when choosing a quilting design. Don't just look at each block or fabric, but select a design that suits a large area, and will bring the whole quilt together.

Though each quilt project suggests a quilting design, you're free to experiment and choose a design that may work better for your particular quilt. You can also decide to stitch what would have been a hand-stitched design by machine, or take on the challenge of approaching a typically machine-quilted pattern by hand instead.

STRAIGHT-LINE QUILTING

Lines that run in just one direction (**A**) or in two, to form an even grid (**B**), are simple but effective quilt designs. Usually I allow the seams on the quilt top to dictate the distance between the lines (meaning some of the lines will be stitched in the ditch of the seam); this makes is easier to keep your lines straight too.

CROSS-HATCH QUILTING

This design can be worked over the entire quilt top. Use a long ruler and your chosen marking tool to mark 45-degree lines, in both directions, across the whole patchwork (**C**). As with straight-line quilting, cross-hatched lines can be stitched closely together, matchstick style.

VERMICELLI QUILTING

This is an all-over, free-motion quilting design that is worked by machine over any patchwork pattern. Set up your sewing machine by lowering the feed dogs (or, if your machine is a slightly older model and doesn't have the capability to do this, by setting the stitch length to "0") and install an open-toe darning foot. The quilting pattern is "self-guided", as you control the size of the 'swirls' and the density of stitching yourself (**D**).

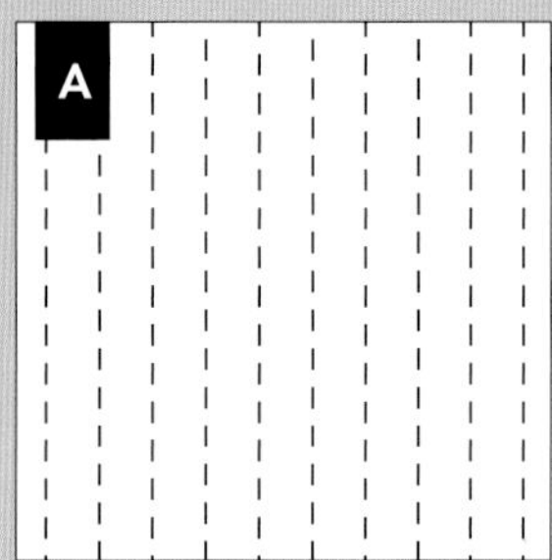

Straight lines, one direction.

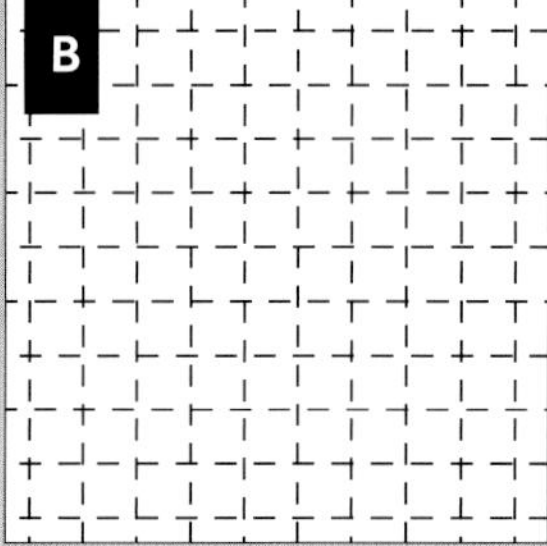

Straight lines in an even grid.

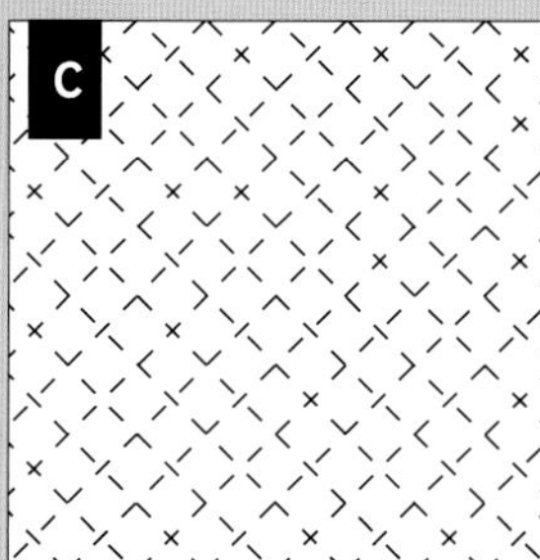

45-degree angle cross-hatching.

Vermicelli quilting.

Top left:
Straight lines, one direction; machine stitched (left) and hand stitched (right).

Top right:
Straight lines, even grid; machine stitched (left) and hand stitched (right).

Bottom right:
45-degree cross-hatching; machine stitched (left) and hand stitched (right).

BAPTIST FAN

This design goes by various names thanks to the many church groups and individuals who used the design frequently. These names include elbow quilting, Mennonite Fan and Amish Wave. There may be different approaches to the size or the way the pattern is made, but they all have the same result.

Historically, they were designs quilted out of necessity: they were quick to quilt compared to elaborate feathers and wreaths, and the designs could be created from items that were common in most homes, such as cups, saucepan lids, and the length of the quilter's arm from hand to elbow for the really large waves. They were popular in quilts of the Depression era, and typically quilters used thicker threads to hold the layers together.

The design could be quilted from the outside edge of the quilt working in toward the center (**A**), or in rows from bottom to top (**B**). If a quilt was positioned in a square frame and being quilted by a group of people, one person could sit on each side and quilt the design, working in toward the center of the quilt. If you quilt on a frame with rollers, you would quilt the design in rows, starting at the bottom of the quilt and working toward the top as you rolled the next part of the quilt on.

This is a popular design for a number of reasons.

- The fan is quilted on the bias of the fabric, which seems to give more readily under the needle and so makes it easier to quilt.
- The design covers the quilt all over, ignoring the piecing and so acts as a unifying feature.
- It can be stitched by any level of quilter and so is a good choice for a beginner.
- It can be quilted by groups, or easily by a single quilter.

A template makes it easy to create even waves. You can make your own to any size you require by using any circular household object— see opposite. Alternatively, you can use the template on page 189.

To quilt, stitch parallel arched lines within each wave, working from the smallest arch outwards. You can use a needle or the width of a finger between each line to keep the distance consistent; the template on page 189 has a 1in (2.5cm) distance between each arched line.

Baptist Fan design on the Ric-Rac Baskets Quilt (see page 36).

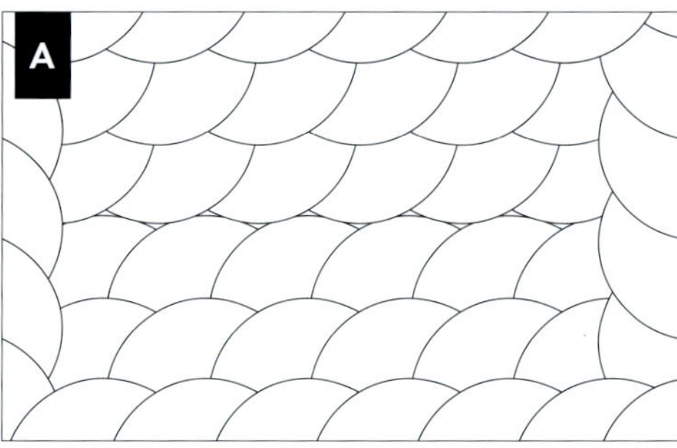

Baptist Fan worked from the outside in.

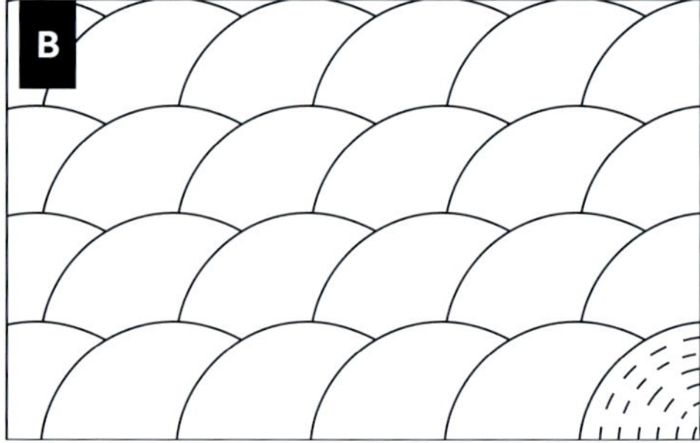

Baptist Fan worked in rows from the bottom to the top. Parallel lines of stitching are then worked inside each wave.

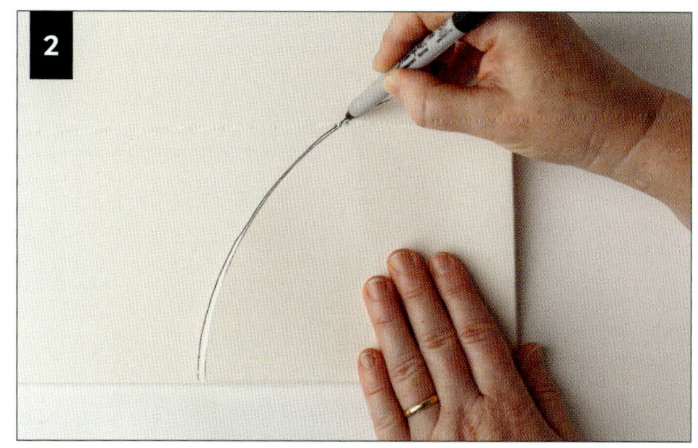

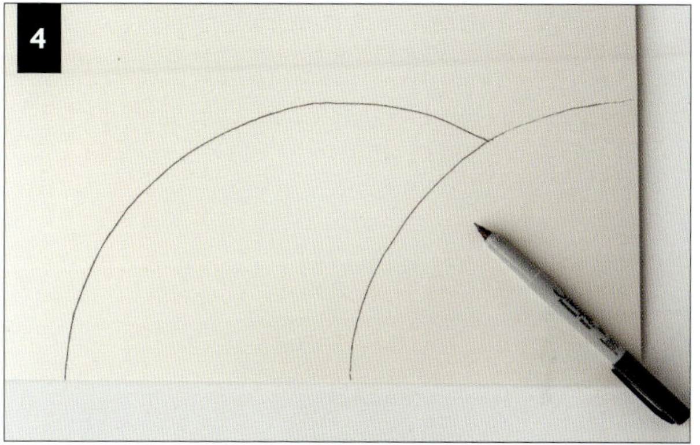

MAKING A WAVE TEMPLATE WITH A PLATE

Step One Draw around a round object such as a plate, saucepan lid or pan onto a piece of paper. Cut out the circle and fold it into quarters, as shown.

Step Two Aligning the straight edges of the quarter circle in the bottom right-hand corner of a sheet of card or template plastic, draw carefully around the curve to create the first arc.

Step Three Unfold the paper to make a half circle and align with the bottom and right-hand edges of the paper. Draw around this shape, from the bottom left upwards, until the line of the second arc meets the line of the first arc.

Step Four Remove the paper circle, and cut out the second shape, which is the template for your fan quilting.

Adding extra curves

To work the design speedily and in one fluid movement, machine quilters have adapted the design so that the next arched line in the wave can be quilted simply by rotating the quilt then sewing up and in the opposite direction, creating a curved end to each row.

Marking

EQUIPMENT

There are several ways to mark a quilt, including a chalk wheel, chalk pen, a sliver of dried soap or soapstone pencils.

I prefer to mark my quilts with a Hera marker (see right), which leaves a crease in the fabric that you can follow with your quilting stitches. This method is non-invasive and uses no inks, so there is no worry about harmful chemicals or needing to get rid of the marks afterwards. When the quilt is washed, any creases that weren't quilted over will disappear. Bodkins embedded in a cork for ease of holding, or even your fingernail, can do the same job,

With any method you use, do make sure that it will erase after it has served its purpose, and that it does not leave damaging chemical residue on your work.

HOW TO MARK STRAIGHT LINES

- **Marking tool and ruler**. Use these over areas where there may not be seams to follow. The Hera marker (or chalk or soap pencils) will make a crease or line for you to follow with the quilting.
- **Painter's / masking tape and ruler**. If you want a more definite line, mark it with some masking tape instead of a marking tool. It's then just a matter of stitching along its edge and then removing the tape as soon as you finish (so it doesn't leave residue). You might even be able to re-use strips of it, so it's quite economical.
- **Use lines already there**, either the ditch of the seam for in-the-ditch quilting or with "shadow quilting" (also known as "echo quilting", which involves stitching ¼–½in (0.5–1.25cm) away from the seams). You can use the width of your machine foot as a guide along the seams.
- **By eye**. If you feel confident, you don't need to mark lines and can just eyeball your quilt lines. Usually this takes a bit of practice, but can save time. I use this method when I want to create wavy lines deliberately.

HOW TO MARK CURVED DESIGNS

Run your marking tool around a template (like the ones on pages 186 and 188); this will help make these more organic lines precise enough for you to use as a guide line.

HOW TO MARK FREE-MOTION DESIGNS

By definition these don't need marking, as free-motion quilting has a more organic, free-form appearance. However, your designs will really benefit from you doodling with pencil and paper beforehand, so you can work out what kind of pattern you'd like to make. Take a sheet of blank paper and a pencil. Starting in one corner, doodle the design without lifting the pencil off the paper until the sheet is completely covered. If you can do this successfully, then you are ready to doodle on fabric with your sewing machine!

If you need help getting started, it may be useful to mentally—or even physically—mark out a grid of some sort, even if this is the actual block structure of your patchwork. The idea then is to focus on filling in one section before moving on to the next. Don't follow the grid too rigidly though: if your pattern has lots of loops or a similar all-over design, allow yourself to quilt into the next space a little too; this will prevent blank "borders" between sections.

Hand quilting

As noted on page 44, the hand quilting designs during this period were really not very different from those that had gone before—utility quilting (such as big-stitch quilting) being the most commonly used for speed. Quilts that featured fine hand quilting tended to be designed for display rather than practical purposes, as often they featured more elaborate and intricate designs, showing off the skills of the maker. Some of the quilts presented at the Sears Roebuck quilt competition feature very fine designs and attractive motifs that have been hand quilted.

There are two kinds of hand quilting I like to use: fine hand quilting and big-stitch quilting. The method for both is the same; the only difference is the thickness of the thread and the size of the needles used.

Before we start stitching, make sure you know how to securely start and stop stitching (see page 172). This will stop you wasting time going back over stitches that have come undone.

As you quilt, you can remove the basting / tacking stitches or pins.

SETTING UP

The length of thread you work with should be no longer than your arm, the same as when hand piecing. This may not seem very long, but it will make it easier to stitch with. The thread is less likely to become tangled and knot, and creates a more ergonomic arm movement when stitching: instead of having to pull a long thread skywards, you will be pivoting from the elbow, which is a lot less tiring.

Many of us will be hand quilting using a hoop. When you lay your quilt over the inner hoop and place the outer hoop on top, you will need to tighten the screw enough to hold the quilt firmly. As you tighten the screw, make sure that the quilt is flat with no pleats around the edge. You will also need to check that the quilt is not tight like a drum. There must be some movement in the quilt, so if you poke your finger up from underneath you will be able to make a hill and see the indentation of your fingernail. All of this will help you to be able to make the stitches.

When I work, the hand under the quilt, wearing a ridged thimble (shown on page 145), pushes the quilt layers up to make a "hill", which the needle will push against to make the stitch (see the center-right and bottom-right images on this page).

STARTING THE STITCH

Start by cutting a length of thread as long as your arm. Tie a knot in the end you just cut. Thread the free end into the needle. You need to insert the needle down through the top layer of fabric and batting / wadding then come up where you want to start, pulling on the thread so that the knot pops through the top fabric and is embedded in the batting / wadding. The embedded thread will be quilted over, securing the thread further.

If the knot gets stuck

If the knot is stubborn, use the point of your sewing needle to poke open the weave of the fabric to expand the hole where the knot needs to go through. Gently pull the thread until the knot goes into the batting / wadding and then, using the needle again, push the threads back into place.

FINISHING THE STITCH

Whether the thread is running out or you've finished your stitching, you will need to finish off securely. Make sure you leave a long enough tail of thread for this—about 5–6in (13–15cm) long.

Step One Make the last stitch, going all the way through to the back of the quilt with the needle. Bring the needle up at the beginning of the stitch.

Step Two Pull the thread through and wrap it around the needle two to three times, keeping the thread close to the quilt. The number of wraps will depend on how thick the thread is, and how densely woven the fabric is too. Essentially, you are making a knot that will pull through easily.

Step Three Push the wrapped needle back through the fabric and into the batting / wadding, just underneath the middle of the last stitch, and traveling a needle's length away from the stitching. As you pull the thread a knot will form that needs to be gently pulled through to embed it in the batting / wadding. Snip the tail of thread close to the quilt top.

BIG-STITCH QUILTING

This style of quilting uses a relatively thick thread and big stitches. The stitch length is often longer on the top surface of the quilt and smaller on the bottom. Big-stitch quilting is a bold style of quilting and the designs are usually fairly widely spaced, therefore needing fewer lines, and taking less time to quilt.

Big-stitch quilting looks great in straight lines. If you're working across the whole quilt top, you'll need to mark the lines with a ruler and your chosen marking tool to start with (see page 170). You can also work into the ditches / seams of your quilt top; For this I recommend using a bold, contrasting thread, for greater impact.

- Follow the sequence on starting the stitch (see opposite), and continue on. As you make the stitches, try to work with a rhythm to create even but large stitches that go through all three layers.
- I keep the needle hand still with the needle horizontal, moving only the finger that is on the underside of the quilt to create the stitches. Try different motions to see which is comfortable for you and creates the even stitches you want.
- When you have about 6in (15cm) of thread left in the needle, finish off and then start a new length of thread, as described opposite.
- For the needle, use a size 6 Embroidery, Betweens (quilting), Chenille or Sashiko needle. For the thread, use 12wt coton perle, size 16 coton à broder or 12wt cotton thread.

FINE HAND QUILTING

This is the traditional form of hand quilting with the emphasis being on making small, even running stitches to hold the quilt sandwich together, and with it create a subtle, textured design all over the quilt. It's very similar to big-stitch quilting, except a smaller needle and finer thread is used.

Historically, it was considered important to make your stitches as small as possible, perhaps up to as many as 14 stitches for every 1in (2.5cm) area. Nowadays, this "rule" is less adhered to.

- Follow a similar process described in the first three bullet points of big-stitch quilting, left.
- If you're new to fine hand quilting, you may want to use a larger size needle to begin with, like the size 8. As you become more experienced, you can move on to one of the smaller sizes, such as the size 11. If these smaller needles prove harder to thread then look out for "easy thread" needles, which will have a long eye.
- For the needle, use a size 6, 8, 9 10, or 11 Betweens (quilting), needle. For the thread, use 28wt quilting thread.

Machine quilting

Quilts can be quilted on your domestic machine or sent out for long-arm quilting. There is no shame in having a professional long-arm quilter quilt for you; it's getting it finished and closer to being used. Some of the quilts in this book were professionally quilted, often with a design you could emulate at home on your own machine if you wished. The vermicelli quilting on the Endless Chain Quilt on page 66 was professionally worked, and the same applies to the cross-hatching quilting on the Embroidered Linen Squares quilt (shown left), but everything else was made by me. It is nice to work in this way—having the professional tackle what you may not feel you could have achieved on your machine, then adding your own signature to the rest of the quilt.

If you're keen to do the quilting yourself, here are some pointers.

SETTING UP

Generally, you'll need to fit your sewing machine with a quilting or "jeans" needle, and with a machine quilting thread—for more information about which weight to use, see page 132.

The foot you use will depend on which kind of quilting pattern you choose:

- For **simple lines** that go in one direction, or a grid of straight lines or diagonal lines, a walking (dual- / even-feed) foot will make the quilting process easier.
- **For in-the-ditch quilting**, a stitch-in-the-ditch foot will ensure you follow seam lines as accurately as possible.
- **For free-motion quilting (like vermicelli stitching)**, it's necessary to use an open-toe darning foot, in conjunction with dropped feed dogs.
- **For shadow quilting and gentle wavy lines**, you can use a standard presser foot or walking foot for quilting, depending on the thickness of your batting / wadding.

It's worth taking the time to practice your stitching on a scrap of fabric or left-over unit—ideally layered over both an oddment of batting / wadding and backing fabric, so you can re-create the layers. This then gives you the opportunity to not only experiment with quilt designs, but also to test thread colors, thread thicknesses, stitch lengths, and various machine feet.

TYING OFF AND JOINING IN THREAD

At the end of machine quilting, or when you run out of thread and need to join in more, you'll need to tie off and sew in your threads.

Personally, I like to have as few ends of thread to tie off and sew in as possible. The easiest way to achieve this is to start your stitching on an outside edge of the quilt—in the batting / wadding—and finish this way too. This means the thread ends are not on the quilt top, and can be trimmed off and/or hidden in the binding later.

However, if you run out of thread halfway through stitching, it's good to know how to tie off your thread in the middle of your design and rejoin in a new thread, ready to carry on quilting.

The following steps show how I've fastened off, sewn in and rejoined the top thread on the quilt-top side of the quilt; you can use exactly the same process if you've run out of bobbin thread—the only difference is, at Step 2, you won't need to flip over your quilt.

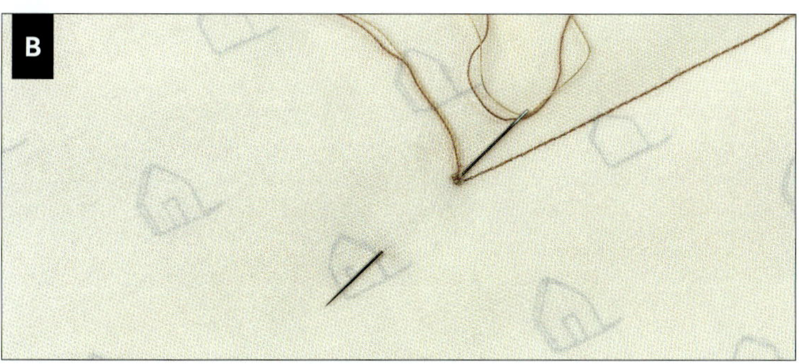

TYING OFF THREAD

Step One When you're close to running out of thread (avoid running out completely), stop stitching then pull the quilt away from your machine until you have at least 4in (10cm) of thread. Snip away from the machine.

Step Two Flip your quilt over, so the backing side of the quilt is facing you. With the help of a hand-sewing needle, pick up and draw the top thread through to the backing (**A**).

Step Three Bring the bobbin and top threads together then tie a knot with them, close to the backing. Thread the two threads onto your needle, then take the needle back into the quilt, through the backing only, close to where the two threads emerge. Bring the needle back up about 1in (2.5cm) away (**B**). Gently pull the threads until the knot "pops" through the fabric, between the batting / wadding and backing, then trim away the excess thread.

JOINING IN THREAD

Step Four Re-thread your sewing machine as necessary, referring to your machine's manual if required.

Step Five Flip your quilt over to the quilt-top side, and move it under the needle until you're a stitch away from your ending point. Manually turn the hand wheel to lower the needle into your quilt, then manually lift it again, until the bobbin thread pops up. You'll need to hold the end of the top thread in your hand and keep it taut as you do this. Thread the top thread through the bobbin thread (**C**), then carefully draw the loop of the bobbin thread back down through the quilt by pulling it on the underside (backing side) of the quilt with your hand. You're then ready to start stitching again.

Hand tying a quilt

Technically this is not quilting, but it's one of the simplest ways to secure a quilt without using a sewing machine. The ease and thriftiness involved with this technique appealed to some makers in the 1930s—the quilt on page 8 is one example of hand tying being used.

Tying can be done with a single thread and a simple reef knot, or more elaborately with multiple threads and more complicated knots. Experiment with different threads, thicknesses, and thread-tail lengths to see which work best with your project. I most commonly use doubled thread and a reef knot.

When tying the quilt, you can start with a long thread in the needle, often twice the length of your arm. Generally, these ties or tufts will be at the seam junctions of the patches, giving an easy grid to follow. If, however, you do not have such a pattern to follow, here is a simple method to create a grid.

This vintage scrap quilt has a soft, thick batting / wadding and the layers have been tied at regular intervals with thick cotton thread.

MAKING A GRID

Take a piece of quilters' graph paper measuring at least 18in (45.75cm) square; if you don't have a piece large enough, tape sheets together to create one. With a pencil and using the lines on the paper, mark an even grid—the distance between lines can be either your hand span (about 6in / 15cm) or your closed fist (about 4in / 10cm). When you are happy with your grid, fold the paper along the rows of marks and snip out a diamond at each point. Continue until all the marks are replaced by a hole. You can now place the paper over the quilt and, using a pencil, mark through the holes where you want to tie the quilt.

This method will also work with a piece of checked gingham cloth and will give you a larger sheet of grid to work with.

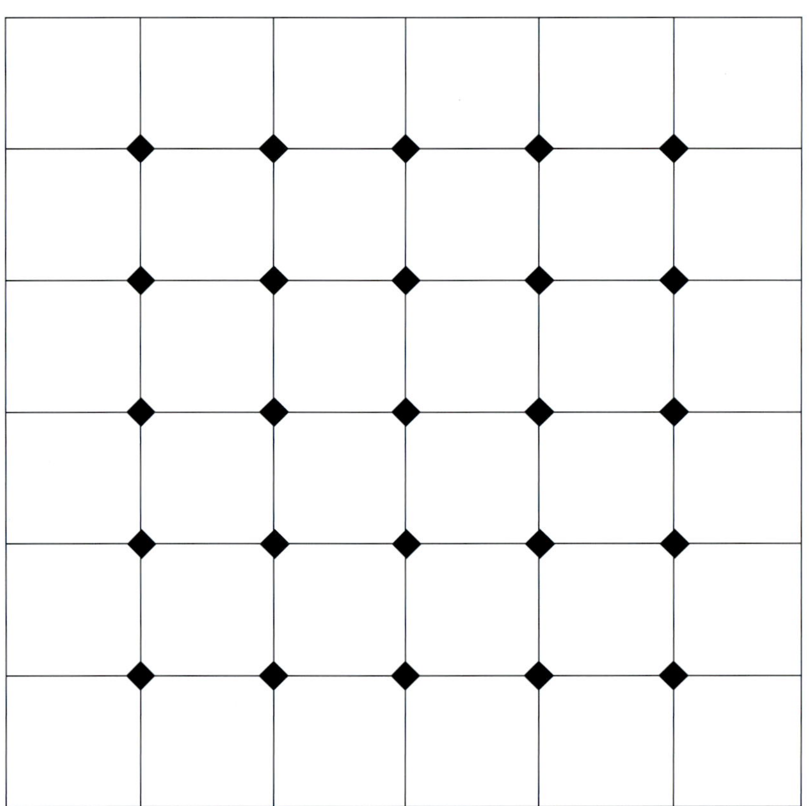

Diagram demonstrating the diamond-shaped cuts in your grid template.

MAKING A REEF KNOT

Also known as a square knot, this is the most common tying knot and most of us will be familiar with it. The length of thread you stitch with is dictated by the size of the tails you wish to leave—you must leave enough for knotting. I like my tails to be roughly 2in (5cm) long.

Step One Insert the needle through all three layers of the quilt, from the front of the quilt and coming up ¼in (5mm) away from the start. Don't pull the thread all the way through.

Step Two Re-insert the needle at the starting point, through all the layers, then bring the needle up where you came up in Step 1.

Step Three Pull the thread tightly.

Step Four Loop the left thread over the right and through the loop.

Step Five Pull tight and repeat, this time passing the right thread over the left and through the loop.

Step Six Repeat across the quilt. Once all the knots are in place, snip the excess thread to finish.

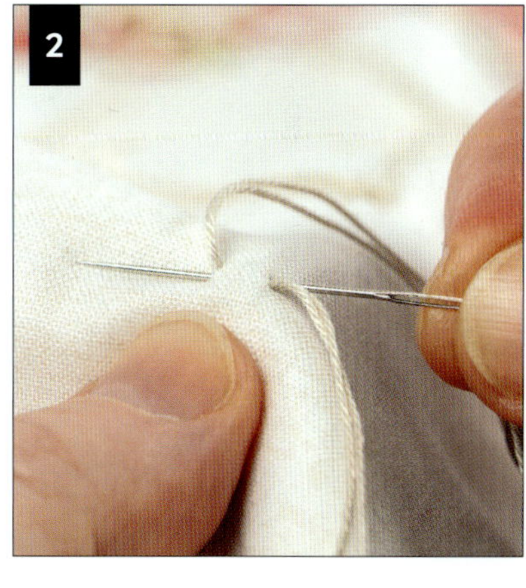

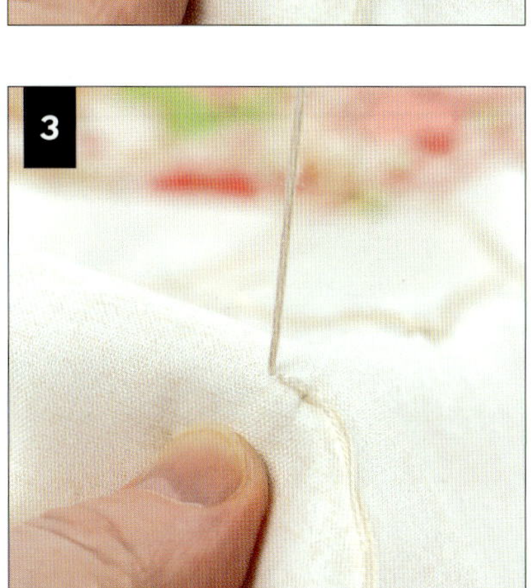

BINDING

Preparing the quilt for binding

Once the quilt is quilted and the basting / tacking stitches are removed, the backing and batting / wadding can be trimmed.

Some quiltmakers like to start binding the quilt without trimming the batting / wadding and backing; they leave it in place, add one side of the binding, then trim. Personally, I like to trim my quilt before binding, as often it means I can square up the corners at the same time, and make my quilt as neat as it can be before the binding goes on.

Important note: For the "Wide square-corner binding" method you will need to leave some batting / wadding allowance; see page 183 for details.

The excess backing and batting / wadding can be trimmed with fabric scissors; just make sure they are sharp. Be aware that batting / wadding will dull their blades, so sometimes it's good to keep a pair just for cutting batting / wadding. I like to tie a spare strip of batting / wadding around the handle of those scissors, so I know which pair they are.

If you want to use a rotary cutter, again it may be wise to set aside a cutter just for trimming batting / wadding, as this too can get easily dulled. A bigger cutter will work better due to the depth of the batting /wadding, so opt for a 60mm or 45mm if you can.

Any left-over pieces of batting / wadding can be kept for smaller projects, used as stuffing or joined to make new "Frankenbatting" (see page 133). The left-over backing fabric can be kept for more patchwork, or added to a scraps bag for scrap and string quilts.

METHOD

- Trim the edges of the batting / wadding and backing from the front of the quilt (i.e. the side with the quilt top), cutting through both at the same time, so they line up with the raw edge of the patchwork.
- I like to use a square ruler for the corners and adjacent sides. You can use the 12½in (31.75cm) square ruler you used to make your quilt blocks, or a bigger one if you have it. Place the square ruler on the untrimmed corner, making sure the adjacent sides are as straight as you can get them, then trim the corner. Now repeat at the next corner. There will be batting / wadding and backing still attached between these two corners, along the side. Now trim this side with a straight ruler, matching up from cut to cut. Repeat on the remaining corners and sides.

Making binding tape

The binding for my quilts is most often made from strips cut across the width of the fabric; this is an economical way to cut the binding and gives it a strong straight edge. Once joined into a continuous length with a bias or cross-wise join (which eliminates bulk when the binding is sewn to the quilt), the strips of fabric will be folded over to make what is known as a "double binding", which is very durable and gives a nice clean edge to your quilt.

Step One Open out one short end of two strips. Lay one strip over the open end of the other strip, RS together and at a 90-degree angle. Allow an extra ⅜in (1cm) of fabric along each short edge. Pin across the diagonal, or mark in a stitch line with a pencil or a Hera marker. Stitch along this line.

Step Two Cut off the excess fabric, leaving a ¼in (5mm) seam allowance. Repeat Steps 1 and 2 to join together the remaining strips. Open out the strips then press the SA open.

Step Three Fold the length of joined strips in half, WS together, then press.

Slip stitch

To achieve a neat finish, for some of the binding methods you'll need to hand-sew the remaining edge of the binding to the back of your quilt with slip stitch. Refer to the diagrams, right, for a reminder on how to slip stitch.

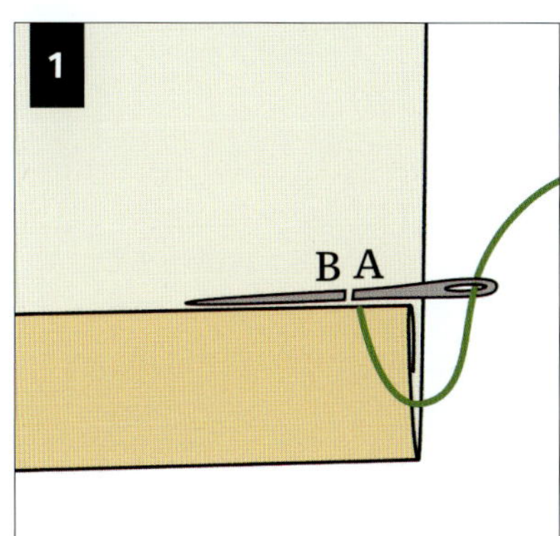

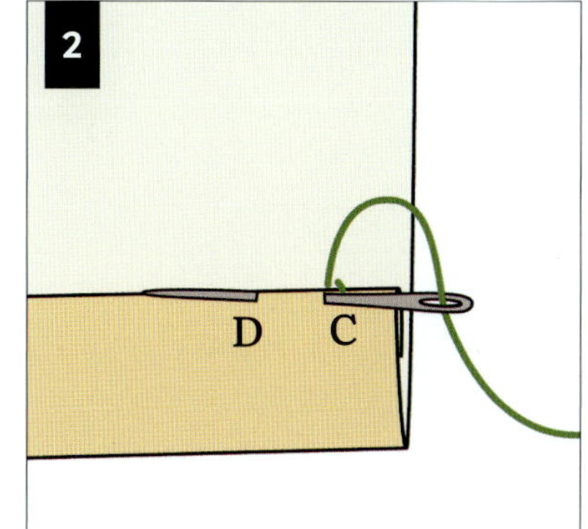

Continuous mitered binding

This is a traditional way to bind a quilt, leaving it with a narrow binding that's approximately ⅜in (1cm) wide. I recommend using a walking (dual- / even-feed) foot if you have one. You will need to finish off the binding by hand with slip stitch (see page 179).

Step One To start, make a mock bias join at one end of your binding: fold over one end of the strip by 90 degrees, creating a mitered fold as shown in the photograph above.

Step Two Trim off the excess fabric at the end of the strip, leaving a ¼in (5mm) seam allowance.

Step Three Pin the mock bias end of the binding to the quilt top, about one-third of the way along one edge (see the black arrow), and with raw edges aligned.

Step Four Sew the binding along this edge with a ¼in (5mm) SA, then stop ¼in (5mm) from the first corner you meet. To make stopping at this distance easier, fold your binding toward your sewing machine (as in Step 5) then lay it back down again as shown; this crease (highlighted with the dark-green line) is your ¼in (5mm) mark—when your needle hits this crease, stop sewing.

Step Five Reverse stitch, then move the quilt away from the foot. Fold the binding at a 90-degree angle, away from the quilt and so the free long edge of the binding aligns with the next, unbound edge of the quilt.

Step Six Fold the binding back down along the next unbound edge, aligning the raw edges and creating a fold at the corner. Start sewing from the folded edge and then stitch down to the next corner (see the dark-red dashed line).

Step Seven Repeat Steps 4–6 to sew the rest of the binding to the quilt top. When you get to the last side, stop 6in (15.25cm) away from your mock bias join.

Step Eight Ensuring that there is an overlap of about 1in (2.5cm), trim away the excess binding at an angle.

Step Nine Tuck the trimmed end inside the end with the mock bias join.

Step Ten Continue to stitch along the binding as before, to finish stitching the last section of the binding and to secure the ends to the quilt top.

Step Eleven Turn the long, folded, unstitched edge of the binding over to the back of the quilt. Pin the binding to the backing side, so the folded edge covers your stitching. At the corners, the fabric should "magically" miter, but you'll need to help it sit neatly by tucking one side under the other, as shown.

Step Twelve Slip stitch the binding in place by hand, along the fold. You can stitch right along the miter too, as shown, but this is a personal choice.

Hacked mitered binding with a square-corner finish

Since seeing an antique quilt with a binding consisting of three mitered corners and one square corner, sometimes I'll use this method instead of the classic "Continuous mitered binding" approach (see page 180). With this technique, there is no worry about neatly joining the ends of binding together; at a glance the casual observer won't notice one of the corners doesn't look like the rest.

Step One Start with one binding end lined up along one edge on the front of the quilt, raw edges matching and from one corner, as shown in the photograph.

Step Two At the next three corners, fold and stitch as you would for a mitered corner (see page 180).

Step Three As you approach the last corner, fold the already stitched binding along the next edge away from the quilt, as shown.

Step Four Lay the rest of the binding along the edge, then stitch right to the edge. Trim off the excess binding.

Step Five On the back of the quilt and at the square corner, trim away the surplus fabric (and batting / wadding, if necessary) to make the corner less bulky.

Step Six Turn the binding to the back of the quilt, and cover the raw edges and stitch line of the binding worked from the front of the quilt. Fold and pin the mitered corners as per Steps 11 and 12 on page 181; for the square corner, fold and pin as shown, so the corners are "stepped". Then slip stitch in place along the fold.

1

2

3

4

5

6

Wide square-corner binding

This is great way to create a border-like binding around your quilt, and add more depth and color too. The steps that follow are almost the same as those you would follow for a regular square-corner binding; the only differences are you will need to trim the quilted batting / wadding and backing to extend ¾in (2cm) from the quilt top, and you're left with a wider finished binding.

Make the binding in the same way as described on page 179, this time cutting 4½in (11.5cm) wide strips.

Step One Trim the batting / wadding and backing fabric, leaving a ¾in (2cm) allowance around the quilt top.

Step Two Sew a strip of binding to one side of the quilt top, raw edges matching and with the tape facing toward the patchwork top. When you have finished sewing, trim the binding to the size of the batting / wadding and backing fabric. Repeat on the opposite side.

Step Three Finger-press the strips away from the quilt top. Now stitch the remaining strips of binding to the top and bottom of the quilt top. Start by matching the raw edge of the binding to the raw edge of the quilt top, but make sure you start the strip at the fold of the binding already in place. Once the strips are sewn, finger-press away from the center of the quilt top.

Step Four On the back of the quilt, trim away the surplus backing fabric and batting / wadding from each corner, as shown, to make turning the binding to the back easier and to reduce bulk.

Step Five Starting in the middle of a straight side, turn the binding over to the back of the quilt and pin in place along the line of stitching made from attaching the binding to the front of the quilt (see the dark red stitching). As you approach the corner, fold the binding so it encases the raw edge. Pin in place and repeat at each corner.

Step Six Slip stitch the binding in place, stitching down each end/corner completely to secure it.

Labeling and aftercare

LAUNDERING QUILTS

Once your quilt is finished, it may need laundering. This will freshen the quilt after so much handling and remove any markings and residue from the quilting process. Also, depending on the batting / wadding used, laundering will shrink the quilt a little and emphasize the quilting stitches.

Quilts are quite sturdy and can easily be washed in a washing machine. Only fragile quilts (particularly ones using vintage fabrics) are best washed by hand. I put my quilts in the machine on a gentle cycle at 86°F (30°C) with detergent specially formulated for colors. If you've pre-washed your fabrics there should not be an issue with color bleeding. If you are concerned about color bleeding, put in a few color catchers.

Most of the time, I will only wash my quilts when I can dry them outside, especially on a windy day. This is an obvious way to save resources, and avoid needing to tumble dry. If I cannot do that then I will put the quilt in the tumble dryer long enough to take out the excess water, then I'll put the quilt in the airing cupboard or over a clothes airer to finish off. Once the quilt is dry it can be used, and will not need ironing.

LABELING YOUR QUILT

Once your quilt is sewn and bound, it's worth giving a thought to labeling it. If we think about how many lovely vintage and antique quilts that there are to inspire us, then look to see who made them, many are anonymous. It is a shame to think of all that work, and yet there is no acknowledgment of the maker.

The label can just be your name and the date. If the quilt is a gift, perhaps include a short message and the recipient's name too.

Re-using fabrics

It is worth thinking about using discarded vintage embroidered coasters or doilies as fabric for labels (see the photographed examples below). These can often be bought cheaply in thrift / charity / op shops. Choose designs to which you can add your name and the date at the very least. Wash and press them first, pin them in position on the back of the quilt, then hand-sew in place with slip stitch (see page 179).

Handwritten

The labeling can be written directly onto the back of the quilt with a permanent marker pen, or onto a muslin / calico label that is then stitched to the quilt.

Pre-printed labels

Many craft shops sell fabrics consisting of decorative blank labels. Buy these by the yard or meter to cut out and use on your projects. Labels can also be ordered from name-tape suppliers, and you can customize these with various motifs and phrases. If you find that you have labels that were cut out of school uniforms over the years and saved, you can use these as part of the labeling process.

Embroidered and cross-stitched labels

Many talented quilters embroider too. Consider embellishing your written label with simple stitching such as backstitch, split stitch or stem stitch. With a little planning and some graph paper, you can also work a cross-stitch label. A special canvas, known as waste canvas, can be used on top of the muslin / calico and the threads pulled away afterwards to leave your stitching on the muslin / calico.

Printed computer labels

If writing your label is proving a little daunting, then you can produce one on the computer instead. Simply create your label as a document and then print it out on to special fabric sheets. Just follow the instructions to make the printing permanent, and stitch the label to the quilt.

Templates

The following templates are provided at 100% scale. Note that the seam allowances for some templates are not included, and will need to be added where necessary. For templates that have the letter "R"included in the name, this stands for "reflect" and means you will need to flip the template to create a second template that is a mirror image of the original. All the cutting templates in the book feature a grain line arrow, which should be aligned with the fabric grain line before the shapes are cut out.

Digital templates

These templates are also available to download free from the Bookmarked Hub website:

www.bookmarkedhub.com

Search for this book by title or ISBN; the files can be found under "Book Extras".

Membership of the Bookmarked online community is free.

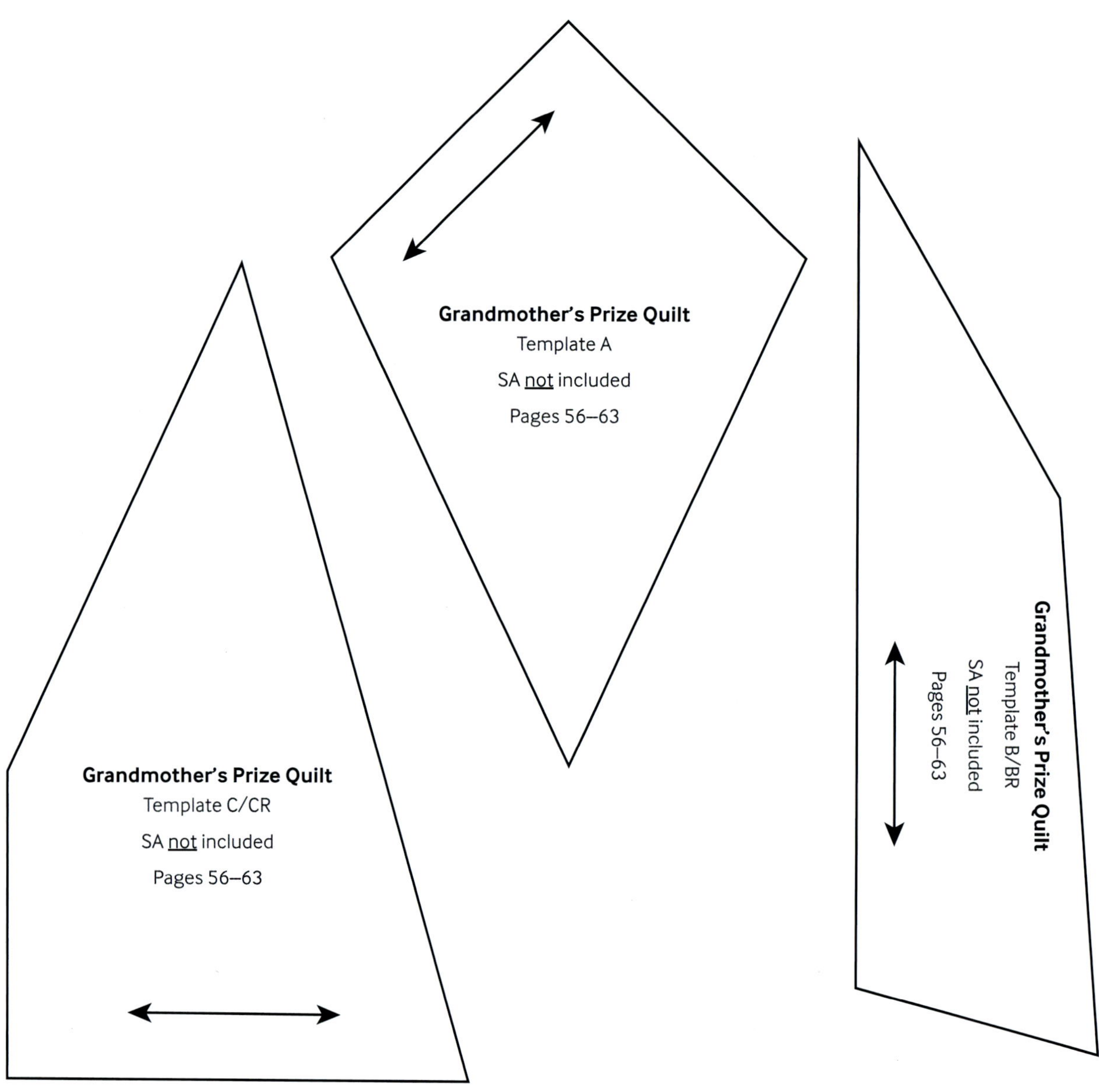

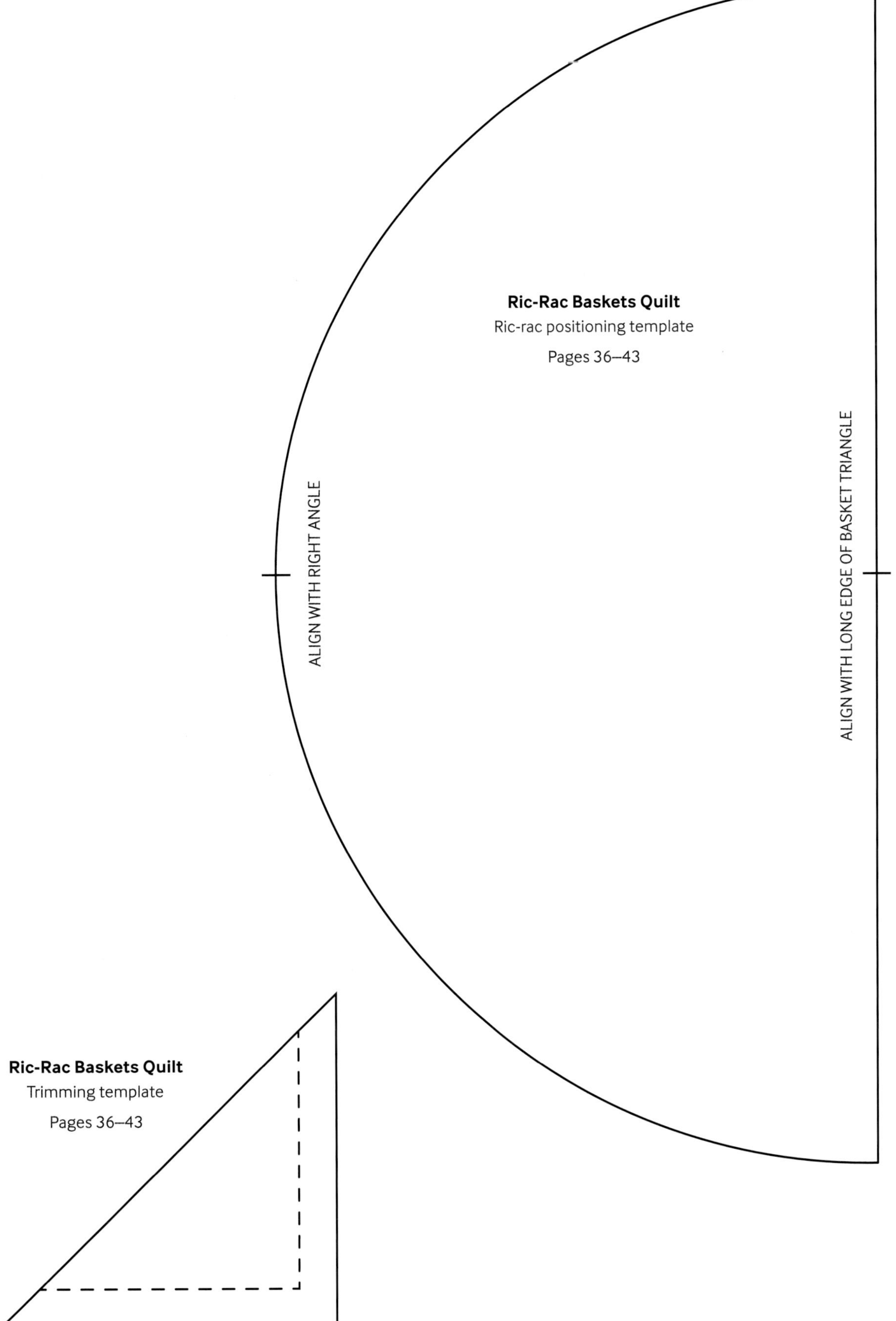
Ric-Rac Baskets Quilt
Ric-rac positioning template
Pages 36–43
ALIGN WITH RIGHT ANGLE
ALIGN WITH LONG EDGE OF BASKET TRIANGLE
Ric-Rac Baskets Quilt
Trimming template
Pages 36–43

Scrap Baskets Quilt

Quilting design templates

NOTE: The dotted lines are to help with positioning only; do not transfer to fabric

Pages 46–53

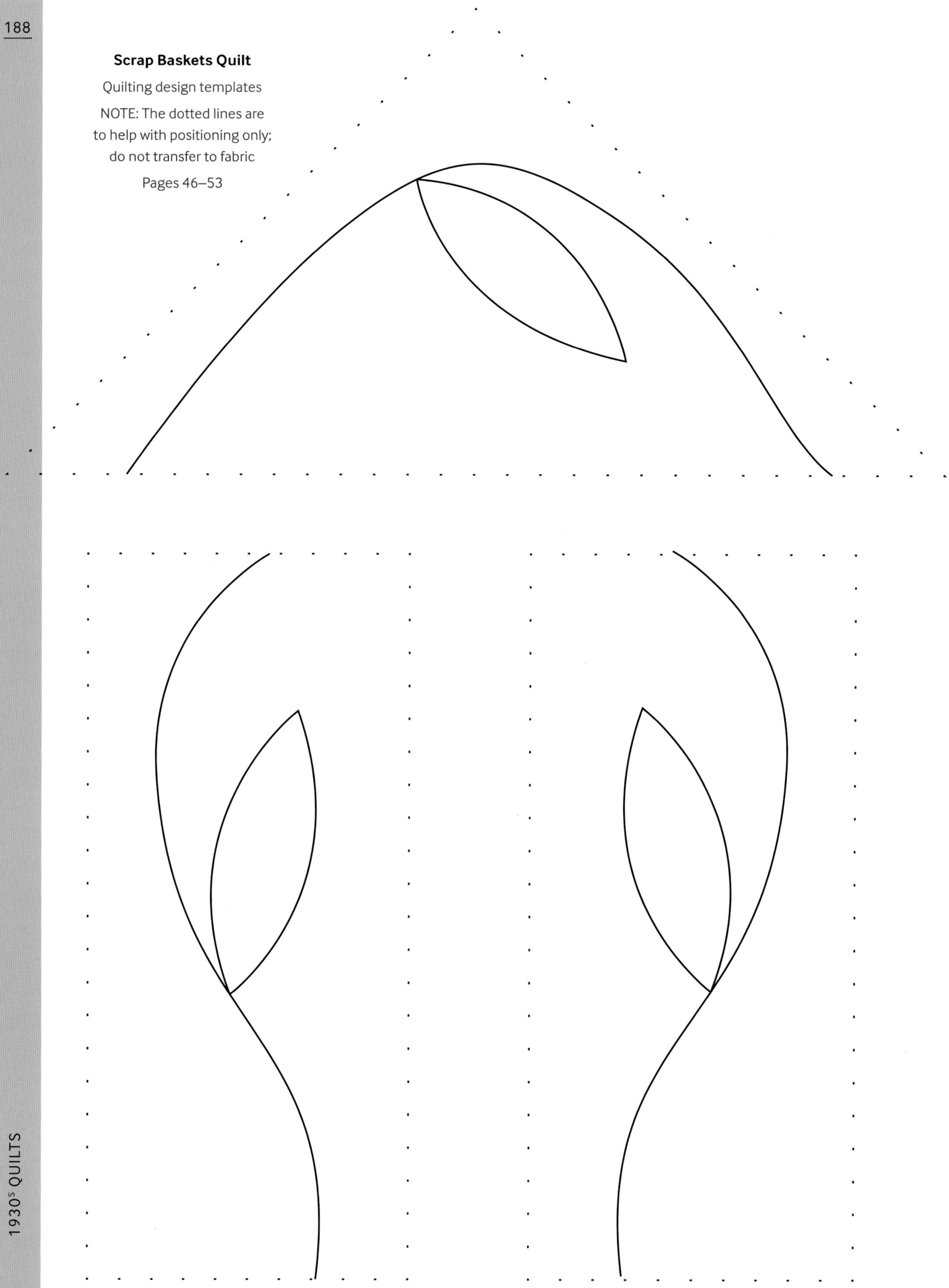

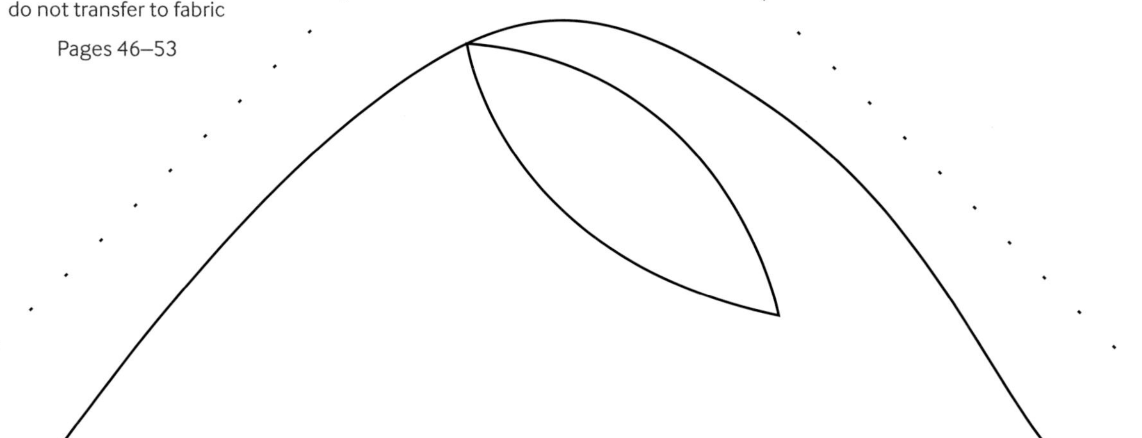

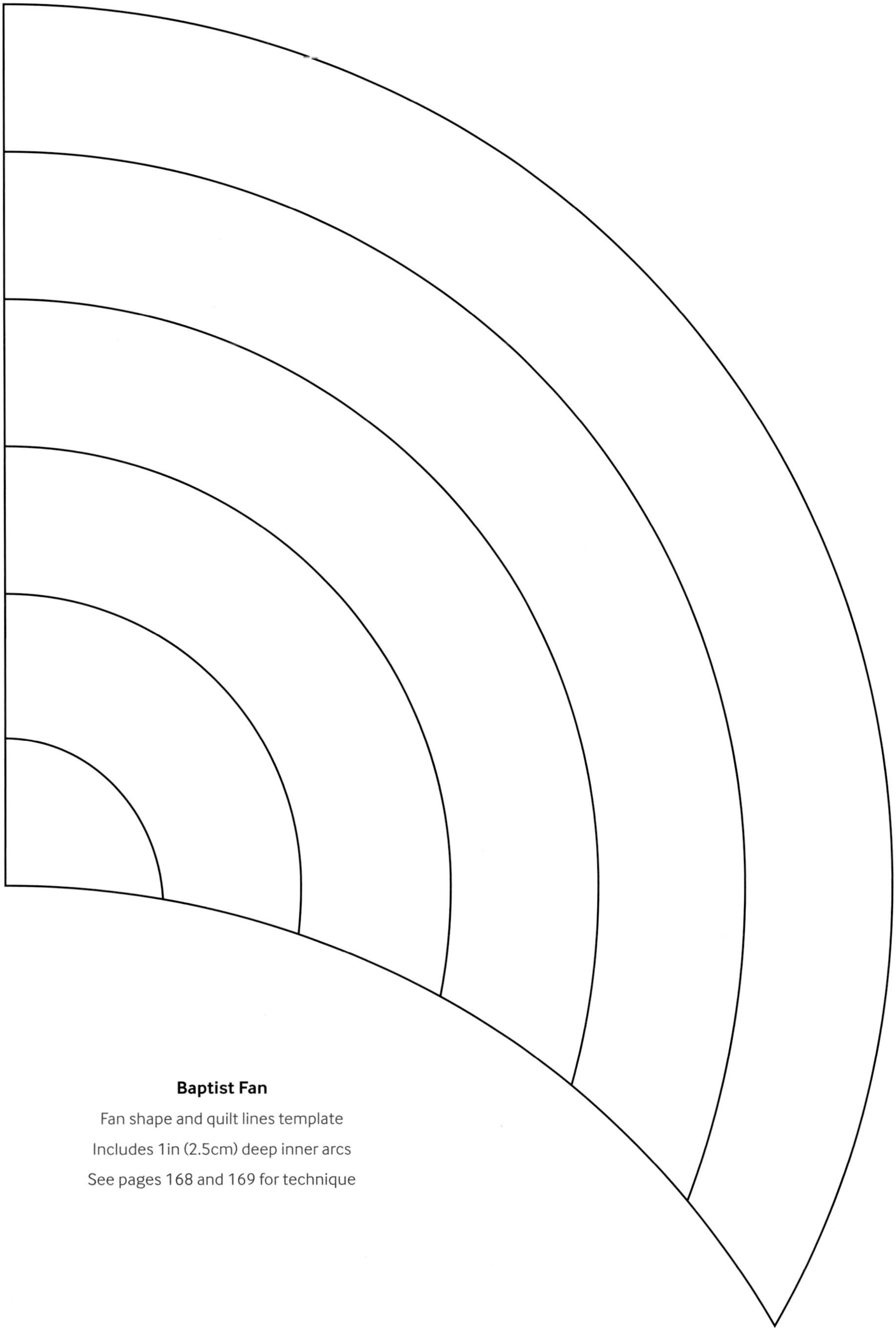

Baptist Fan

Fan shape and quilt lines template

Includes 1in (2.5cm) deep inner arcs

See pages 168 and 169 for technique

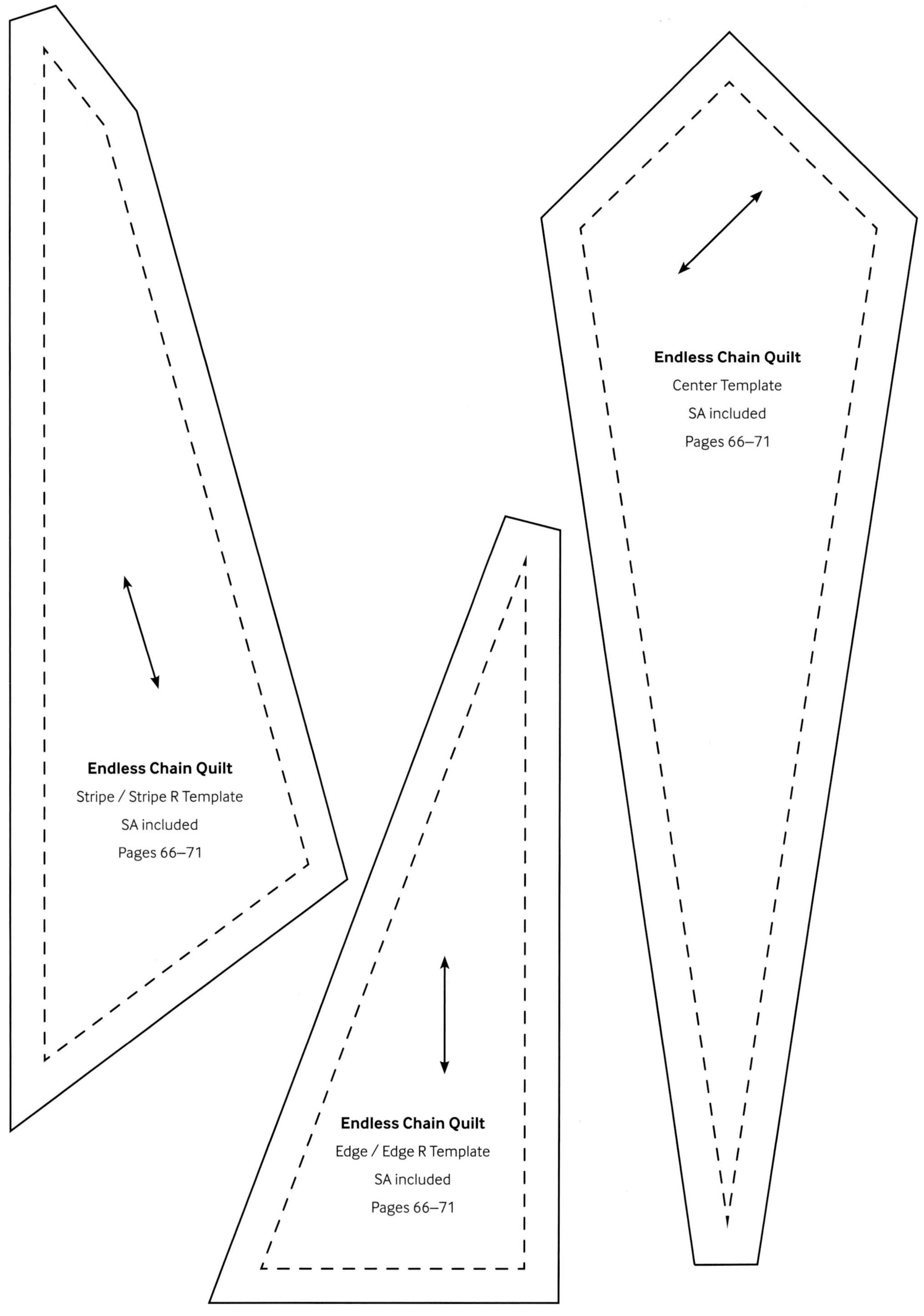
Endless Chain Quilt
Stripe / Stripe R Template
SA included
Pages 66–71
Endless Chain Quilt
Center Template
SA included
Pages 66–71
Endless Chain Quilt
Edge / Edge R Template
SA included
Pages 66–71

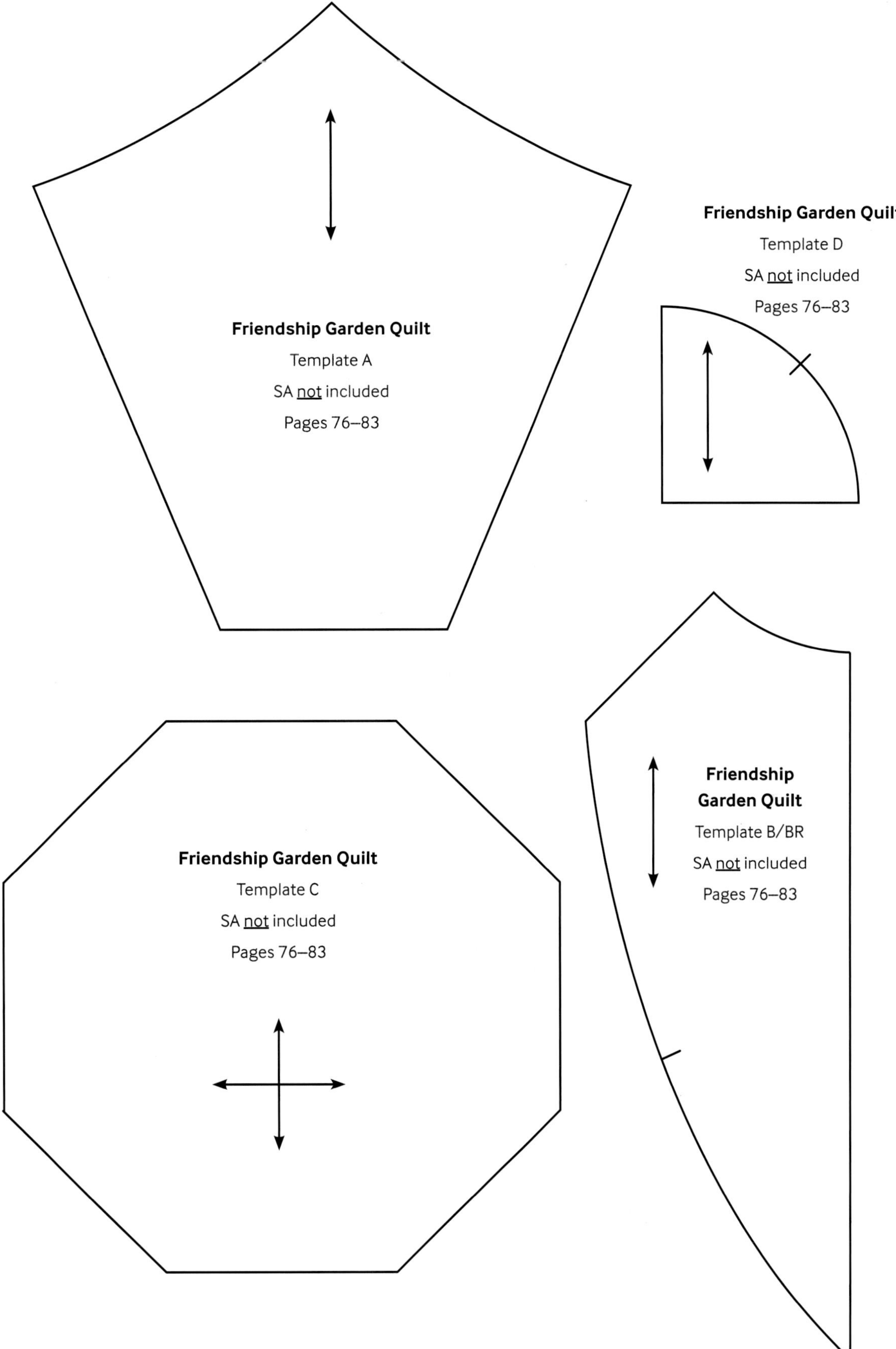

Friendship Garden Quilt
Template A
SA not included
Pages 76–83
Friendship Garden Quilt
Template D
SA not included
Pages 76–83
Friendship Garden Quilt
Template C
SA not included
Pages 76–83
Friendship Garden Quilt
Template B/BR
SA not included
Pages 76–83

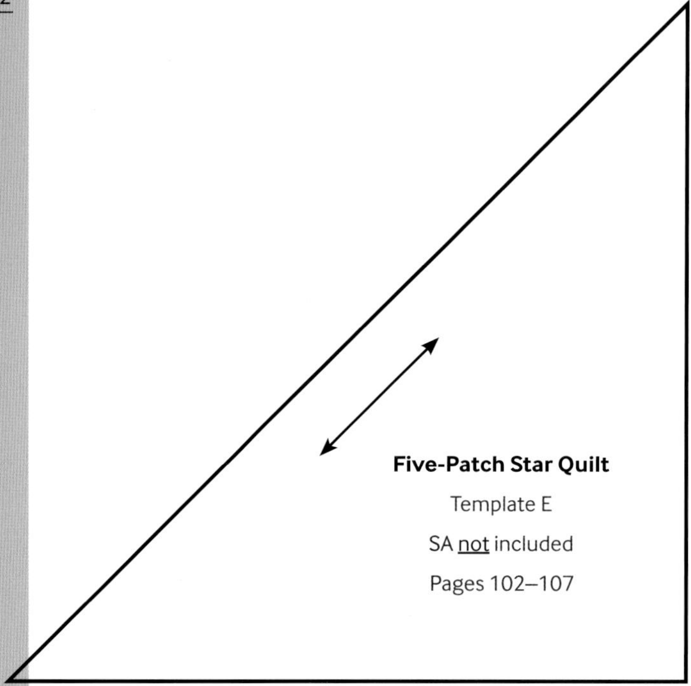
Five-Patch Star Quilt
Template E
SA not included
Pages 102–107

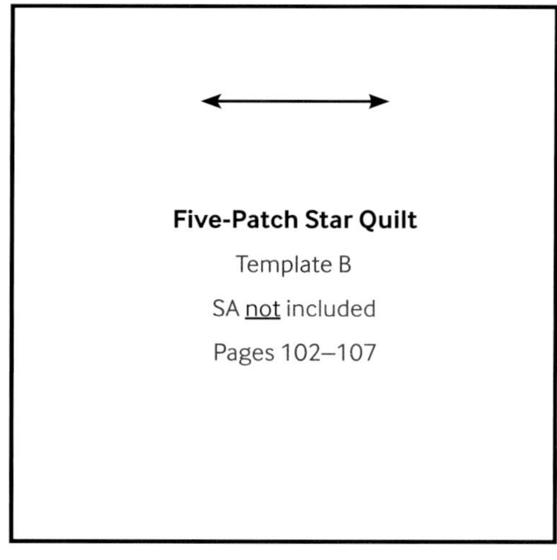
Five-Patch Star Quilt
Template B
SA not included
Pages 102–107

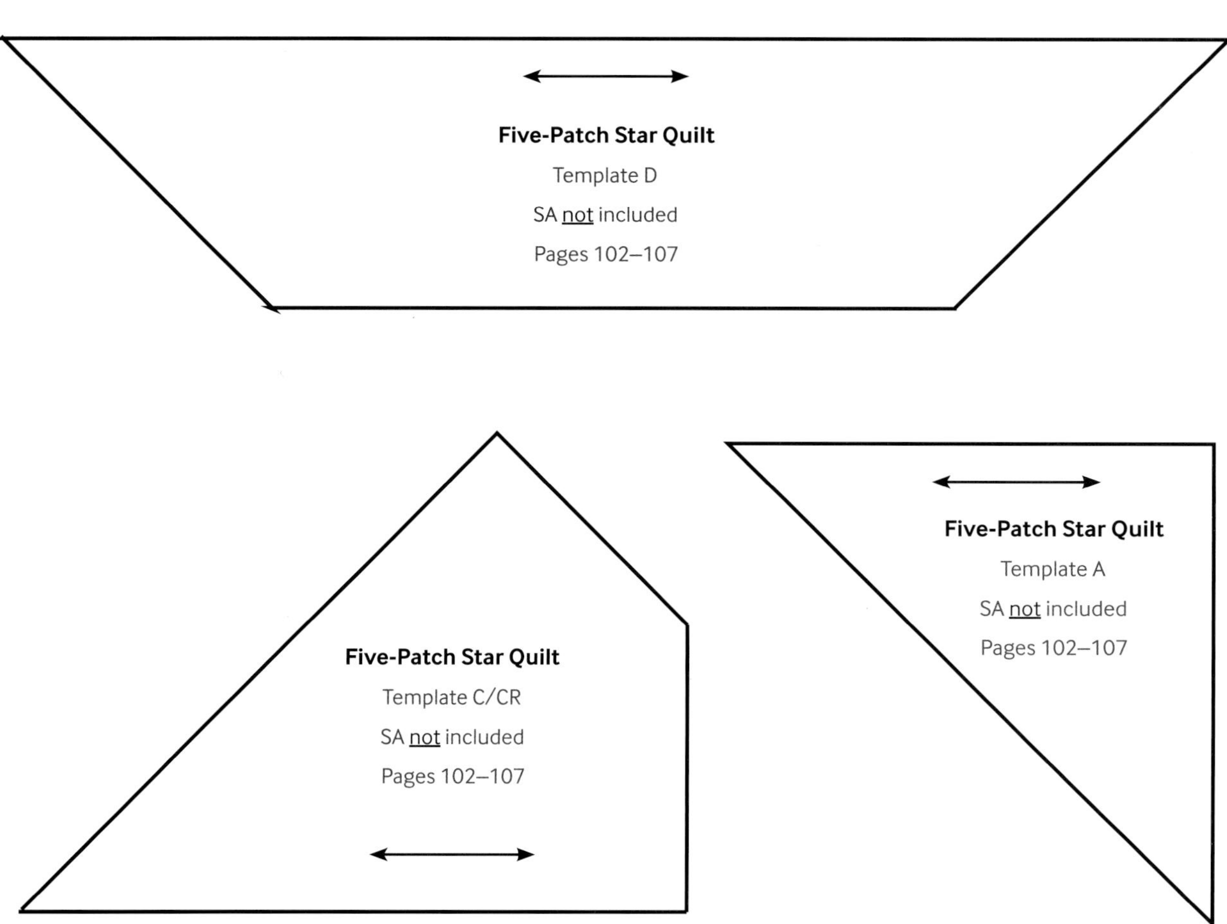
Five-Patch Star Quilt
Template D
SA not included
Pages 102–107
Five-Patch Star Quilt
Template C/CR
SA not included
Pages 102–107
Five-Patch Star Quilt
Template A
SA not included
Pages 102–107

Embroidery Template B positioning diagram (20% actual size)

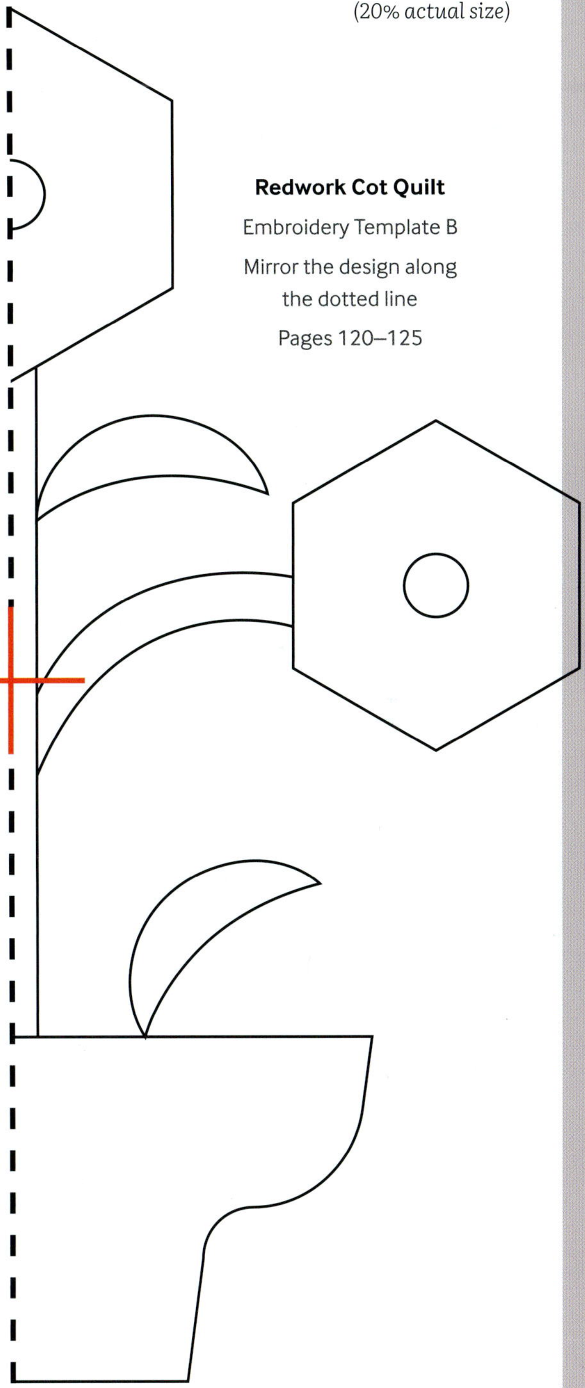

Redwork Cot Quilt

Embroidery Template B

Mirror the design along the dotted line

Pages 120–125

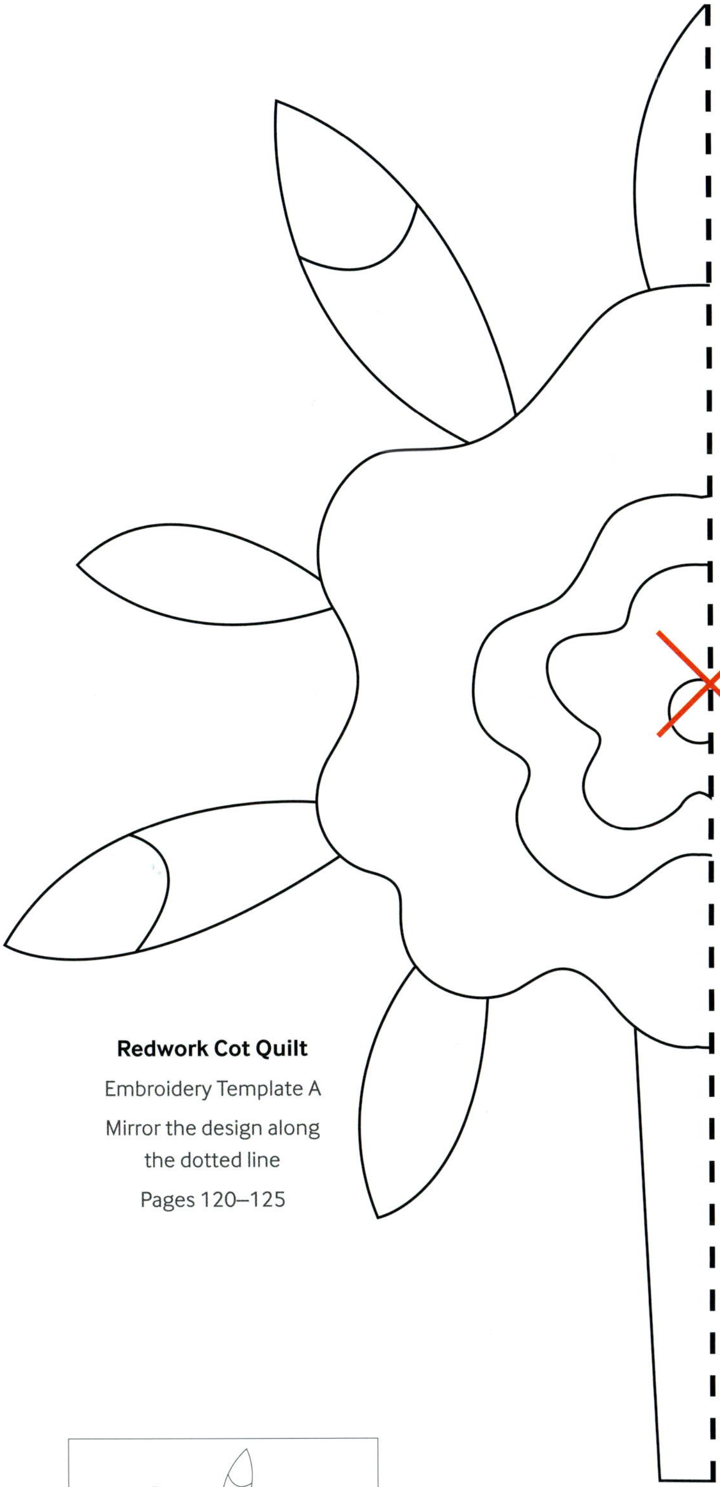

Redwork Cot Quilt

Embroidery Template A

Mirror the design along the dotted line

Pages 120–125

Embroidery Template A positioning diagram (20% actual size)

Redwork Cot Quilt

Embroidery Template C

Mirror the design along the dotted line

Pages 120–125

Embroidery Template C positioning diagram

(20% actual size)

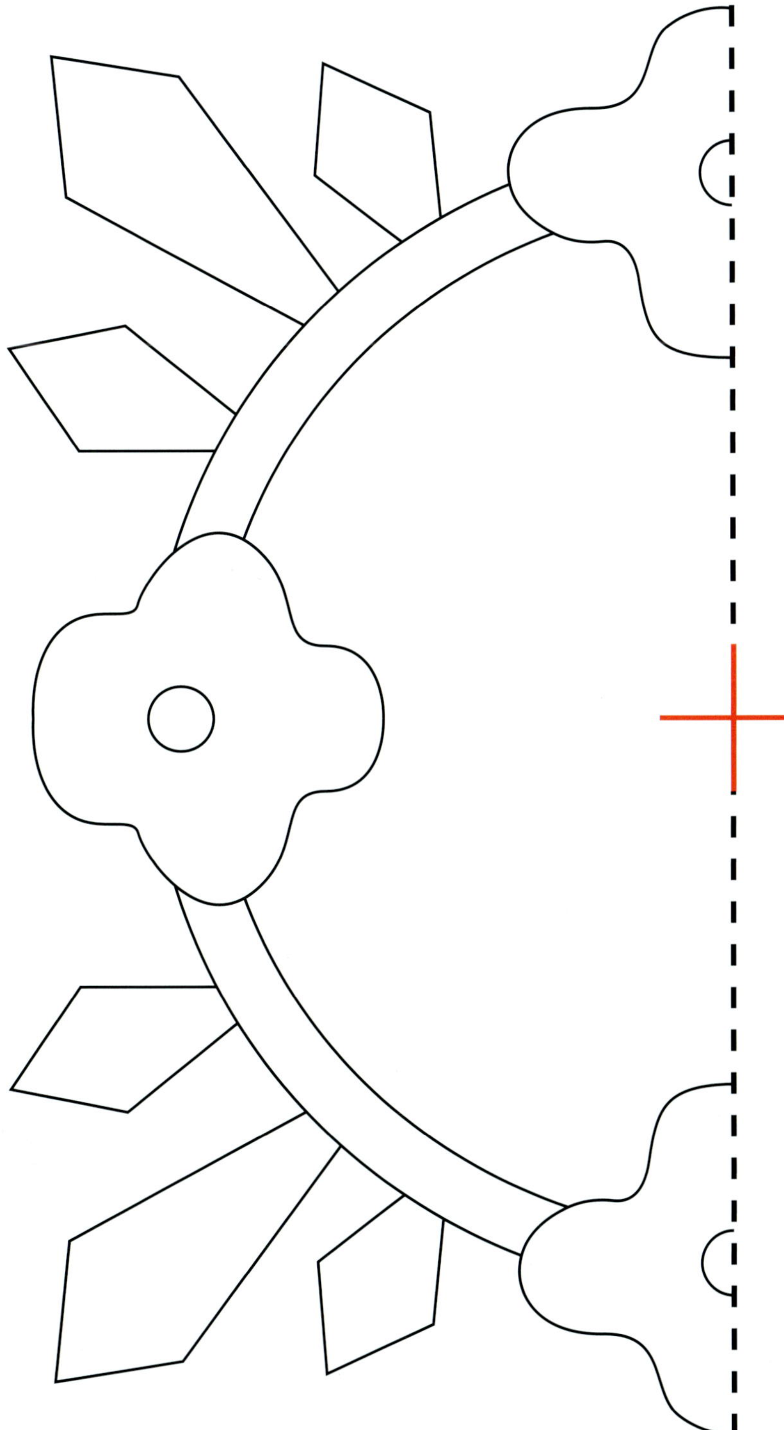

Redwork Cot Quilt

Embroidery Template D

Mirror the design along the dotted line

Pages 120–125

Embroidery Template D positioning diagram

(20% actual size)

Redwork Cot Quilt

Embroidery Template E

Pages 120–125

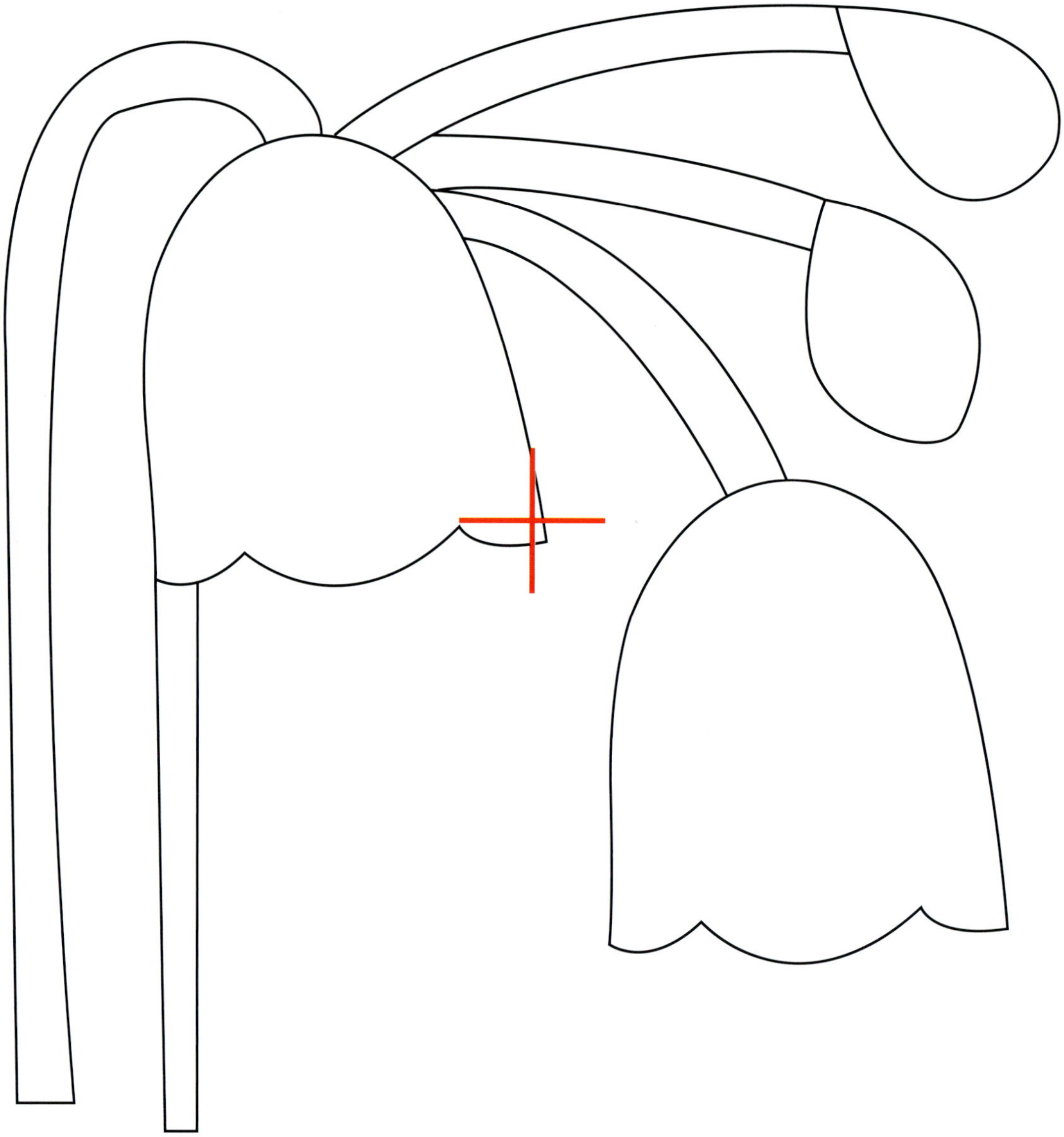

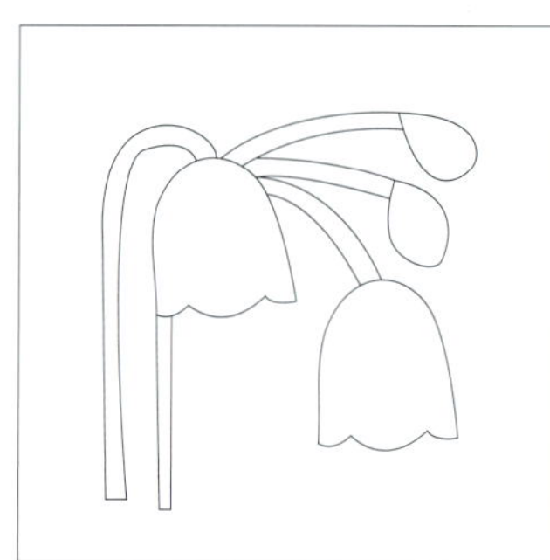

Embroidery Template E positioning diagram

(20% actual size)

Redwork Cot Quilt

Embroidery Template F

Pages 120–125

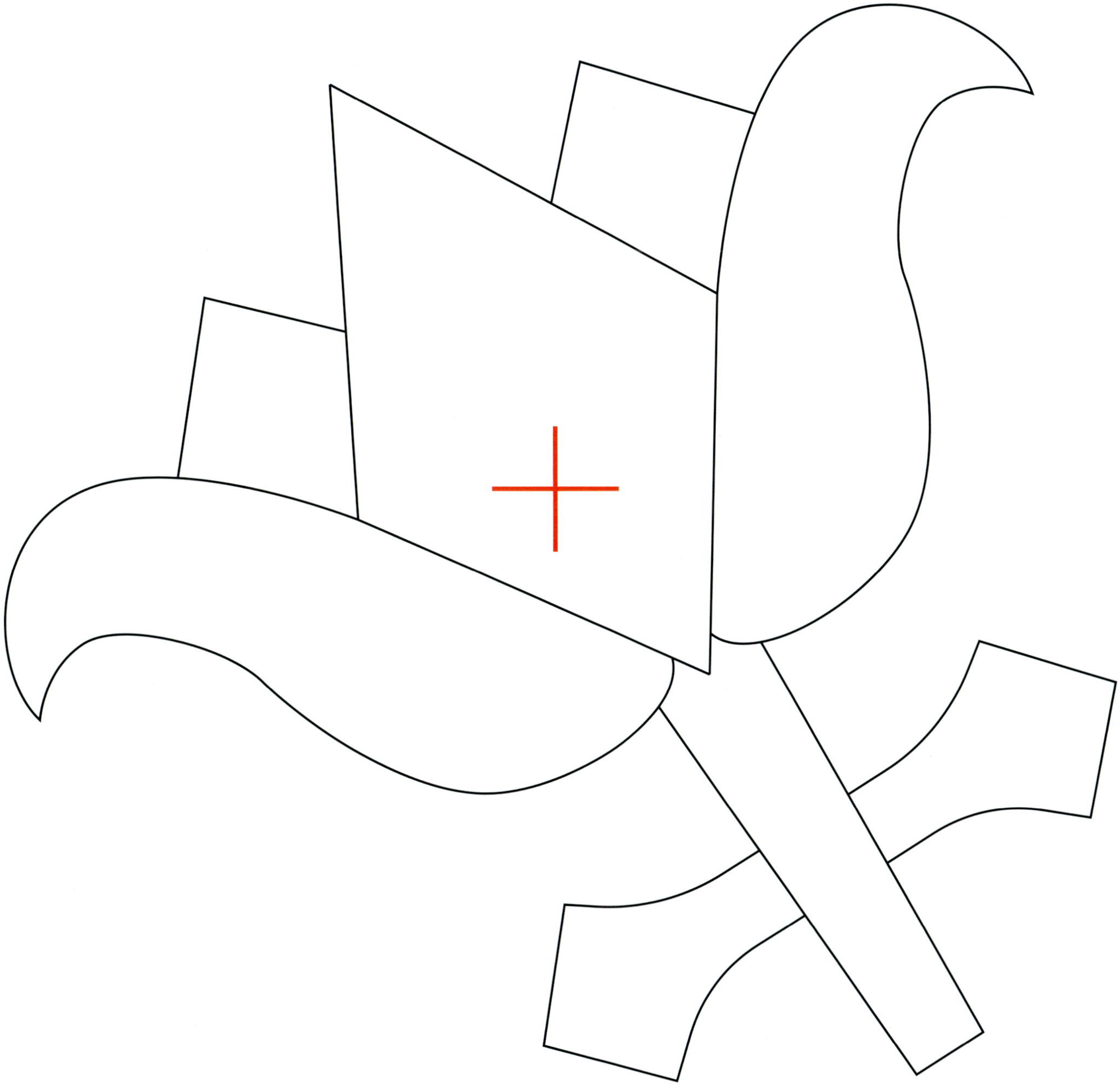

Embroidery Template F positioning diagram

(20% actual size)

Thanks

Thank you to Search Press for having such a vision for this book; it's more than I could have thought possible.

Thank you to Kate Hebert for her valuable contributions to this book, with both her foreword and the descriptions of the museum's quilts throughout, and the involvement of the American Museum & Gardens (AM&G) in Bath, UK. Little did I know when I saw my first American quilts at the museum in my teens, that they would have such a lasting impression on me.

Many thanks to Heather Audin, Curator of the Quilters Guild Museum Collection, for her support and guidance.

I'm incredibly grateful to Marion Drake, who so generously shared her quilts with us here; she was a real treasure in the quilt world.

Many thanks to Mark Davison and Lisa Brown, who photographed and styled the quilts; you really brought them all to life.

Thanks also due to the behind-the-scenes folks who I could not stitch without, especially all the staff and engineers at World of Sewing in Tunbridge Wells, UK; you are always so great with my last-minute sewing-machine crises and panics.

Index

A

appliqué 23, 25, 32, 34, 35, 37, 45, 55, 64, 72, 85, 92, 93, 119, 121, 134

B

backing fabric 9, 28, 39, 49, 59, 69, 79, 89, 97, 101, 102, 105, 112, 115, 123, 131, 159, 160, 161, 164, 165, 174, 175, 178, 181, 183

basket quilt(s) 36–43, 46–53, 168, 187, 188

baste(ing) 43, 53, 62, 71, 82, 91, 99, 107, 114, 125, 137, 160, 171, 178

- grid system 57, 160, 161
- hand 160, 161, 162
- safety-pin 134, 160, 163,
- table-top 164–165
- thread 132

batting 7, 9, 25, 32, 35, 39, 49, 59, 69, 79, 59, 97, 105, 112, 115, 123, 133, 134, 160, 161, 165, 172, 174, 175, 176, 178, 182, 183, 184

binding 39, 49, 57, 59, 69, 79, 89, 93, 97, 105, 112, 123, 132, 134, 153, 175, 178, 179

- continuous mitered 180–181
- hacked mitered 115, 182
- tape, making 179
- wide square-corner 57, 62, 183

border(s) 9, 17, 45, 55, 64, 65, 67, 69, 71, 73, 76, 79, 82, 94, 97, 99, 119, 123, 125, 140, 170, 183

C

chain piece(ing) 152, 153

color palette, Thirties 6, 7, 8, 10, 11, 13, 15, 17, 18, 20, 24, 29, 32, 33, 34, 35, 44, 45, 55, 65, 72, 73, 74, 75, 84, 85, 92, 93, 101, 108, 109, 119, 121, 128, 129, 130, 131

cornerstone(s) 64, 89, 90, 102, 105, 107, 156, 157, 158

cutting (fabric) 9, 67, 86, 135, 138, 139, 140, 141, 142, 143, 178, 179, 183

E

embroidery 9 ,10, 14, 15, 21, 23, 32, 35, 37, 39, 40, 45, 73, 84–85, 86–91, 92, 116–119, 121, 123, 124, 185, 193, 194, 195, 196, 197

equipment, quiltmaking 134, 135, 136, 137, 154, 162, 163, 164, 170, 178

F

fabric(s) 10, 11, 12, 18, 20, 23, 28, 29, 32, 35, 37, 39, 57, 64–65, 67, 74, 76, 84, 86, 92, 93, 94, 102, 109, 123, 128–131, 138
see also feedsacks

- scrap(s) 12, 28, 29, 44, 46, 57, 59, 69, 76, 79, 105, 108–109, 110, 112, 115

fastening off (thread) 172, 174

feedsack(s) 12, 25, 27, 28, 29, 64, 67, 100–101, 102, 121, 130, 131, 166

flour sacks *see* feedsacks

frames, framing strips 46–53, 86, 59, 90, 155

H

hand-tying (quilts) 9, 44, 71, 132, 166, 176–177

historical quilts *see* vintage quilts

HST (Half Square Triangle) 39, 40, 49, 138, 142

- units 49, 50, 98

J

joining in (thread) 172, 175

K

kits 15, 20, 23, 26, 28, 30, 44, 45, 119, 166

L

label(ing) 72, 73, 74, 75, 185

M

marking (quilting designs) 35, 53, 57, 59, 62, 69, 79, 82, 99, 107, 123, 125, 136, 137, 166, 170, 173, 176, 184

N

needle(s) 39, 49, 59, 79, 123, 134, 137, 144, 145, 161, 162, 165, 171, 172, 173, 174, 175

P

pattern(s), historical block or quilting 7, 10, 11, 12, 18, 20–23, 25, 26, 27, 29, 35, 37, 44, 45, 46, 54, 55, 57, 65, 67, 75, 85, 86, 94, 102, 109, 116, 119, 121, 166

- penny squares 84, 85, 119, 121

piecing, pieced 17, 24, 45, 55, 65, 72, 134, 138

- hand 59, 102, 132, 134, 136, 138, 143, 144–151 ,154, 171
- machine 35, 86, 94, 110, 120, 132, 134, 138, 143, 152–153

post(s) *see* cornerstones

press(ing) 86, 147, 138, 154, 159, 179, 185

Q

quilting (designs) 35, 44, 45, 91, 119, 166–169, 170, 174

- Baptist Fan 99, 107, 168–169, 189
- big-stitch 43, 57, 59, 114, 125, 132, 134, 171, 173
- cross-hatch 57, 82, 91, 125, 166, 167, 173, 174, 199
- fine hand 35, 44–45, 46, 53, 55, 64, 85, 99, 116, 134, 171, 173
- outline (echo) 7, 13, 17, 45, 46, 53, 91
- straight line 82, 93, 166, 167, 170, 173, 174
- vermicelli 71, 166, 170, 174

quilter's grid 110, 112, 113, 115

R

redwork 23, 84, 116–119, 120–125, 193, 194, 195, 196, 197

reef knot 177

Ruby Short McKim 10, 11, 23, 25, 26, 37, 84, 109, 116, 119, 121

S

sashing 64, 102, 105, 107, 123, 125, 140, 156–157, 158

slip stitch 179, 180, 181, 182, 183, 185

spoon 9, 134, 137, 161, 162, 163, 165

square knot *see* reef knot

tack(ing) *see* basting

technology 6, 16, 18–19, 24, 29

template(s) 39, 40, 43, 49, 53, 57, 59, 60, 67, 69, 76, 79, 99, 105, 107, 123, 124, 136, 168, 169, 170, 176, 186–197, 200

- how to use 143

Thirties quilts, original
see vintage quilts

thread(s) 49, 57, 59, 79, 119, 121, 123, 132, 135, 144, 168, 171, 172, 175, 176

thread saver(s) 152, 153

V

vintage quilts 7, 8, 13, 15, 17, 33, 34, 35, 44, 45, 55, 65, 72, 73, 74, 75, 84, 85, 92, 93, 101, 108, 109, 117, 118, 121, 127, 176

W

wadding *see* batting

First published in 2026
Search Press Limited
Wellwood, North Farm Road,
Tunbridge Wells, Kent, TN2 3DR
United Kingdom

1 2 3 4 5 6 7 8 9 10

IMAGERY
Photographs of quilts on pages 7, 8, 13, 15, 17, 45, 65 (BR), 84 and 118 are printed with kind permission of the American Museum & Gardens in Bath, UK
www.americanmuseum.org

All remaining photographs by Mark Davison (www.markdavison.com)
copyright © Search Press Ltd., 2026
Styling by Lisa Brown (www.lisa-brown.co.uk)

Illustrations by Bess Harding
copyright © Search Press Ltd., 2026

ISBN: 978-1-80092-253-2
ebook ISBN: 978-1-80093-252-4

DIGITAL TEMPLATES
The templates in this book are also available to download free from the Bookmarked Hub website:
www.bookmarkedhub.com
Search for this book by title or ISBN; the files can be found under 'Book Extras'. Membership of the Bookmarked online community is free.

PUBLISHERS' NOTES
Imperial measurements are used in this book; the metric conversions are rounded to the nearest 0.25cm. Always use either metric or imperial measurements, not a combination of both.

The Publishers and author can accept no responsibility for any consequences arising from the information, advice or instructions given in this publication.

For errata, please visit the Search Press website (www.searchpress.com) or the Bookmarked Hub (www.bookmarkedhub.com).

GPSR information can be found at www.searchpress.com

Printed in China, AP032026

FSC www.fsc.org MIX Paper | Supporting responsible forestry FSC® C136333